Abandoned

Recent Titles in Practical and Applied Psychology

The Powerful Bond between People and Pets: Our Boundless Connections to Companion Animals
P. Elizabeth Anderson

Sexual Enslavement of Girls and Women Worldwide
Andrea Parrot and Nina Cummings

The Global Muslim Community at a Crossroads: Understanding Religious Beliefs, Practices, and Infighting to End the Conflict
Abdul Basit, Editor

Living in an Environmentally Traumatized World: Healing Ourselves and Our Planet
Darlyne G. Nemeth, Robert B. Hamilton, and Judy Kuriansky, Editors

The Psychology of Black Boys and Adolescents
Kirkland Vaughans and Warren Spielberg, Editors

Lucid Dreaming: New Perspectives on Consciousness in Sleep
Ryan Hurd and Kelly Bulkeley, Editors

The Myth of Black Anti-Intellectualism: A True Psychology of African American Students
Kevin O. Cokley

Borderline Personality Disorder: New Perspectives on a Stigmatizing and Overused Diagnosis
Jacqueline Simon Gunn and Brent Potter

Ecopsychology: Advances from the Intersection of Psychology and Environmental Protection
Darlyne G. Nemeth, Set Editor, with Robert B. Hamilton and Judy Kuriansky, Volume Editors

Weapons of Mass Psychological Destruction and the People Who Use Them
Larry C. James and Terry L. Oroszi, Editors

The Psychosocial Aspects of a Deadly Epidemic: What Ebola Has Taught Us about Holistic Healing
Judy Kuriansky, PhD, Editor

LGBT Psychology and Mental Health: Emerging Research and Advances
Richard Ruth and Erik Santacruz, Editors

Abandoned

How Children Suffer When a Parent Deserts Them

Andrea Francis

Practical and Applied Psychology
Judy Kuriansky, Series Editor

BLOOMSBURY ACADEMIC
NEW YORK • LONDON • OXFORD • NEW DELHI • SYDNEY

BLOOMSBURY ACADEMIC
Bloomsbury Publishing Inc
1385 Broadway, New York, NY 10018, USA
50 Bedford Square, London, WC1B 3DP, UK
29 Earlsfort Terrace, Dublin 2, Ireland

BLOOMSBURY, BLOOMSBURY ACADEMIC and the Diana logo are trademarks of Bloomsbury Publishing Plc

First published in the United States of America 2023

Library of Congress Cataloging-in-Publication Data

Names: Francis, Andrea (Child psychologist), author.
Title: Abandoned : how children suffer when a parent deserts them / Andrea Francis.
Description: 1st edition. | New York : Bloomsbury Academic, [2023] |
Series: Practical and applied psychology | Includes index.
Identifiers: LCCN 2022059998 | ISBN 9781440877964 (hardback) | ISBN 9781440877971 (ePDF) | ISBN 9798216170747 (ebook)
Subjects: LCSH: Abandoned children. | Children of divorced parents. | Attachment behavior in children. | Child psychology.
Classification: LCC HV873 .F693 2023 | DDC 305.23086/945—dc23/eng/20230224
LC record available at https://lccn.loc.gov/2022059998

ISBN: HB: 978-1-4408-7796-4
ePDF: 978-1-4408-7797-1
eBook: 979-8-2161-7074-7

Series: Practical and Applied Psychology

Typeset by Westchester Publishing Services, LLC

Dedicated to the children who suffer when a parent leaves them behind.

Disclaimer: The Use of Cases in This Book

The cases discussed in this book, *Abandoned, How Children Suffer When a Parent Deserts Them*, are not the exact stories of individuals and their families but representations of stories told to me in the over twenty-five years I worked as a psychologist and school counselor. All the names are fictional, and the scenarios are a mash-up of several cases with common themes. Any similarities are coincidental. For those that are a direct telling, the names have been changed and signed permission has been obtained for any story that is identifiable. Direct telling includes the stories of my own life experiences.

Contents

Preface

I grew up in the Caribbean, experienced parental abandonment, and saw firsthand the effect of parental abandonment on children both in the Caribbean and later in my work with children in the United States. My story will be referenced throughout this book and serves as an anchor for my exploration of how children suffer regardless of race, culture, or socio-economic status.

Acknowledgments

This book is for the traumatized children who grieve the absence of their mother, father, or both parents, a story I share. The deep pain of our abandonment is difficult to fully capture in a book. However, I tried to put words to our suffering, and to understand and explain why our parents left us. I also offer some solutions so that we can heal, thrive, and live happy lives.

My deepest and sincerest gratitude to Dr. Judy Kuriansky, who encouraged me to write this book. Dr. Judy supported, guided, corrected, and mentored me through the initial writing process to the point of submission and subsequent acceptance for publication. Judy, thank you for your hard work, absolute belief in me, and your kind and single-minded insistence that the stories of abandoned children must be told, even when I doubted I had a book in me. This book would not have been written had you not come into my life at that Wellbeing conference in St. Maarten. Thank you, Olga Mussington-Service, for organizing that conference and making the meeting between Judy and me possible.

To editor Jessica Gribble, thank you for taking on this project with me. I appreciate your expertise, wisdom, and nudging me to make this book the best it can be.

To my dear friend Kathy, who patiently read and reread my thoughts and helped me to express myself clearly, since sometimes my own emotional response to the subject got in my way. Thank you, K., for your unwavering support, encouragement, and hard work.

My sister Marsha, thank you for your clear-mindedness, your help with editing, and the important research on our family history. I appreciate you being a sounding board as we discussed your interviews with relatives, and your recollections of our life without our father and then the years without our dear mother.

Rene, sister, thank you for your insight, and younger-sister perspective into our lives without our parents. Your experience as well as that of our brothers Robert and Richard and cousin Humphrey contextualized and enriched the stories I shared in this book.

Thank you, mom Dolorita, for fighting hard to give us the best you could first as a single mother and then as a mother who made the heart-wrenching decision to leave us in pursuit of work in the United States. We understand that you did what you had to do, to provide for us.

To my father, Dennis, whose abandonment traumatized and sensitized me to the suffering of children abandoned by one or both parents. Dad, your behavior still mystifies but did lead me to a deeper understanding of the critical role of parents, in particular the father's, in their children's lives. Your behavior also led me to discover that healing comes with understanding, acceptance, and forgiveness.

To my children, including their spouses—thank you so much. I love you. Ayanda and husband Hang; Danjuma and wife Stephanie; and the youngest, Imani—thank you for your love and absolute support for this book. I am so grateful for your looking out for me—with "mom you need to rest now"—when I was fading. I so appreciate your computer help and technical advice. A special shout-out to Imani, who in pursuing her own degree in clinical counseling gave me wise counsel, technical intervention, and guided me to clarify the butterfly–metamorphosis model as I tried to find my way through this book.

Finally, to my dear husband, Henry—my life companion, ever at my side watching over me with patience, encouragement, support, and enduring love.

Introduction

Very few experiences can be more traumatic for a child than being abandoned by a parent, whether by a mother or a father. In 2016, this is what happened to over twelve thousand children in the United States. In addition, the statistics about the number of children in foster care in the United States are shocking. Of the 273,000 children who entered the foster care system in 2016, 5 percent were abandoned by either mother or father.[1] The number of children in foster care for any reason has been steadily increasing, from over 390,000 in 2012 to 437,000 in 2019.[2] Parental abandonment affects children across all races and ethnicities. Although trends in the number of Black children in foster care indicate a leveling off, the numbers have climbed for White and Native American children.[3] Thirty-three percent of children in foster care are African American, but they make up only 15 percent of the child population in the United States.[4] In addition, although the majority of America's near 74 million children under age eighteen live in families with two parents (69 percent), from 1960 to 2016 the percentage of children living with only their mother nearly tripled from 8 to 23 percent, while the percentage of children living with only their father increased from 1 to 4 percent. The percentage of children not living with any parent increased slightly from 3 to 4 percent.[5]

Given these grim statistics, it is clear that people of no race or ethnicity are untouched by the absence of children's lived experiences of abandonment by one or both parents. Children of all races suffer the pain of loss and grief. This book, multicultural in approach, addresses how separation from one parent or from both traumatizes children. The book also explains the impact on all affected children and explores the intentions of and impacts on parents and the suffering of the whole family. Such trauma becomes the responsibility of counselors like me to help these children and their families cope.

Children suffer when they are deserted by either parent—though the specific dynamics of the impact can be different whether it is a mother or a father who leaves the family. While many children these days grow up without a father in the household, less discussed is the pain of children growing up without a mother in their lives. With the absence of just one of the primary caregivers, children are at risk for distress and adjustment problems. This situation contributes to the disturbing statistics about the increasing number of children suffering from depression, anxiety, and other mental conditions. In this book, given my vast experience with these family situations, I argue that family instability with an absent father or mother is a matter of considerable concern for the child and the entire family as well as the school system and by extension the society. With real-life case stories and my analysis, the book exposes the intensive and extensive distress of children from the loss of the parent as well as from the parental discord and separation that lead to that outcome.

Reports affirm the resilience of children today regarding being raised in single-parent families.[6] While this resilience presents a positive force, the opposite response to the trauma of parental abandonment cannot be downplayed or ignored. In this book, research and professional clinical experience of children missing dad or mom is presented. In addition, children's pain and grief are shared through narratives in their own voices from their lived experiences. The stories told are true representative narratives of children and adolescents who shared their stories with me over my twenty-two years as a school counselor and extensive experience as a therapist. It is important to note that changes were made to names, contexts, and specific identifiers to protect the children and their families.

For many of these children, parents' fights and the exchange of hateful words are like storms that never pass from the child's experience. Fears, anxieties, worries, and feelings of abandonment that these children suffer have been expressed and shared by youngsters sitting in my office, either in my role as a school counselor or in private practice. I see these children suffering from separated and divorced parents as walking survivors of parental distress that are essentially experienced as emotional earthquakes, with the youngsters struggling to survive the disaster caused by parental discord, disappointment, breakdown in their relationships, and abandonment. What is worse, the pain can last throughout the children's lives and spill over into many relationships with peers, teachers, and others. Sadly, this trauma can even affect their future relationships.

MY THEORY OF TWONESS

While some children may seem to adjust and cope—the essence of resilience—many children still emerge from these disasters traumatized, emotionally dazed, shaky, out of sorts, and off-balance. In these current times, when resilience is touted so strongly in the clinical community, the distress of many of these children is going unnoticed.[7] Many of these children are so emotionally shaken they have to focus on simply putting one foot in front of the other in order to keep moving. I have come up with a theory of my own that has been influenced by W. E. B. Du Bois's theory of duality[8] and from my years of experience in the field. I define the children's situation as a split, experiencing "twoness." That is, they are at once "here"—in one place and in one mental state—seeming to function but also still "there"— in a sort of no-man's-land, withdrawn and stuck in the internal pain and loss of their parents' stormy relationship. They're in a sort of dazed disaster/survivor state, picking through the emotional wreckage left by a mother or father missing from their lives. Children bounce between these two mental and emotional states, which depend on children's internal states as well as their external circumstances.

In their most withdrawn states, these children relive moments of grief or fantasize an alternate ending of what happened to them that led to their fractured family during times of daydream and mental escape. This strategy, although painful, has its positive aspects, since it can be seen as a way of coping with pain. These states are described by children in their own voices in Chapter 9 of this book.

The turmoil in the hearts and minds of these children in distress, missing mom or dad, will not quiet without intervention. Left untreated, these are the children who are greatly at risk for maladjustment, including school-related problems that are increasingly being recognized by the educational community (e.g., acting out, school phobia, aggression, withdrawal, excessive online activity), and personal maladjustment in emotional (e.g., fears, anxieties, depression), cognitive (e.g., lack of concentration, confusion, poor school performance), and behavioral functioning (e.g., poor tolerance for distress). Worse yet, these problems persist later in life if early intervention is not received.

The factors that impact the reactions to feelings of abandonment are also explored in this book. I explain the roles and of the father and the mother and some of the reasons either of them abandons their children. As I explore in this book, there are many versions of how and why each parent may leave, but each reason has its own effect on the children left behind. These scenarios will be explained and compared.

In addition, children's reaction to parent loss are influenced by their own traits, character, and personality, as well as their defense and coping mechanisms. It is important to note that children's reaction to missing a mother or father is generally related to the extent and degree of the loss, meaning the degree to which their parent is out of the picture. Some children perceive that their dads make an ineffective or half-hearted attempt to see them or to be with them, while others believe that their mothers want to be free of them and that they are in her way to freedom and happiness. This book focuses on the children's experiences of their parent's absence as abandonment and experiences of trauma as a result. In addition, the psychological dynamics of both mothers and fathers who leave their children are explored in this book.

Another factor explored in the book is the relationship between the parents, and how that affects the child. For example, dad's perceived abandonment is greatly influenced by the role of the mother in the child's separation from dad. In other words, mom plays an important role in many situations, where it is not all the decision or choice of the dad to separate from the child. Mom is presented as a "gatekeeper"—controlling the father's contact. Moms play a powerful role as gatekeeper to dads' presence and continued contact with his child or children. Initially, children often have little understanding of this powerful role and the barrier placed by mother's gatekeeping, preventing father's access to the children. By the same token, factors that keep mothers away from their children will also be explored in this book. The absence of some mothers is often made possible because of the extended family, usually grandmothers who assume responsibility for the children, allowing mom to go away.

While parents usually make an effort to separate "with the best interest of the child in mind," sadly, this intention is not always realized. Instead, personal and interpersonal dynamics are acted out between the parents often consciously or unconsciously, without any intended primary concern for the best welfare of the child, or awareness of the immediate and long-term impact on the child or children. For example, mother's feelings of hurt from how she was treated by dad can forbid her own forgiveness for the nonresident father's behavior—and children are used as weapons against the fathers, pawns in economic and emotional bargaining, that ultimately keeps dads away. Research conducted by the U.S. Department of Health and Human Services[9] confirms that long-term effects emerge when dads are missing from their children's lives.

In this book, the word "mom" and "dad" is used, but it is noted that today many couples may live together who are not married. Thus the "dad" figure can be a (stable or transient) boyfriend, which complicates the stability of the union for the child. Similarly, "mom" can be a (stable or transient) girlfriend. And in some cases, the parents may be of the same gender.

ASSESSING OTHER FACTORS THAT IMPACT TRAUMA

Other factors have to be taken into consideration in assessing the impact of missing dad or mom on children. This includes the age of the child, which determines issues of child development. This means that the times of the separation from dad or mom are significant, for example, does it happen at the time when the child is experiencing individuation? Or does it occur when same- and opposite-sex identification takes place? Also included is the availability of other children with whom the child can bond, as research has shown that siblings can cope with parental problems by bonding with each other. Another factor is the availability of other adult figures who can serve as mother or father substitutes. Other loving caregivers help children cope with the pain of loss.[10] Interventions in all these situations are critical for the health of the child at the time of separation and also in the long term.

As a veteran clinician who has treated many of these children, I include advice for these youth as well as for their parents, to interrupt the negative cycle of this never-ending pain. There are many issues pointed out in this book that are important not only to the children but also to the adults, as the advice will address not only how parents relate to their children but also how they relate to each other as parents. Since not every story is the same, I will explore angles, feelings, and strategies for healing. The interventions derive from several sources, including my personal journey through the traumatic experience of being abandoned by both parents—a story I will return to throughout this book—and my clinical training and experience both in private practice and in the educational system. The strategies are described in detail so they can be applied by parents and caregivers. I also give advice to educators and teachers, including how to recognize children suffering from feelings of abandonment and rejection from either their mother, father, or both, and how to care for these children in school.

PART I

Mother and Father Roles and Child Development

1

Abandoned

MOM AND DAD

"It was a dark and stormy night" when my father walked away from us for good. At least that's the way I remember it. I remember my four-year-old self looking out the window as he walked away into the night. He grew smaller and smaller and soon became lost in the darkness. He never really came back home, but popped in and out of our lives intermittently and surprisingly. I spent a great deal of my young life mostly happy, playing with my younger siblings, neighborhood friends, and cousins. But that night never left me, and I wondered for a long time why he stayed away. I brooded on my self-worth and, although the eldest of five, with four younger companion siblings, created an imaginary friend. That friend, Jerry, my protector, was blamed for many of my four-year-old misdeeds.

Growing up in Jamaica with a single, angry, and emotionally hurt mother, I heard her version of the tale of my parents' failed marriage—many times. And as I matured, I soon learned that my siblings and I were not unique. Several of my friends lived with both their moms and dads; however, there was another group of kindred souls who lived with a single mom like I did or with grandparents, or were being raised by an aunt or distant relative or lived in a boardinghouse, with a paid caretaker. The common bond among our motley crew was that we were missing either mom or dad or both parents. During those years, I do not recall discussions about parents gone AWOL among us, the tribe of "the one-or-two-parent-less," but there was a common yearning and struggle to understand why we were left behind. This experience shaped my curiosity about the role of fathers in children's lives. Does it really matter if a father leaves his children? Why did it hurt my siblings and me so much? Later, I was intrigued by the role of mothers. What happens when a mother leaves? And what is the effect when both parents leave? We appeared on the outside to manage well, but like me, I know my siblings and friends were brokenhearted.

Family systems theory is a helpful framework to understand the relationship between parents and children. Family systems pioneer Murray Bowen explained that the family is an emotional system—independent yet interdependently connected like a spider's web. As an emotional system, the family is the primary source of its members' emotions and personality.[1] For example, it is in the family that its members learn how to behave and emotionally respond to traumatic or stressful situations. Responses are passed from one generation to the next. Bowen uses the family diagram—which is a graphic display—to understand and explain how family members relate to each other and to capture complex connections.[2] I use the family genogram, a derivative of the family diagram,[3] in this book to describe complex relationships between children and their parents; and to explain patterns of behaviors over generations. I will show the genogram in more detail in Chapter 6.

The family is also described by another family systems pioneer, Salvador Minuchin, who notes that: "A family is a special kind of system with structure, patterns, and properties that organize stability and change. It's a small human society whose members have face to face contact, emotional ties, and a shared history."[4] He continues, "People in a family have a special sense of connection with each other: an attachment, a family bond that is both a perception and a feeling. They know that 'we are us,' and they care about each other. . . . The individual is the smallest unit in the family system—a separate entity but a piece of the whole."[5]

Minuchin further argues that while both the mother and father are critical to providing a child a stable environment, it is "the entire family—not just the mother or primary caretaker—including father, siblings, grandparents, often cousins, aunts and uncles [who] are extremely significant in the experience of the child."[6]

This statement has arguably limited application. The children I work with still suffer when mother or father leaves despite close relationships with extended kin. For my part, my heart was broken when my father left, despite the hard work of my single mother and the support of my extended family. While the extended family plays a critical role in helping abandoned children cope with their missing parent, the pain of abandonment is nonetheless still there. When my father left, I felt a part of myself went with him. "Something" was taken away—half of my heart—as explained by fourteen-year-old Talia as she described her feelings of her father's absence. This sentiment of the "missing piece" is echoed by many of the children I grew up with in Jamaica as well as the children and adults I would later work with both in the Caribbean and in the United States. When a mother or father abandons their child, the pain of being left behind is life altering, lasts a long time, and has traumatic impact on the abandoned child, because the mother and father are critical to a child's normal development.

2

Moms and Attachment to Their Children

We are familiar with the figure of the "deadbeat dad" that has been explored and excoriated in the media—namely the man who lives away from his children, forced by the courts to pay for their sustenance, but who neglects these responsibilities. What if the father leaving and staying away from his family is a more nuanced act than his irresponsible behavior suggests? What of the mother who lives away from her children? She evokes another kind of outrage; dads may leave but mothers are expected to stay. Perhaps the mother left her children because she just could not stay. What of the children left behind when mother rather than father leaves? Do the children interpret this differently? Is one situation more traumatic than the other?

We expect parents to stay with and nurture their children—to follow the ideal of loving mother and father who from conception care, provide, protect, and plan for each child. Ideally, at birth the child enters the world joyfully from and to mother and then father, who remain a constant source of love, protection, nurturing, and socialization. Ideally, too, the loving, stable mother and father are supported under the watchful eyes of caring extended families and friends who, along with the parents, nurture the child's maturation and interaction with society. In a holistic understanding of the family, we recognize the role of the extended family of grandparents, aunts, uncles, family friends, teachers, and spiritual guides who bolster and encourage the parents' work in raising compassionate, grateful, and productive citizens, fully cognizant of their rights and responsibilities to their family, society, country, and the world.

In this nurturing situation, the child in turn experiences the joy of growing up with unconditional love, with feelings of self-worth, self-confidence, optimism, fair-mindedness, compassion, empathy, humility, and prudence—embodying the virtues of character strengths. The nurturing of character strengths, according to positive psychology practitioners, encourages flourishing and well-being.[1]

Character strengths, a concept that grew out of the work of psychologists Chris Peterson and Martin Seligman, are pathways to individual thriving. With the help of other psychology scholars, Peterson and Seligman studied the tenets of Eastern and Western traditions and beliefs. The result was the identification of six virtues regarded universally by cultures and societies across the world.[2] The virtues are wisdom, courage, humanity, justice, temperance, and transcendence. Twenty-four character strengths emerged from these six virtues. The virtue of transcendence, for example, aligns with the character strengths of spirituality, appreciation of beauty and excellence, gratitude, hope, and humor.[3] Psychologist Neal Mayerson[4] further explains that when we deploy our character strengths we experience positive emotions, bolster resilience, and build positive relationships, all of which nurture our well-being and the well-being of those in our lives.

A child will thrive knowing that their character strengths are recognized, encouraged, and nurtured by their parents, by the extended family, and the community. This child's life is permeated with unconditional love. As a result, the child is secure, copes with challenges, has grit, is resilient, and is not afraid to take risks. This child receives love and so can give love—securely attached to their parents and therefore secure to make connections with others, looking bravely toward the future with excitement and hope. This is healthy child development.

We know, however, that reality does not always allow for this ideal. Parents are human with complicated lives; as a result, children's lives are complicated as well. Although 69 percent of children in the United States live in two-parent homes, these parents include biological parents, adoptive parents, and stepparents.[5] Twenty-three percent of children live with their single moms, while 4 percent live with their single dads. In addition, the latest national census report[6] indicates that the number of single fathers has increased since the last census, suggesting that the number of mothers who live away from their children has also increased. Many children suffer separation from a parent by death or service in the armed forces. The grief suffered here is contextualized by the somber finality of death and relief from worry when mom and/or dad return home from active duty. The longing, worry, doubt, and grief a child experiences is different if the parent is somewhere else and is perceived as having made the choice to stay away.

Both mother and father absences are keenly felt by their children left behind. Yet children experience the mother's absence differently from the father's absence. In child development,[7] while the father is the first "other, not mother" in a child's life, the mother or mother figure is the first to provide unconditional love. Our understanding and expectations of mothers are that they nurture and care for their child. Even if the father leaves, we expect the mother to stay. We visualize the single mother toiling to put food on the table, being emotionally and physically ever present, caring for and nurturing her children with superhuman effort, being both mother and father, sacrificing her own needs for those of her children.

But mothers are human, far from perfect. They often do not measure up to these high expectations. Some mothers fall short of society's gendered expectations. Psychologist Peggy Drexler[8] discusses this issue, concluding that mothers who choose to walk away are on the increase and are receiving the harshest criticisms. The number is unclear, but, according to recent census reports, approximately 18 percent of custodial parents are fathers,[9] which implies a corresponding percentage of noncustodial mothers. In addition, a Web search for noncustodial mothers reveals support for "walkaway" moms in blogs such as *Filter-Free Parents*,[10] while Christina Munroe of the *Rebel Circus* blog discusses the reasons moms walk away.[11] Kathy Parker, a mother who walked away from her four children, explained that "support" was exactly what she needed to help her manage her overwhelming feelings of failure. Parker described the events that led to these feelings as she tried to live out an unrealistic and unhealthy devotion to her children.[12] Single mothers feel pressured to fulfill the role foisted on them—that of supermom.

For the mothers themselves, Web searches indicate that for many, walking away from their children was a very difficult decision. Leaving goes against their own expectations of themselves as women and as mothers. In addition, the social expectations of a mother is that she will stay with and nurture her child. This expectation is fostered by the perception that there is a natural attachment based on physiology and therefore a natural bond irrefutably forged between mother and child. However, we know that these perceptions of mother–child bonds do not reflect the reality or the complexity of this relationship.

Our understanding of the power of the mother in her child's life fuels popular culture. Literature and other media draw attention to mothers who act outside of gendered expectations through horror or comedic stories. For example, Hollywood poked fun at mothers refusing their established roles in the popular *Bad Moms*[13] movies. Thus, even if the father leaves, the mother's stable presence ensures that the child will benefit from unwavering, dependable love and care. This ideal of the mother—the one who stays, sacrifices, and nurtures still dominates our understanding of motherhood. Mother is naturally attached to her child because of biology and societal expectations.

CLASSICAL STUDIES ON MOM–CHILD ATTACHMENT

One main source of our understanding of mother–child attachment comes from Konrad Lorenz's work with nonhuman mothers. Lorenz was the founder of ethology, which is the science of studying animal behavior and applying it to human behavior.[14] One of his most celebrated insights into mother–offspring attachment is the concept of imprinting. This is based on his work with goslings. At birth, the new incubator-hatched gosling identified "mother" as the "first large moving object it met."[15] The incubator-hatched goslings which when hatched first saw Lorenz immediately attached to him and followed Lorenz around his Austrian estate. Lorenz even mixed "his goslings" with the goslings hatched with their goose mother to see if they would switch attachment. The young goslings hatched with the goose followed their goose-mother, and the incubator-hatched goslings followed Lorenz. Lorenz concluded that the process of an offspring imprinting or attaching to its "mother" is innate, genetically programmed, natural and instinctive."[16] Through imprinting the offspring learns how to behave socially and how to survive.

Lorenz applied imprinting as attachment to human beings and argued that attention must be given to the critical role of the mother. The mother, he argued, is naturally the first object the baby meets after birth. "Maternal care was a matter of instincts, as [is] the behavior of an infant towards its mother."[17] Lorenz further explains that "imprinting has consequences, both for short-term survival, and in the longer term forming internal templates [in the offspring] for later relationships. Imprinting occurs without any feeding taking place."[18]

For human beings, imprinting is bonding; the connection between parents and their newborn.[19] Children can become attached to other caregivers who were first attachment objects. For example, a father who is present at his child's birth and holds and bonds with the baby before the recovering mother would be the first attachment figure, or first source of child–parent imprint. Does that make this first-object–father bond closer than the later mother–child bond? I will discuss later the role of the father as an attachment figure. Lorenz is described as the "foster mother of ducks"[20] and is famous for his focus on the critical nature of the mother–child dyad. Lorenz could really be described as the "foster father of ducks," and in effect provided the basis for later arguments that "mothering" does not have to be gendered and that fathers provide parenting for their offspring that's similar yet different from the mother's.

HARRY HARLOW AND JOHN BOWLBY

The concept of mothering for scientists Harry Harlow and John Bowlby is inextricably linked to mother–child attachment. In the late 1950s on two different continents but almost simultaneously, American animal psychologist Harlow and British child psychiatrist Bowlby recognized the negative effects that separation from mother or mother substitute had on their young.[21] Through their work, the two identified the critical role mothers play in the development of their babies, and both agreed that without mother or mother substitutes their young offspring would not thrive. Harlow's (now surely unethical) work with young rhesus monkeys was encouraged by Bowlby's emphasis on maternal bonds, while Bowlby referenced Harlow's experiments with the young monkeys. Harlow separated baby monkeys and placed them in a wire enclosure with two fabricated "mothers": both were made of wire, but one was covered in warm terry cloth and had no food, while the other had food but nothing covering the cold wire frame. In Harlow's experiments, it was observed over and over again that young monkeys would consistently choose the warm terry cloth–covered wire mother without food over the cold wire mother with food. The frightened little monkeys clung to the cloth-covered "mother" and, driven by hunger, only left the cloth mother to drink quickly from a bottle attached to the cold wire mother. After quickly drinking, the young monkeys would hurry back to cuddle with the warm mother.

Mother Love

Observing the behaviors of the young monkeys, Harlow identified maternal "love"[22] and noted that "[a]ffection in infants was long thought to be generated by the satisfactions of feeding. Studies of young rhesus monkeys now indicate that love derives mainly from close bodily contact." Further, Harlow described how the young monkeys interacted with and soothed themselves from the safety of the cloth mother. When they ventured away and were frightened, they ran and clung to the cloth mother—the object of contact-comfort. After calming themselves, the young monkeys tentatively explored, then with increased confidence, knowing they could run to the warm, safe cloth mother, eventually played with a strange, loud object—such as a mechanical teddy bear beating a drum.[23] In contrast, young monkeys kept in isolation or who interacted with the wire mother only for food had poor social skills and kept away from other monkeys. These sad, young monkeys also had physical ailments and poor emotional regulation when they were frightened or under stress. For example, they shrieked, flung themselves to the floor, and did not seek soothing from the cold wire mother when they were frightened.[24]

Mother as Safe Haven

On the other hand, Bowlby's clinical work with human patients guided his emphasis on the power of the attachment between children and mother or mother substitute. He also focused on the importance of attachment to the child development. Bowlby[25] identified four characteristics of attachment—safe haven, secure base, proximity maintenance, and separation distress. He described mother or substitute as safe haven, being physically close, cuddling and hugging, and giving warmth, in symbiotic harmony with the child. Safe haven is critical for the young child's experiences of security and connections, all of which form the basis for the child's future relationships. The second characteristic of attachment is secure base, from which the child explores and understands their world, and is closely linked to the third characteristic, proximity maintenance. As the child matures, they explore their world within an ever-widening range, close enough to mother or mother substitute, learning to regulate anxiety while gaining independence.

The fourth characteristic, separation distress, describes how the child responds to and tolerates separation from the mother. Bowlby created the term *separation anxiety*[26] to describe the crisis a child experiences when separated from their mother figure. Separation anxiety is a grief response with three stages of mourning—protest, despair, and finally detachment fueled perhaps by sad acceptance.

A securely attached child, however, understands that when their mother leaves the room she will return. The child comes to understand that the mother or mother substitute keeps her word and will return, not "forget" or abandon them. The consistent stability of the mother's return to the child relates to Piaget's concept of object permanence.[27]

Object permanence means a child comes to understand and believe in the stability of his or her world. It fosters trust as children rely on caretakers to be consistent and dependable. The child learns to become trustworthy themselves by learning about loving trustworthiness modeled by mother or father or caregiver. The concept of trust is critical in a child's development, as it is one of the emotional pillars of their belief in a stable world, in establishing confidence, and in overcoming adversity. Children learn to trust their abilities, their worthiness, and to believe that they matter. Trust is also important in creating, establishing, and maintaining positive relationships with significant others in childhood and as they mature into adulthood. Thus, healthy bonding and attachment between mother and child are critical physical, emotional, and psychological needs in a child's development. When a mother or mother substitute leaves, deep scars are formed as an essential trust is broken. The work of psychologist Mary Dinsmore Ainsworth helps us identify the importance of the quality of mother–child bonding and attachment.

Mary Dinsmore Ainsworth: The Strange Situation Classification

Ainsworth, an American-Canadian developmental psychologist,[28] expanded on Bowlby's theory and became known for the attachment assessment technique called the strange situation classification (SSC). Ainsworth investigated how child–parent attachment might vary between children. Originally based on previous work in Uganda in 1967, the strange situation experiment assessed how children reacted to their mother's presence before and after a stranger enters the room and how the child reacts after she returns after leaving the child alone with the stranger. The resulting attachment styles were observed: secure, anxious-avoidant (insecure), anxious-ambivalent/resistant (insecure), and a style later identified as disorganized/disoriented.[29]

Ainsworth's work expanded Bowlby's description of child–mother attachment and mothering styles. The type of attachment a child has to their mother is related to her style of mothering. Children who demonstrate secure attachment will manage distress when separated and frightened, assured of their mother's consistent, loving attention to their needs. Mothers who ignore or rebuke their anxious children, are insensitive and not in touch with their children's emotional state, create an insecure/resistant attachment in children to their mothers. Children whose mothers interact with them with distracted, inconsistent attention and affection are often ambivalent/resistant in the attachment to their mothers, anxious and unsure of how their mothers will respond.

Critics of attachment theory argue that too much emphasis is placed on the mother when a child's own innate temperament and changes in circumstances could, for example, change a securely attached child into an ambivalently attached one if, say, their mother becomes ill and unable to attend to the child's needs. Jerome Kagan laments that "a serious limitation of attachment theory is its failure to recognize the profound influences of social class, gender, ethnicity, and culture on personality development. These factors, independent of a mother's sensitivity, can be as significant as the quality of the early attachment."[30]

Criticisms, however, do not negate the fact that a mother's or mother substitute's closeness with their child nurtures the child's feelings of being loved and wanted. Indeed, pediatric clinicians Yoo Rha Hong and Jae Sun Park recommend parents adjust their parenting styles to better fit their child's temperament and so buffer the child's feelings of unworthiness and inadequacy.[31] In private practice and as a school counselor working with grieving children, I see how they yearn for their absent mothers. A caring mother or mother substitute has proven critical to a child's well-being. What happens when a child is abandoned by her? The sad images of children in orphanages, deprived of physical touch and closeness to nurturing mothers or mother substitutes, were evident after the fall of the Berlin Wall. The BBC reports that even now as adults, many of these deprived children still suffer cognitive, social, and emotional problems.[32]

MARGARET MAHLER

Symbiosis and Separation–Individuation Theory

Psychiatrist Margaret Mahler confirmed the importance of attachment, showing that the most important dyad in the family system was the mother–child relationship.[33] Mahler identified the first three years of life as critical for setting the foundation for healthy, stable psychological development and well-adjusted adulthood. First, from birth to one year of age (identified as the autistic stage), the child receives the satisfaction of care and nurturing from the mother, who the child experiences as part of themselves; there is no distinction. The child seeks equilibrium, unaware that nurture comes from outside of them. Second, at the "normal symbiotic" stage, ages one year to five months, although still interconnected, the child recognizes the mother as the source of nurture and care. However, according to Mahler, now the child is truly developing a bond with another human being. This connection is confirmed by the child's closeness to the mother and the mother's loving care and attention to the child.

The third stage of "separation–individuation" consists of three distinct phases corresponding with the child's increased mobility, now that they are crawling, standing, and walking. The first two phases of this stage, "differentiation/hatching" and "practicing," are the child's increasing awareness of the world outside themselves and their mother. The child initially tentatively explores, but often from the safety of their mother's arms, or within her close proximity. The child's confidence is bolstered by the mother's consistent closeness and encouragement. By ages sixteen to twenty-four months *rapprochement* occurs. This is the first true crisis the child experiences in both seeking independence and at the same time clinging to the mother. At this stage, the child may demonstrate frustrations at the limits on independence by throwing temper tantrums or helplessness, but the stable, available, consistent, caring mother provides the child the opportunities for learning the limits of their independence.[34]

The classical theories discussed above emphasize the critical role of the mother or mother substitute in the social and emotional well-being of children. Mothers provide warmth, safe haven, mother-love foundations for thriving and overall well-being in their children. Available loving mothers foster secure attachment and at the same time allow their children to safely explore the world, thereby promoting healthy mental states in their children especially during infancy and early childhood. The tremendous value of loving connections transmitted by mothers' warm physical touch and emotional bond cannot be ignored.

Parental Attachment to Child Before Birth

So far my discussion on attachment has centered on attachment between mother-caregiver parent after the birth of the child. However, modern technology, specifically the ultrasound machine, has made it possible for parents to see their child before birth and to develop a connection to the child prenatally. Reva Rubin, a nurse in Chicago, laid the groundwork for theoretical understanding of a woman's connection to her unborn child, although she did not use the term "attachment." Rubin states: "By the end of the second trimester, the pregnant woman becomes so aware of the child within her and attaches so much value to him that she possesses something very dear, very important to her, something that gives her considerable pleasure and pride."[35]

Criticisms of prenatal attachment suggest that it is a one-way relationship, predicated only on the experience of the mother carrying the unborn child in her womb and not true attachment as attachment must necessarily involve both child and mother. It is a relationship in which the child seeks connection to the mother, who in turn provides the responses that nurture secure attachment. Anna Brandon comments: "During pregnancy, attachment seems to have the goal of *providing* security; emotions and cognitions seem to be stimulated by the mother's feeling of responsibility for the well-being of the fetus. It has been proposed that prenatal attachment is more appropriately viewed as an 'emotional bond' that bears similarities to attachment but is not the same as traditional infant and adult attachment."[36]

Despite this criticism, because of modern technology, the concept of attachment is extended to the relationship between parents and the unborn inside the womb. "Fetal imaging, for example, provides the context for the expectant mother to assign reciprocity to the fetus in terms of movement and activity."[37] Further, studies have found that through fetal quickening, or the mother feeling movement in her womb in response to her voice and touch, the bond between mother and her unborn is strengthened.[38] Thus, recent studies based on advances in technology give evidence of attachment between mother and child before birth. Since prenatal attachment to mother is real, children are born connected to their mothers. So while attachment is real, it is the mother's response to the baby after it is born that determines the quality of the attachment between mother and child.

RECENT THEORIES OF ATTACHMENT

Recent theories about the mother–child attachment reflect the social changes in modern society. In particular, current understanding is that parents may not be limited to male-female pairings since same-gender parents are gaining more acceptance and prevalence. In "The Attuned Therapist," Wylie quotes family systems pioneer Minuchin as arguing against the intense focus on the mother as the central figure in child development, pointing instead to the family system.[39] Structured family theory views the family as a whole system, freeing "family members from stereotyped positions and functions, and enabl[ing] the family to mobilize resources inherent in all members."[40] Family members are therefore not limited by gender or tradition. This freedom from gendered roles, for example, helps the family "mobilize underutilized resources and improve its ability to cope with stress and conflict."[41]

As a result, the mother–child dyad is replaced by the child's relationship with other members of the family and the corresponding interdependence between the members. This departure from the mother as the primary source of child–parent bonding allows attachment to fathers and other caregivers such as grandparents, "cousins, aunts and uncles."[42] While indeed viewing the family as a system as a whole, we must not lose sight of the purpose of this book, which is to give voice to the grief children experience when a parent walks away from them, regardless of gender. In my experience as therapist and school counselor, the child–mother connection is significant, and the pain children feel when mothers walk away from them is deeply felt, despite the availability of other caregivers. Classical theorists discussed in this chapter argue that the mother–child bond is instinctive and provides the critical foundation for healthy child development and well-being. Mother love means providing not only food but bodily warmth, physical touch, security, and soothing. When a mother abandons her child, the experience is truly traumatic, and abandoned children suffer and struggle to mature in a healthy, balanced way.

Jadah: Mother Leaves

When she was four years old, Jadah's mother left her in the care of her father. In middle school, her teachers noticed how sad and anxious she was after her return from spring break. As her school counselor, I asked about her sadness and anxiety. Jadah explained that she loved her father, did not want to hurt him, but that she wanted to live with her mother. She continued that she knew that when she was young that her mother made the choice to leave her and be happy. Jadah's unhappiness without her mother contrasts with her perception that her mother is happy without her. Twelve-year-old Jadah cannot comprehend why her mother would not want to be with her. Other girls had their mothers—maybe she was just not good enough.

When I called Jadah's father, Jack, to discuss concerns about Jadah's feelings, he explained that he realized that Jadah's sadness was because she wanted to live with her mother. Jack described the difficult decision that was made when Jadah was very young. When he and Jadah's mother decided to divorce, it was agreed that Jack would be the primary custodial parent. He further added that Jadah's mother was not prepared to be a mother. He was the willing and capable parent. Jadah's mother wanted to pursue her career.

Jadah sees a therapist outside of school and is being treated for depression, *but how do we mend [her] broken heart?*[43] Jadah suffered loss and experienced trauma from her mother's initial rejection of her at four years old. Jadah's grieving is never abated as she experiences repeated rejection with each visit to her mother. Despite her loving father's consistent care, Jadah questions her own worth and why she is unlovable to her mother. Nothing else matters. She was not good enough for her mother to stay with her when she was a baby nor now as a preteen.

My work with children like Jadah who experience their mothers' leaving as abandonment and who suffer grief and trauma as result confirms for me the value of the classical approach to the role of the mother. Jadah's sadness and sense of not being worthy suggest that an absent mother cannot be completely replaced by the present father. To Jadah and children like her whose mothers have walked away, mother and father are not interchangeable. Perhaps the pain of rejection would not be so keenly felt if Jadah did not know or have contact with her mother, who consistently rejects Jadah by sending her away.

ATTACHMENT TO MOTHER IMPORTANT TO THEIR CHILDREN

Attachment theorists, bolstered by robust research, hold that the mother–child bond is critical to child development. This attachment, they argue, provides the child a myriad of critical neurological, physiological, emotional, and psychological benefits essential to healthy development from the womb prenatally to adulthood.

In contrast, critics of emphasis on the mother–child attachment bond, argue for a more balanced perspective, since this emphasis on the mother in effect diminishes the role of other family members in their child's development and well-being. Critics, in particular family systems theorists, remind that the child is born into a system of influential and interconnected relationships.

However, while theoretical approaches may disagree about the role and influence of the mother on her child, the mother abandoned children I work with experience deep grief and profound feelings of rejection. Like Jadah mentioned above, these grieving children feel the bond between themselves and their mother was broken when she left them behind.

3

Dads and Attachment to Their Children

There is a dearth of literature on fathers and attachment. Indeed, Ahnet and Schoppe-Sullivan noted that "attachment theory and research have been slow to more fully consider and investigate father–child attachment. Perhaps this relative neglect of fathers, especially during infancy, was once understandable given fathers' lesser involvement in parenting of infants and toddlers relative to mothers. But dramatic increases in fathers' early involvement in parenting in many societies around the world demand greater attention to the meaning, development, and consequences of father–child attachment from infancy onward."[1]

Not surprisingly, fathers, like mothers, become attached to their unborn children, although they are less likely to show their feelings, perhaps because of gendered expectations of "male" behaviors. Condon found that fathers were equal in their feelings and thoughts about their unborn child.[2] While expectant mothers feel attached to their unborn children because of movement in their abdomens, Von Bakel's research team found that with each visual of prenatal growth made possible by ultrasound technology, the expectant fathers felt more attached.[3]

Further, Condon found that fathers' attachment continued after their children's birth.[4] In addition, fathers who experienced skin-to-skin contact with their children after birth experienced feelings of closeness to their children, as the personhood of their children became real. Skin-to skin contact involved touching, stroking, hugging, and cuddling with their children—actions of "father love" that fostered bonding, and although different, complemented "mother love."[5] Tarabulsy explained that actions such as "smiling, caressing, and eye contact [displays of attention and appreciation] were expressions of love necessary to satisfy the emotional needs of an infant."[6]

The father's involvement is critical at each stage of his child's development. The particularly "fathering" perspective helps children navigate conflicts and crises, as he balances the mother's perspective. As the first man in a boy or girl's life, fathers are very important role models. Girls, for example, are less likely to engage in risky behaviors that negatively affect their lives and development, such as having unprotected sex, when fathers are involved in their lives.[7]

The generalizations of gender roles, though changing, still hold true. Mothers interact with their children primarily through nurturing. Fathers' care is different but complementary. Because they exist outside of the mother–child maternal circle, fathers help their children manage and cope with the world outside the home. Dads encourage independence and risk-taking as they are usually more physically playful and engage in rough-and-tumble play. Lamb notes that while mothers play with their children more than fathers, the type of play is different. Fathers' play is "particularly boisterous, stimulating, and emotionally arousing."[8] The rough-and-tumble play characteristic between father and child serves very important developmental needs of the child. Such play fosters bonding and teaches children how to lightheartedly manage and cope with distress, and how to take risks.

ROUGH-AND-TUMBLE PLAY—CRITICAL FOR DEVELOPMENT

Fletcher[9] examined the interaction between children and their fathers, and concluded that rough-and-tumble play is crucial to the psychological development and well-being of boys as well as girls. In the study, thirty children were told to get their dad's sock off his foot. As the children attempted to get the sock, they were subject to all manner of exciting interactions with their fathers, including being tickled, put in playful headlocks, somersaulted, playfully squeezed, pinned, chased, and spun. Amidst the squeals of laughter, the children learned to regulate their myriad emotions, including feelings of anticipation, anxiety, challenge, frustration, excitement, elation, and delight as dads tried to evade capture. Children had to think of and figure out ways to get the sock at the risk of a variety of thrills such as being tackled, tickled, or thrown on their fathers' back for an impromptu "horsey ride."

In the rough-and-tumble play experiment, children trusted their father and knew they were safe as they interacted with dad. Yet, through this type of play, children also learned competitiveness, how to lose and how to win, while having fun in safety. Dads help children to safely take risks, building courage, hope, trust, and resilience. Dads are also physically bigger than their young children. When a father allows his child to win, the child experiences the elation of conquering a force larger and more powerful than them. This experience builds hope, creates optimism, and plants the notion of being able to overcome future barriers and obstacles. As children mature, these skills of resilience and grit[10] are crucial to problem-solving and well-being. In addition, fathers engaging in rough-and-tumble play with their children strengthens their confidence as they learn strategies toward goal attainment.

FATHERS PROMOTE PRO-SOCIAL BEHAVIORS

Fathers close to their children help their sons maneuver maturation by modeling and teaching the rules of formal play and social skills. Fathers also model the appropriate use of physical power and aggression for both their sons and daughters to emulate.[11] Girls close to their fathers avoid sexual promiscuity,[12] experience more positive social relationships, are more likely to achieve in academic areas involving risk-taking, and develop interests in subjects traditionally male, such as math.[13] Fathers model respectful, caring treatment of women when they have a positive relationship with their children's mother. Boys with fathers who are caring and respectful are less likely to act aggressively toward women, and girls learn how to expect to be treated in relationships with men.[14] Further, while attachment to mother predicts that a child is optimistic about the world and trusts others, attachment to father predicts high self-esteem, with a sense of possessing innate goodness and feelings of being lovable.[15]

Dad is the other half (other not mother) of the attachment object for a child. A look at a basic genogram[16]—which is a way of organizing family relationships and information using symbols, with squares to the left representing males and circles to the right for females, joined by lines to indicate relationships[17]—show the father as "other not mother" (Figure 3.1). The father is the matched but different anchor in the family systems graphic

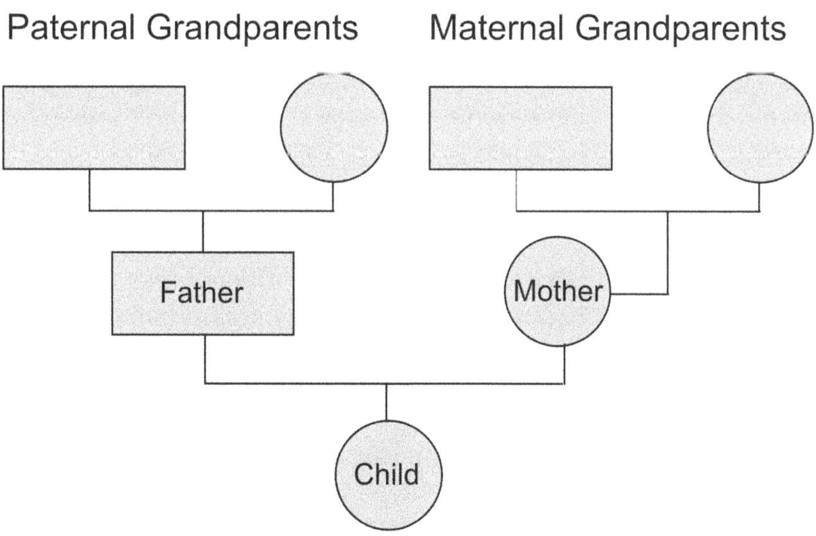

Figure 3.1 A basic genogram of a female child including the extended family (maternal and paternal grandparents).

model, symbolizing his equal but different role from the equally matched mother. The father navigates, mediates, and interrupts the outside world's influence on the family in a way a mother cannot. The father both represents and interprets the world outside the home from a different lens from that of the mother. Children need the balanced perspective of both the mother and the father to cope with the world inside and outside the home.

The idea of "inside" the home immediately addresses what is described as "home training," learning social norms of behavior such as respect, obedience, responsibility, and the six virtues underlying character strengths.[18] But "inside" also has implications for psychological well-being such as confidence, introspection, grit, and optimism. In addition, the father plays the critical role of mediating the world outside the mother's own perspective, and outside the home. Therefore from infancy it is the father, who with the mother, in partnership, helps the child understand how to navigate the outside world. But even more so, it is the father who provides an understanding from a uniquely "fatherly" point of view.

James: Do Dads Live with Their Kids?

Six-year-old James reported to his mother that he had a great time at his friend's house. "The funnest part," James explained excitedly, "was that Josiah's dad played with us. He lives there. Do dads live with their kids' mom?" His mother was devastated by the question. For the first time it dawned on her the James did not know that fathers live with their children. James's father left home a few weeks after James was born. Although hoping for a reconciliation, James's mother reluctantly accepted that her soon-to-be ex-husband was in a committed relationship with another woman.

Psychologists Lawrence Kohlberg[19] and Carol Gilligan[20] agree that both father and mother provide the framework from which a child's moral reasoning is established. The child learns the family values, including socially appropriate behaviors, when interacting with the world outside the home. The father's role in interpreting the world outside the mother is critical for the child not only to understand their family values, but to understand the norms of the outside world. The outside world includes not only the extended family of grandparents, uncles, aunts, family friends, and other relatives, but also all social interactions, including those within the community and the world. Children benefit from their father's different but complementary parenting from their mother's,[21] most importantly from their father's rough-and-tumble play and the close loving, caring interaction with them.

While fathers can never experience the maternal bond between mother and child, a mother in turn, can never experience the unique bond of attachment that children feel toward their father. Children have a bond to their father even when they have never met him. When dad is absent, children grieve the loss of connection with dad, of being anchored, feeling safe and protected.

Children abandoned by their father, even if fortunate to have a caring, loving mother, still experience an emotional blunting in response to their father's absence.

The "mother love"[22] of the caring mother or mother figure helps to mitigate the child's feelings of not being loved; but while assured of mother's love, the child struggles with "am I worthy of being loved by the 'other not mother?'" A father's care and nurture provide the child the integrated layer of core emotional stability, of being safe. A father's constant love assures the child that they are indeed worthy of love, that they are lovable, and will be loved by others. A father's consistent care fosters attachment and strengthen bonds of trust. A child trusts in "father love" because he is emotionally available and cares, recognizing that his child matters. When a father leaves, his going away is perceived as abandonment and experienced as broken trust. Why this happens is a mystery. Why should a child wonder about or yearn for a father they never met? Logically quite inexplicable. Yet emotionally very real and tangible. Perhaps the yearning or sense of loss comes from father-abandoned children being aware, like James in the vignette above, that other children have fathers in their lives, and then like James's implied query, asking themselves "Where is my father?"

Sasha: Broken Trust: He Said He Would Come Back

Sasha's behavior changed from happy and outgoing to surly, defiant, and disrespectful. I asked Sasha what was going on. Her teachers were baffled and deeply concerned about her change in behavior. She explained that nothing really mattered anymore. Her dad and her mother broke up two years ago, he moved out and will never come back home. Sasha explained further that when her dad first moved out, she visited him and he promised his move was temporary and that he would come back home. It has been two years and no change. Recently, her dad told her he could not and will not return home. He refused to tell her why, except that it was between himself and her mother. Sasha is sure it's her fault. She is sure it's something she said or did. Her father and mother tried to assure her that the breakup has nothing to do with her. She does not believe them and is very sad that her father lives away from her. Sasha started to cut her thighs, enjoying the sting each time. She often thinks about dying. She cannot live without her dad at home. She yearns for him and for her family to be restored. At Sasha's request and with mother's permission, her father visited Sasha at school. However, to help her manage her suicidal ideation and self-injurious behavior, Sasha was taken for psychiatric evaluation and is in treatment. Her parents consented to family therapy aimed at helping Sasha heal through forgiveness, understanding, and their coparenting.

A father's role in parenting differs from mother's as he provides loving relational perspective outside of the mother. A father provides another kind of safety for his child—one that complements mother love. A father is very important to a child's understanding of how to relate to others. Girls abandoned by their dad, for example, had a high rate of sexual activity and high rates of adolescent pregnancies.[23] Children miss their father whether they have met him or not. The pain is particularly keen, as in Sasha's story, she knows and loves her father and experienced his leaving as a rejection of her. His silence about why he left and his adamant refusal to return hurt her deeply, making her question her worth. Father is very important to a child's understanding of relationships with others.

4

Child Development and the Importance of Parents

Who better to teach their child about how to behave in, understand, and manage social relationships in this ever-changing, complicated world than consistent loving parents? Parents are the primary caregivers and the first models in a child's life. Social learning theorist Bandura noted that children learn by observing, imitating, and modeling the behavior they see.[1] Children are likely to repeat a behavior if it is reinforced, and learn from the models around them. As a child's first attachment figures, parents model responses to social situations, and children learn how to behave in similar circumstances.[2] Later, as children mature and interact with others outside the home, they observe and learn from the behaviors of consistent models, such as family members, teachers, peers, and actors through technology—like television, videos and social media.[3]

A child learns by observing and receiving feedback from a parent—in the form of either punishment or reinforcement. Through the learning process, the child makes mental transformations on how to behave: what is appropriate, what will cause mom or dad's disapproval, and what will illicit praise and encouragement. Children develop feelings of confidence, of competence and agency—in other words, self-efficacy. Bandura explains that "self-efficacy is concerned with people's beliefs in their ability to influence events that affect their lives. This core belief is the foundation of human motivation, performance accomplishments, and emotional well-being."[4]

Mothers foster feelings of independence and competence by encouraging their infant children to explore their world from the securely attached safe haven of mother and to work through fears, worry, and fright knowing that their mother is nearby. Fathers also give their children a sense of security, and teach through the unique nature of rough-and-tumble play where their children learn the give-and-take of relationships, understand power dynamics of others, and the limits to their own influence.

Among other things, as primary models then, parents are critical nurturers of their child's feelings of self-esteem, self-worth, self-knowledge, and identity. When parents model pro-social behaviors and engage with their children, children are less likely to engage in risky antisocial behaviors. For example, when parents provided sons with social and emotional support, there was a reduction in early sexual activity and violence among sons.[5] When either parent abandons a child, the child is left vulnerable to other models for guidance and explanations of how to behave, and as a result, often makes decisions that are detrimental to their well-being.

The parent who is left behind by the abandoning parent suffers too. They have the burden of managing double parenting tasks and often must rely on other caregivers for support. Single-parent families are often less likely to keep daily routines for young children than are two-parent families. Some reasons include time constraints, financial pressure, fatigue and lack of support. Indeed, single parents are overwhelmed, even more so during times of stress, including worry about work, childcare, and schooling.[6] With their single parent distracted and exhausted, abandoned children perhaps unwittingly seek to fill the void left by the missing parent. They use technology to distract themselves or to self-soothe. The American Pediatric Association, concerned over children's ever-increasing screen time, noted that twenty four and thirty six months old children who had an excessive amount of screen time had developmental delays at thirty-six months and sixty months respectively. In the report, Madigan emphasized that "excessive screen time can impinge on children's ability to develop optimally."[7]

When questioned, parents explained[8] that they allow their preschoolers screen time because it was convenient, their children lacked entertainment, or that they were too exhausted to pay close attention to their children. In addition, parents stated that they needed to get things done, or that they needed time away from their children and technology provided that respite. The ideal parent's role includes nurturing and guiding positive physical, social/emotional, psychological growth and development in their children, and when a parent leaves, abandoning their child, the remaining parent is left to manage on their own. Often exhausted and overwhelmed, the single parent needs help to cope. Technology provides that support; however, without a parent's vigilant monitoring, the result is a detrimental increased amount of screen time for children.

Social learning theorists identify the influence of screen models on children. On-screen models teach viewing children ways of interacting with their peers and their social environment. Children watch and learn and mimic the behaviors of on-screen models.[9] Without monitoring and close controls, on-screen role models become substitute parents. Streyer describes technology with its on-screen models as the "other parent."[10]

Distracted parents forget that the "other parent" may not model behaviors that are in keeping with their own family values. For example, online gaming, YouTube and TikTok stardom, and provocative programming are alluring. Children could become entrapped through pleasure, affirmation, and consistent interaction with on-screen models who give them examples of behaviors that may not be developmentally appropriate. Screen time is the way many children are connecting with school, peers, teachers, and family, with some children engaging in interaction online that is harmful to social and emotional development.[11] In addition, during the COVID-19 pandemic although more children were online for the sake of school, many schools reported that children were not logging into classes or had fallen behind in their academic work.[12]

Children need their parents to help them to manage social situations by modeling balanced behaviors. This means modeling managing screen time with online social interactions. Children also need their parents to help them manage the psychosocial crises that are natural to human development. Erikson identified eight crises that occur during the life span from infancy to old age.[13] The first is trust vs. mistrust that occurs between birth and around two years of age. At this time the child learns how to place faith in parents who consistently keep their promises. Through loving care of their children, parents and caregivers teach what trust is by being trustworthy. Parents, for example, will feed the child, will be consistently available to protect and soothe, will return when out of the child's sight. Trustworthy parents model behaviors that children understand as characteristics of care and love. When a parent breaks trust, children question their own worth and experience anxiety and worry.

The psychological and social challenges that children face continue through to adolescence. Without consistent loving parental guidance and protection, children are vulnerable to managing psychosocial crises with less than ideal outcomes. For example, according to Erikson,[14] children who are between two and four years old will try to do things on their own, for example, putting on their shoes or clothing without help from parents. At this stage, the child is seeking and developing autonomy from their parents or caregivers. Patient, supportive parents will allow the child time to master the attempts to dress themselves. Through this experience, the child begins to learn independence, self-confidence, and self-efficacy. In contrast, there is the child whose parent is under stress and impatient, consistently hurrying the child along, inadvertently fostering the child's doubts and insecurities about self-management and self-worth. Each subsequent psychosocial challenge builds on the previous one and continues up to adolescence, where the child will face an identity crisis, asking "who am I?" A child who was fortunate to receive loving nurturing and guidance will come through the adolescent years with a clear sense of self—confident in their ability to take risks, secure in self-worth and self-efficacy. The alternate outcome is likely for the child without parental support and guidance—a life plagued by feelings of guilt, self-doubt, inferiority, and at adolescence unclear as to self-worth and their place among their peers.

When a parent abandons their child, the single parent left behind is often exhausted and overwhelmed. Single parents struggle to manage tasks without a supportive caring partner. It takes a single parent extreme effort to complete all the responsibilities of parenting alone, and they often suffer from burnout[15] When a single parent is tired and distracted, they are unable to fully pay attention to their children. Their children are therefore vulnerable to a variety of models of behavior, for example, being exposed to and learning from the precociousness of on-screen actors.[16]

PARENT–CHILD ATTACHMENT

As we have discussed, parents are not perfect. Single parents in particular are often overwhelmed, anxious, and stressed. Many carry the scars of their own trauma story. Psychiatrist and brain researcher Daniel Siegel argues that in spite of parents' own imperfections, their most critical role is to nurture their children's well-being by fostering a healthy attachment between themselves and their children. Evidence shows that children with secure attachment to their caregivers are confident risk-takers, who demonstrate agency over their lives. They are "better emotionally regulated, [with] higher self-esteem than those [children] with histories of anxious (insecure) attachment."[17]

Siegel encouraged parents to examine their own lives and to recognize their attachment to their own parents or early caregivers, because our "earliest attachment experience is perhaps the single most important influence on human development."[18] Siegel describes how to foster secure attachment by using the "four S's attachment [model]"[19] Parents are encouraged to first build a relationship with their child that includes making sure the child is "seen." Parents should work at sensing their child's inner thoughts, feelings, and the meaning behind their child's visible behavior. This means really trying to understand their child. Second, parents should make sure their child is: "made to feel 'safe'—a parent protects a child from harm, and is not the source of terror for the child.

[Third,] the child is 'soothed'—the parent helps the child regulate emotions in times of distress; and [last, the child is] 'secure,' developing a clear, resilient sense of self."[20]

Siegel's four S's approach requires parents' honest appraisal of their own attachment history; they may be able to recognize patterns of behaviors that interrupt their child's secure attachment to them. Through this recognition, parents can purposefully repair the relationship with their child and identify their actions that created insecure, avoidant, or ambivalent attachment.

It is interesting to note that Siegel does not focus on the mother–child attachment dyad, but consistently speaks of parents, including fathers in the important role of creating thriving children who are securely attached. This inclusive approach embraces the tenets of both classical attachment theory and family systems, which take a holistic view of the child's experience—recognizing the importance of both parents. Parents are, in fact, critical to their children's well-being. They foster healthy development by interacting with their children, modeling appropriate behaviors, teaching, nurturing, guiding, supporting, and providing unconditional love.

PART II

Why Parents Abandon Their Children

5

Why Moms Leave

Mothers leaving their children is not a new phenomenon. Women who leave their children in the care of others—fathers or extended family—do so despite the pressure of societal judgment and criticisms. This chapter explores reasons mothers leave their children. Factors such as career opportunities, economic forces, and the pull of wanting to be free draw some women away from the traditional gendered role of a mother staying with their children. Some mothers leave their children to find self-fulfillment, while others, ironically, abandon their children to find work to feed their children. Others leave for safety reasons to escape domestic violence. Incarceration, mental illnesses, or immaturity add to the list of external and internal forces that cause some mothers to desert their children.

It is important to explain that leaving discussed in this chapter describes a mother's physical act of separating from her child for a prolonged or permanent period. When a mother leaves her children, it not only impacts the children, but as Cathy Schen notes, the toll it takes on the mother's psychological well-being is mitigated only by whether or not she had control or choice over leaving them.[1]

CANNOT DO MOTHERING

Some women decide to and do walk away from their children because they cannot "do mothering" and so resist gendered role expectations. The increase in single fathers raising their children[2] indicates that mothers are not at home. Three million children or 4 percent of children in the United States under the age of eighteen are being raised by their dads alone,[3] while 2 percent of children in the United States are being raised by their grandparents.[4] The increase in single fathers parenting and the numbers of grandparents raising grandchildren indicates that the number of women who live away from their children has also increased. Women have choice. Accounts of liberation such as the memoirs *Eat, Pray, Love*[5] and *Wild*,[6] and accounts from ES of "Eat, Love, Migrate,"[7] inspire and support a woman's desire to try unexplored paths, take personal risks and to step out of the expected gendered roles of carers of their children. Some mothers are able to resist the idea that because she was biologically connected to her child, she should conform to maternal duties. Mothers who feel they have choice leave their children with relatives and or the fathers of their children.[8]

How many are walking away is unclear, but a Web search for noncustodial mothers reveals both support for "walk away" moms—such as "MommiFried"[9]—and commentators discussing the reasons moms walk away such as Christina Munroe on her Rebel Circus blog.[10] Some bloggers however, still struggle to understand why a mother would walk away from her children. Their comments express confusion, empathy, and appeals to mothers to pay attention to their mental health and to practice self-care.[11] Implicit in some of the comments is that a woman must be mentally unstable or just needing time away from the strain of mothering, since no mother would naturally want to leave her child or children behind.

Additional Web searches. however, reveal that for many mothers, the decision to walk away from their children was agonizingly difficult. Leaving goes against their own expectations of themselves as mothers. Many suffer from guilt and shame and experience rebuke and scorn from family and friends.[12] Around the world, women who leave their children for love or happiness pay a high price. In Australia,[13] the United Kingdom,[14] Nigeria,[15] Ireland,[16] and the United States,[17] women who leave are vilified.

Mother: I Wanted to Do Other Things

As a school counselor, I called father Jack to discuss concerns about Jadah's sad, detached behavior at school since her recent return from spending time with her mother, Katelyn. Jack explained that he realized that Jadah's sadness was because she wanted to be with her mother. Katelyn, who lives in another state, did not seek custody after the divorce from Jack when Jadah was four years old. Jadah's mother wanted to pursue her career and did not want to be a mother. She left the marriage and Jadah in his care. He was the capable parent who has taken care of Jadah since she was four years old.

Katelyn knows herself and her limits as a mother. Her decision to leave Jadah with competent father Jack was really an act of love. However, the reality for daughter Jadah is the lingering sadness and yearning for her mother despite the care of her capable dad.

WOMEN WHO WORK: RACE AND GENDER CONTEXTS

The increasing number of women who work and are breadwinners in the home is discussed as a recent phenomenon in the United States,[18] and it is a challenge to traditional gender relations.[19] But women across the globe in other cultural and social contexts have worked for centuries. Arguably, then, this much-discussed rise in women in the workforce is from the perspective of the traditional role of white women in America.[20] As such, feminist calls for women rights and liberation have "discount[ed] the lives of women of color by assuming that the experiences of white women were representative of the lives of all women."[21] For example, in former slave societies such as the United States, Black women worked the fields alongside Black men. Hallam explains, "On small farms with few slaves, women were more likely to perform the same labor as men. Usually, however, especially on larger farms and plantations, fieldwork was divided along gender lines, with more physically demanding tasks assigned to male gangs. Men, for instance, might chop the wood for a fence, while women were put in charge of its construction. Men generally plowed the fields, while women hoed."[22]

Women worked in slave societies in the Caribbean and South America. "Planters across the Americas forced enslaved women and men to perform exhausting work in the fields with little regard for sex.[23] In addition, and equally important, slave societies embraced and [enforced] a profound division of labor between enslaved women and white women: enslaved women were expected to show strength and stamina in the fields, while white women ideally did little or no outdoors work."[24]

In modern-day United States, women of all race and ethnicities work. A diverse group of women workers make up 47 percent of the workforce in the United States. Seventy percent of these women are mothers with children under eighteen years of age.[25] Mothers are also the primary or sole breadwinner of 40 percent of the households with children under eighteen years of age.[26] Despite this, however, women are reluctant to move to find work. They worry about care for their children and the loss of support systems.[27] Interestingly, women who live with their male partner are most reluctant to move. If they live in a household separate from their male partners, women were more willing to relocate for work.

Guy Standing coined the term, "feminization"[28] of the workforce, arguing that while women have increased in the labor force, rather than gender equality emerging, the conditions in the labor market are still trending "towards greater uncertainty and inequality."[29] Even as uncertainty and inequality persist, women still work.

Immigrant women make up roughly 14 percent of all the women in the United States.[30] In fact, women from Asia, Europe, South America, and the Caribbean make up the majority of immigrants to United States, while the majority of men are from Central America and Mexico.[31] Immigrant women tend to be over eighteen years old, married, and come to the United States to work, leaving their brokenhearted children behind.[32]

IMMIGRANT PARENTS LEAVE LOOKING FOR WORK

Children suffer when they are deserted by parents—whatever the reason. For several decades, large numbers of parents migrate from the Caribbean to Europe and North America to find work. Post–World War II was a particularly marked period of migration to England. In the 1940s after the devastation of World War II, Caribbean men and women—British commonwealth citizens—responded to an appeal from Britain to help with rebuilding the colonial motherland. Caribbean men and women left in droves and worked on rebuilding Britain in all critically important areas such as infrastructure, construction, transportation, and coal factories. They left their children and families behind and became known as the "Windrush" generation.[33] *Windrush* was one of the main passenger ships that transported Caribbean men and women to the United Kingdom between 1948 and 1973.[34]

In the Caribbean post-independence era of the 1960s, the number of parents leaving the Caribbean for work in United States and Canada increased in all categories of workers, especially the professional classes. The steady flow of educated, skilled, and trained professionals, such as civil servants, nurses, teachers, and doctors was so pronounced, there was general outcry against the devastating effects of the "brain drain" on the Caribbean region. An International Monetary Fund report concluded that "the migration rates [were] particularly striking for the high skilled. Many countries have lost more than seventy percent of their labor force with more than twelve years of completed schooling. [This was] among the highest emigration rates in the world."[35]

MOTHERS WHO LEAVE—THE CARIBBEAN EXAMPLE

The factors that push both men and women away from their children are well documented and include fleeing violence and poverty and seeking work to create a better life. Psychologist Crawford-Brown argues that Caribbean women took over from men as migrant workers to the United States, Canada, and the United Kingdom in the 1960s and 1970s seeking opportunities to support their children and families by sending money and goods and services back home.[36]

The frequency of parents leaving and the large numbers of children left behind were so common Crawford-Brown called these abandoned children "barrel children."[37] The barrel children phenomenon persists today in Jamaica and other Caribbean islands.[38] Parents, especially mothers who leave to find work mainly in the United States and Canada, send foodstuffs; household items; and clothing in large barrel-shaped storage containers back home to their children. Caregivers and children eagerly await these barrels full of items such as food and clothing, toys, and other items of support. The quantity and quality of items in the barrels symbolized the progress that the parent was making abroad and usually arrived at Christmas and summer in time for school. For children, the barrels represented a connection to the absent love and attention from their mother who was miles away. But as Melissa Noel comments, "what can't be shipped in these containers and is therefore missing from the lives of these children is emotional nurturance."[39]

When my mother left my four siblings and me to find work in the United States, we joined the thousands of children left behind in the Caribbean. Because of the range of our ages, with me being the oldest at sixteen and my youngest brother six years old, we had varying degrees of understanding of her reasons for going away. We knew that she had to work because it was difficult to make ends meet in Jamaica, and it had to do with her being a single parent, with no support from our father, her ex-husband. We suffered deep longing for her as we tried to parent ourselves. In our minds we knew that our mother did not, could not, would never abandon us, but in our hearts, her leaving us to find work left us bereft of her love and attention. We felt lost, lonely, and abandoned.

My Story (Author Andrea Francis): One of the Barrel Children[40]

Women who leave their children to migrate to another country do so because they must. I experienced firsthand the factors that push some women to leave their home country and their children to seek the proverbial "better life" in the United States. In the 1970s, my mother left me and my four siblings in Jamaica to work in America. My parents separated after many years of married acrimony. My mother gained sole custody of my four siblings and me; and as sole breadwinner, she struggled to make ends meet, living paycheck to paycheck. Although my father was court-ordered to pay child support, his payments were often late and over time nonexistent. My mother explained, "I didn't want him in prison for not paying child support. As much as I wanted to punish him for the hardship on me [to raise you children by myself], I do not want them to kill him in prison. He would not survive, not even one day in there. I did not want your father's death on my conscience. So I had to manage on my own."

Surviving without my father's help meant all five of us and my mother moving in with her sickly sister and her infant child. Together the sisters tried to make ends meet to feed and clothe six young children. Over time, in the 1970s, tumultuous years of Jamaica's economic crisis,[41] marked by political instability, violence, food shortages, and low wages, my mother decided she had to try another way to provide for us. She left us in the care of our well-meaning but overwhelmed aunt—to go to the United States to work.

My siblings and I joined the throng of "barrel children"[42] and waited with anxiety for remittances from our mother, which she sent with some regularity once she started working as a nanny and housekeeper for a well-to-do family. We waited for her to send the barrel—a container with goods and products to keep us fed and clothed. The money and food, however, did not fill the deep void of her absence. My younger siblings and I suffered long dry spells between her paychecks. Emotionally, we yearned for her, our only loving parent; and although we knew why she had to leave, we missed her, felt abandoned and lonely for the care and love she gave us. My aunt struggled between resentment and frustration, which increased our feelings of loss and grief for our mother. During the many lean days in between remittances from our mother, my aunt would voice her anger at having to manage the five of us; especially shaming were her sharp comments about my mother choosing such a "worthless" man as my father.

For my mother's part, feeding five children in Jamaica while paying bills for basic needs in the United States was difficult. On her off days she lived in a small flat in New York—where Caribbean immigrants clustered. As she worked long hours tending to the needs of her employer's family, she counted each penny and every day imagined what we were doing "back home." She waited eagerly for our letters, which she still has—fifty years later. There is one that she holds dear, and which we, now much older, view with amusement. My younger brother, then eight years old, wrote her asking for a pair of shoes and a pony—such were the imaginings of children who thought the United States, the land of milk and honey, provided for their dearest and wildest yearnings.

Away from us, my mother said she also waited for the occasional phone call to cheer her up. With cellphones in the far future, calls made to her from Jamaica were reverse charges to her. The exorbitant rate for reverse charges we knew would be better used buying food for the barrel container she filled

> with food and clothing, or for sending the cash to pay for food, or school supplies or to help Aunty pay the light bill. So as we grew up, we pined for her. The process of establishing herself and integrating into American life took years. The barrel came as often as she could afford to send it—twice per year, usually around Christmastime. The initial excitement over the contents of the full barrel was short-lived as we felt empty without her, suffered anxieties and grieved.

TEEN MOTHERS LEAVE DESPERATE

While some mothers leave their children to find work, others leave because they are not willing to care for or emotionally ready for a child. A woman's lack of readiness may be because she was too young when she became a mother. In 2017, two in every one hundred teen-aged women between fifteen and eighteen years old became mothers resulting in the birth of 194,377 babies.[43] In general, motherhood can be a stressful time for women who have difficulty adapting to the demands of motherhood. Several studies show that teen-aged mothers are particularly vulnerable to experiencing postpartum depression.[44,45] Little more than children themselves, teen mothers indeed do suffer anxiety, worry, and depression, especially if their families are in conflict, they feel unsupported, are frightened, or suffer from low self-esteem.[46]

As a result, frightened, feeling the disappointment and disapproval of family and friends, teen mothers are at risk for experiencing the adverse outcomes of extreme stress. Many young mothers, ashamed and feeling different from their peers, withdraw from friends and family. Unsupported, some feel hopeless, helpless, inadequate, experience panic attacks, engage in self-harm, and have thoughts of death.[47] The tremendous strain from the overwhelming responsibilities of motherhood drive some teen mothers to commit desperate acts to escape. One news story describes a fifteen-year-old mother who abandoned her baby in a trash bin;[48] another article give details of a sixteen-year-old who left her child in an alleyway.[49] In both instances, the young mothers explained that they panicked and could think of no alternative. Other teen mothers walk away from their children, leaving them with caregivers such as adoptive parents or relatives, the most common being grandparents, specifically grandmothers.[50]

The following true account demonstrates the intersection of immaturity that is young teen motherhood and mental health. The narrative is from the perspective of the mother of the young man who engaged in sexual relations with the teen mother. The grandmother's perspective highlights the strain of young unwanted, unplanned pregnancy. The grandmother gave permission for her account to be used in this book. Although her account focuses on the young mother, the impact on her young son, the child's father, is also explained.

A Grandmother Speaks: The Story of the Teenage Mother and Father

The thirty-six-year-old grandmother started with, "She was just too young and so was my son." She continued,

> They were children who grew up together in the same neighborhood. They went to the same school. Saw each other every day. My son was fourteen [Dain] and the girl [Tye] was fifteen.
>
> They were so curious to see what it felt like; they hid in the closet and gave it a try. Not knowing that their first time having sex would result in her getting pregnant.
>
> What were we [his father and I] to do? [we did not even know what was going on]
>
> Let's not speak of this EVER!
>
> Carrying the heavy burden, the two of them decided to keep this secret to themselves for as long as they could. The girl's mother knew but did not tell us until two years later. Then I received a call saying that my son was a father. Devastation, confusion, heartbreak, shock—this could not be true . . . they were too young. Their lives were just getting started.
>
> Weeks passed and the DNA test came back confirming what I had hoped was a rumor and could not be true. Yep, 99.99 percent TRUE!
>
> At that very moment my son Dain's behavior began to make sense. He had become withdrawn and secretive. We put it down to adolescence, but he was carrying a heavy burden. And the girl Tye—her behavior started to make sense too. We had heard that she had started yelling and throwing things, and had been leaving the house for days at a time.
>
> Now that my husband and I knew about the baby, we began to communicate with Tye's mother more. We learned that from time to time Tye would be gone without a trace. She wouldn't call and would not tell anyone where she was. Her mother would call friend after friend, and the police to find her. [Looking back] we realized that having a baby was all too much for Tye.
>
> During those times, baby Juliana cried and yearned for her mother's voice, her touch when she wasn't around. We knew that all Tye would hear from her own mom was, "Do this, do that, stop, don't do that, that is not how you do it, you are not holding the baby right!" Overwhelmed by her new reality, Tye chose to run away to friends to escape it all.
>
> Equally overwhelmed with how Tye's behavior was spiraling out of control, her mother took Tye for psychological testing. The tests concluded that Tye suffered from depression and bipolar disorder. How could she take care of a child when she barely knew how to care for herself?
>
> Tye's mom decided to take over care of baby Juliana. This upset Tye, who did want to care for her child. She couldn't understand why her mother would take

her child from her. Angry and defiant, Tye continued to leave the house. She disappeared without telling a soul.

It wasn't because she didn't love her baby, but it was because it was all too much for her to deal with. So Tye was in and out of the baby's life. Each time she left, she wanted to be free, but at the same time felt too guilty to leave the baby behind. Life just did not seem fair to her. Two years later she agreed to give baby Juliana to my husband and me. She argued, "It's not fair that Dain could do whatever he want[ed]. Why did I have to stay here and take care of a baby?"

Tye struggled with the responsibilities of being a mother and figuring out who and what she wanted to be. It was difficult watching Dain have time to do what he wanted. Tye needed more help from us, but she [did not know] what to ask for. Her own mother was exhausted and frustrated. We were here to support in any way, but saying it just isn't enough. My husband and I had to step up.

We freed both Dain and Tye to explore college and career options—to get on with their separate lives. Juliana knows who her biological parents are but is not close to either of them, not the way she is close to my husband and me. She grew up with them both in and out of her life—more older playmates or siblings than anything else. She does not really see them as her parents.

When it happened, we couldn't understand—why us? But over the years it has gotten easier and easier. We are really glad we have Juliana in our lives. Now in the 1st grade—she is doing well. She brings us so much joy!

From the grandmother's story, we understand fifteen-year-old Tye's confusion and anxieties. She vacillated between escaping from the huge responsibility of raising her child and staying with her, abandoning Juliana for days at a time. Yet she returned each time, resenting her own mother for caring for the baby. Tye wanted to care for Juliana herself, despite the harsh criticisms from her mother. Tye expressed frustration and resentment at Dain seemingly getting away free of responsibilities for the baby. Tye's mother's decision to seek psychological help for her allowed the family to understand the needs of the young mother. She was suffering from mental illness that was further exacerbated by the strain of unplanned motherhood. Mental illness is also a significant factor that keeps mothers away from their children.[51] Tye's experience demonstrates the intersection of mental illness and the strain of teen pregnancy and motherhood. Teen mothers are particularly vulnerable to depression and latent psychosis that emerge from the severe strain of pregnancy and motherhood, compounded by the stressful processes of maturation.[52]

It is likely that Tye had exhibited sign of mental illness before she became pregnant. From Dain's mother's account of events, her sexual encounter with Dain was curiosity and excitement at a first sexual experience. The shock of the resulting pregnancy, with the avalanche of emotions—including coping with the responses of family and friends, the impact on her school career, and changes in her body—no doubt increased Tye's mental instability and depression. She also had to cope with what appears to be a judgmental mother, who no doubt was trying to manage her own strong feelings. Tye's story has a somewhat happy ending with Dain's parents adopting Juliana. Both Tye and Dain are in Juliana's life but free of parental responsibilities because they were both too young. Tye, the teen mother. deserved the chance to benefit from mental health care and to pursue her goals as she matures into adulthood.

SEXUAL TRAUMA AND MENTAL ILLNESS FORCE MOTHERS TO ABANDON THEIR CHILDREN

The World Health Organization ranks mental illness as one of the world's "leading causes of ill-health and disability."[53] Women suffer higher levels of somatic illness such as headaches, dizziness, and fainting, as well as anxiety and depression, than men, Women are also likely to experience post-traumatic stress disorder (PTSD) because they are more vulnerable to sexual violence.[54]

Mental illness and the need for work are factors that push both mothers and fathers away from their children. The behaviors of a mother with an untreated mental illness, however, is particularly traumatizing for children, who struggle to understand their mother's behaviors. An untreated mentally ill mother is unable to protect and care for her children, rendering them vulnerable to dangers as well as to feelings of confusion, anxiety, fear, loneliness, shame, rage, and hypervigilance.[55] Adults who grew up with a mentally ill parent offer insight. They agree that even as they suffered as children, for many, as they matured they began to understand their lives and the life of their unwell mother. As adults, children of mentally ill mothers express gratitude to their extended family who helped them see that there was hope and "provided [respite] and escape from the distress at home."[56]

A Sister's Account of Mental Illness Resulting from Trauma: Not Right in the Head

Christopher's aunt looked past me to the window behind me. Ten-year-old Christopher had recently come to live with her and her family.

> Since he came to live with us [from Jamaica], he stomps around the house, does not answer when we talk to him, he just stays in his room and when he does come out he just stares at us with a smirk on his face, he slams his plate down on

> the table, he has brought such negative energy to our house. He is cold and removed from us. He shows no care or concern for anybody. But at the same time he acts like we had to take him in—like we owe him something.
>
> We thought he would be friends with my son, his cousin. They are about the same age and go to the same school. We were so happy and excited to have him [Christopher] come live with us. But he is not a nice person. Since he has come to live with us our house is completely disrupted. Such negative energy. . . .
>
> We know he had a hard life . . . with his mother being mental sick in her head and everything . . . but we are giving him a chance to have a different life . . . we really did not have to do it.

Christopher's Aunt Cillia provided details of his life, providing context for his behavior.

Christopher's mother Yvette [thirty-two years old] survived sexual violence[57] at twelve years old. She was viciously attacked and raped by an older man who stalked her as she walked home from school, forcing his way as she opened her front door. He lived in her neighborhood and watched Yvette for a long time. He knew the movements of the family and seized the moment when Yvette was alone—the short window of time between when her older siblings returned from school and when her parents got home from work.

The attacker knew and took advantage of the police tendency to blame sexual assault victims. The police were underpaid and overworked, with poor forensic facilities; he knew he could get away with it. The official investigation would be slow. However, in sharp contrast he also knew that inner-city vigilante justice would be swift and fatal should he be found out. He fled the community in Kingston, Jamaica, the scene of his vicious and monstrous attack. He was never brought to justice.

Yvette was found in a crumpled heap on the floor by her older sister. Her mother, however, decided to keep the attack secret and not report the crime nor seek medical help. Her older sister, however, insisted that Yvette needed attention, and three days later took Yvette to the doctor. She had been brutally violated, so her body took months to heal. Yvette did not receive psychological help. While her severe trauma was left untreated, Yvette's mental health deteriorated. Her natural gaiety and spontaneity were replaced by severe mood swings, with loud sudden outbursts of rage or raucous laughter, often made outdoors, in streets of her neighborhood to her family's embarrassment. She was hypervigilant—startled easily—and began using illegal narcotics, and to her family's further shame, became hypersexual. Her pregnancy with Christopher was for a man who demanded proof of his paternity, since Yvette had the reputation for multiple sexual partners. Convinced by DNA, Christopher's father tried to parent him but was unable to manage Yvette's erratic and violently aggressive behaviors. An unskilled laborer, he sent money for Christopher's upkeep when he could.

Yvette's severe mental illnesses made it impossible for her to parent Christopher. She left him with a sympathetic babysitter on several occasions, forgetting to pick him up at the end of the day. The sitter would keep Christopher for extended periods, unable to locate Yvette, who went missing. When Christopher was home with his mother, she would forget to feed and clothe him and would leave him unattended for hours. The neighbors, hearing his cries, would contact her family. Her siblings took turns keeping Christopher, until Yvette would turn up, screaming that they are trying to take her child away from her. This pattern of erratic behavior remained untreated. However, while in a manic state and distracted by another intimate partner, Yvette allowed her older sister to gain custody of Christopher. Christopher had run away from his mother on several occasions and was associating with older boys known for involvement in petty crimes.

Resentful, ten-year-old Christopher now lives with his aunt, her husband, and their son, his ten-year-old cousin in the United States. His aunt reported that he is angry every day. Why was his mother mentally unstable, and why did he have to suffer for so long? Most telling were Christopher's sneering comments, "I hate all of you and most of all I hate her [my mother], that crazy b----." . . .

His Aunt Cillia explained how the family debated when would be the right time to tell Christopher the traumatic events that led to and explained his mother's mental illness. The family ultimately decided it was not necessary for him to know the event that interrupted his mother's life. That decision not to talk about or mention it, in effect, made Yvette's behavior "a family secret."

In his book *Family Secrets: What you Don't Know Can Hurt* You,[58] Bradshaw suggested that this "not knowing" is the source of shame and unresolved grief for family members. However, the reality for Christopher's family was when would be the best time? Would knowledge of the attack on his mother so many years before his birth help him understand and forgive, when his own traumatic grief is so palpable? At ten years old, Christopher was not emotionally mature nor sufficiently healed himself to bear such knowledge of his mother. He only recognized his own experience of abandonment and rage against everyone for taking so long to save him. Any healing for this child would take a long time of unpacking his rage and helping him process his experiences of abandonment and suffering.

He blames his mother for his suffering and for pushing away his father—who, unable to manage Yvette's erratic behaviors and moods, in effect, abandoned him as well. I discussed with Aunt Cillia that one approach to helping Christopher heal would be to acknowledge to him that he has been wronged and that indeed, his mother did not parent him the way he deserved. Perhaps, too, they could ask Christopher to forgive the family and explain how they tried to both support and respect his mother, and intervened when they could. It was important to help Christopher humanize his mother and find compassion for her. In addition, he should have some knowledge of who his mother was before she was attacked and how she changed after. The horrible details could be explained later when Christopher was more mature. Despite his pain, he is not too young to understand the perspectives and experiences of others. The family's patient and loving explanation that acknowledges his suffering, his mother's suffering, and the family's suffering and failings will hopefully lead him to the path of understanding, compassion, forgiveness, and healing.

MOTHERS FLEEING VIOLENCE ABANDON THEIR CHILDREN

While some mothers abandon their children due to their mental ill health, other women flee their homes and leave their children behind to escape domestic violence. The Centers for Disease Control report that domestic violence is common in the United States as one in four women will experience abuse from their intimate partner. Further, "At least five million acts of domestic violence occur annually to women aged eighteen years and older. [Repeated acts include, for example] grabbing, shoving, pushing, slapping, hitting, and serious, sometimes fatal injuries do occur."[59] Women leave their children to escape their partners, often their children's father.

For so many women, leaving their child was the last resort, literally a matter of life or death. The terror that women face is not to be taken lightly, as the grim statistics show domestic violence is often a precursor for murder.[60] The sad reality is that the incidences of domestic violence leading to the killing of women is a worldwide phenomenon. The United Nations 2019 Global Study on Homicide reports that "intimate partner violence in general victimizes women above all, and the same can be said about homicides perpetrated by intimate partners. In homicide cases where an intimate partner was implicated, 82 percent of the victims were women, while 18 percent were men."[61] In addition, a UN study indicated that "one in three women experienced physical or sexual violence mostly by an intimate partner."[62] There was a marked increase in the intensity of domestic violence against women during the COVID pandemic, with increased calls to domestic violence helplines.

Alyce: I Had to Leave My Son

Alyce shared her reflections with me as she explained her feelings of guilt and shame at leaving her son in the care of his father—a man who was loving to his son but abusive to her. She had to flee him and reluctantly abandon her child. In halting words, Alyce explained that she had to get out of the house. She explained that she had planned to leave for a long time but had to make sure that the timing was right. She had to make sure her ex-husband would not find her, and she had to plan how to safely watch over Jason through a neighbor who had become a trusted friend. Alyce's confusion, grief, and guilt were palpable as she further explained that her ex-husband never harmed Jason in any way, but always reserved his anger, mockery, curses, and humiliations for her.

He never "physically harmed" her, but his threats, raised fists, smashing of furniture and household items, and really hard bumps into her kept her in a state of constant anxiety, with the sure knowledge that one day he would really hurt her. She lived in constant fear, feeling off balance and ever watchful. She felt terrorized. Alyce reported that her ex-husband would drop or throw things unexpectedly, startling her when she least expected it. He would wake her out of her sleep just to yell and shout at her for some triviality such as not putting a plate away. With her head bowed, her legs crossed, and her arms folded tightly across her chest, Alyce continued to explain why she had to leave her son. She tried to made sure the house was perfect and she worked part-time. Outwardly calm, she kept her domestic terror a secret from everyone. Alyce became full of self-doubt and shame, and felt herself slipping away Then she started to have tremors, especially when she was around her ex-husband.

With a somewhat bemused expression, she explained the contradiction of how charming her ex-husband is and how well liked by everyone. But, she continued, nobody really knew him or knew the other side of him that was cruel and frightening. She was constantly plagued by thoughts of doing everything "right" to make sure he would not rage at her. She felt frightened all the time, felt like she was losing her mind. So she weighed her options—wait for him to finally kill her or kill herself and find relief. But what about her dear son Jason? What would her death do to him? He needed her alive and needed to remember his mother as capable and strong. One day she will explain and perhaps he would understand; after all, Jason was witness to the terror she experienced daily. He needed to know how to treat a woman, with kindness and respect. With a sigh, Alyce concluded that she yearns for son and is sorry she left him, but she had to leave him or she would be dead.

For Alyce, the decision to leave Jason was a bitter and painful one. She was certain that staying with her husband would one day cost her her sanity or her life, perhaps both. She carried the hope in her heart that Jason's father would not harm him, but the years of physical and emotional abuse left her no doubt that he would harm her, again and again. Women like Alyce who must abandon their children to save their own lives suffer from the wrenching decision they had to make. Many wrestle with agonizing questions[63] such as: What if they lose custody of their children? Will their children resent them? Where will they go? Can they survive financially if they take their children? Will friends and family support the leaving? When Alyce escaped her abuser, she made the choice to survive with the hope that she would reunite with her son, who would one day forgive her for leaving him behind.

INCARCERATION SEPARATES MOM FROM CHILDREN: INVOLUNTARY ABANDONMENT

While some mothers flee their domestic partners and inadvertently abandon their children, other mothers leave their children because of incarceration. Stiffer drug sentencing laws and difficulties with reentry to the workforce place unique burdens on women.[64] The number of incarcerated women was nearly five times higher in 2020 than in 1980. "Over half (58%) of imprisoned women in state prisons have a child under the age of eighteen."[65]

As the number of women and girls who are incarcerated in state and federal prisons increases, so does the number of children who are without their mothers for varying lengths of time. A woman's time in prison is often closely linked to drug addiction. According to the Pew Report publication *Stateline*, "nearly sixty percent of women in federal institutions are serving time for drugs, as are a quarter of women in state facilities. Others have committed crimes such as theft or prostitution to pay for a drug habit."[66] Laws intended to support the "war on drugs" in 1996 included withholding federal benefits from persons with a prison record for drug offenses.[67] The laws ban benefits such as food stamps and Temporary Assistance to Needy Families (TANF) to persons who were incarcerated for drug offenses. Women have a higher rate of felony drug charges than men. The food stamps and TANF ban against a mother with a prison record for a drug offense in effect punishes not only her but her children and her family.[68]

The ban on access to food stamps and TANF is a hardship on mothers returning from prison. In addition, barriers to traditional job entry are overwhelming.[69] The unemployment rate for the formerly incarcerated is high, particularly for Black women.[70] The *New York Times* reports on the downward spiral of formerly incarcerated mothers who because of their record are unable to find housing or pay bills.[71] Without support and steady work, recidivism is high for the formerly incarcerated as they struggle to find work in the first years of release; it is difficult to find work with a prison record. Many wind up going back to familiar ways of making ends meet and are soon back in prison.

Leslie: She Keeps Going Back (to Prison)

Children experience their mother's incarceration as abandonment, especially if her incarceration was due to drug use and not a violent crime. Fourteen-year-old Leslie explained her feelings to me about her mother's incarceration. Sitting across from me, her eyes flashing with anger and hurt, Leslie explained that her mother keeps going back in prison time and time again. Leslie finds her mother's advice of staying on the straight and narrow laughable. She feels her mother threw away her life, is an embarrassment, and cannot be taken seriously. Discouraged and disgusted, Leslie concluded that interaction with her incarcerated mother is a waste of her time, so she decided to stop visiting her mother in prison, because she says that her mother is just going to keep going back.

Emotionally, Leslie turns away from her mother disappointed and betrayed as her mother repeatedly abandons her, returning to prison yet again.

Antonio: Incarcerated for Deportation

Antonio stood fidgeting at my door. I invited him to sit by my desk. I knew this smart, playful, popular student. He was different today, sad and reserved. Antonio was sent to see me by one of his teachers who noticed a change in his demeanor over the past two days. He was not himself and seemed preoccupied. I asked him to share with me what was going on. After a brief hesitation, Antonio explained that his mother was in jail for something to do with her car. He lived with a single mother and does not know where to find his father. He found out that his mother was arrested when she called him from the jail. He stayed home alone, and his aunt will pick him up from school and take him to live with her. He did not know when he will see his mom again; she told him she was going to be deported as she did not have the right papers to stay in the United States: How could he live without his mom?

His eyes filled with tears as he looked up at me for the answer. Antonio is one among the large number of children who were born in the United States but whose parents, in this case his mother, do not have the legal status or documentation to remain in the United States. With over 4 million children under eighteen years of age with an undocumented parent, mothers are likely to make up a significant percentage. Children feel abandoned; even if they understand the circumstances of their mother's leaving as related to her immigration status, their anguish is increased by their helplessness. Children exhibit signs of PTSD, frustration, anger, worry, panic, depression, loneliness, anxiety, and a range of symptoms related to toxic stress.[72]

While not attempting to cover all the reasons mothers abandon their children, the factors discussed in this chapter are the ones that I have been made aware of by the children and families I work with. Some mothers leave their children by choice, seeking independence and resisting mothering as defined by gendered expectations of a woman's role. Mothers who are seeking their own self-fulfillment without their children suffer societal disapproval. However, from my personal and professional experience, most children are abandoned by their mothers because of emotional, social, and economic forces. Figure 5.1 summarizes the main reasons mothers abandon their children.

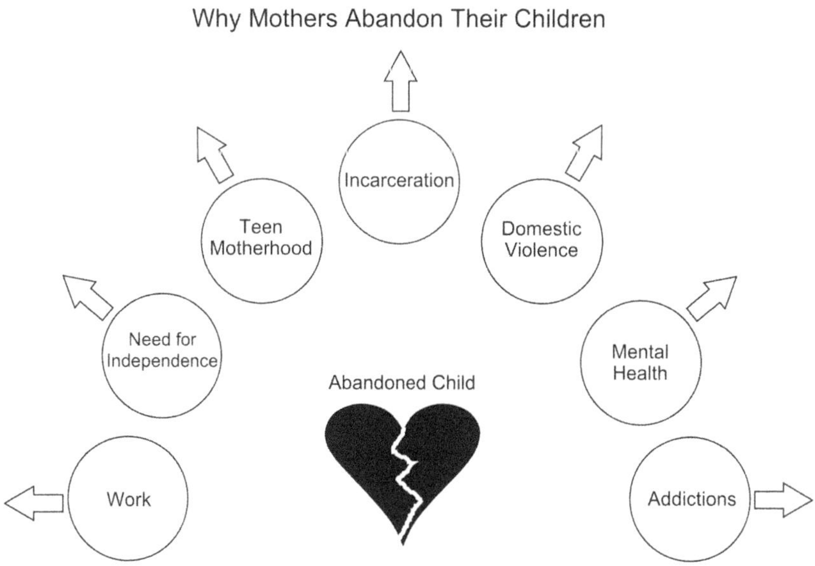

Figure 5.1 Main factors that keep mothers away from their children.

6

Why Dads Leave

Men leave their children for a variety of reasons, most of which are deeply personal and specific to the circumstances of the relationships with the mother. There are, however, certain significant factors common to these men that keep them from their children. These factors in effect, support fathers' abandonment of their children. This chapter explores what, in my view, interfere with fathers' ability to remain with their children: imprisonment, the residue of patterns of fathering prevalent during centuries of Black enslavement, domestic hostilities between fathers and the mothers of their children, the legal social support system, economic stress, addictions, and the availability of artificial means of fathering.

DAD IS IN PRISON

A significant number of fathers are incarcerated, that is, "confined in prison or other facilities under the jurisdiction of the state or Federal Bureau of Prisons."[1] America has more prisons and imprisons more people than any other country in the world.[2] The Bureau of Justice reports that for every one hundred thousand persons in America, 655 are in prison. Both mothers and fathers are locked away from their children, with the resulting 2.7 million children living without a parent. Fathers make up 92 percent of the prison population; two in every ten imprisoned fathers are Hispanic, three out of ten fathers are White, and four out of ten imprisoned fathers are Black. Over 1 million Black children have fathers who are in prison.[3] More disturbing is that the latest 2021 Bureau of Justice report states that over twenty four states, across race and gender, 82 percent of the formerly incarcerated were rearrested ten years after release from prison.[4]

The effect of imprisonment and recidivism and the trauma it causes children is explored in a 2015 ABC News *Nightline* story on incarcerated fathers and their children.[5] In one segment, we are introduced to nine-year-old Amaya and her father, Jeremy Mathews. In and out of prison and incarcerated during the time of the interview, Jeremy, who is white, was serving a twelve-year sentence for burglary. In the interview, he reflected on his feelings about his relationship with his daughter, saying that when in prison, "I get scared that she'll forget [me]. She told me, I love you dad—but you keep breaking promises, you keep getting into trouble. She was seven years old when she told me this. I don't want to disappoint her."

But it is daughter Amaya's words that are heartbreaking. As she reflected, she explained the basis of her distrust, disappointment and feelings of abandonment: "I told him [dad] I am not gonna trust you no more because You promised . . . promised me that you would be there for me for the rest of my life—and then you go back to jail. . . . I'm not going to trust you no more."[6]

The disappointment that child Amaya expresses is poignant both in her rejection of her father's behavior and in her childlike understanding of his repeated lapses. It is personal. Dad has broken her trust in him over and over again, and has repeatedly abandoned her. Deeply saddened, she has given up hope that he will change. Jeremy's behaviors reject her stated need for him "to stop getting in trouble." She is in effect begging him to follow the rules and stay with her. He repeatedly breaks his promises to be with her "for the rest of [her] life," he lets her down by his frequent incarceration, abandoning her both physically and emotionally time and time again. The emotional turmoil Amaya experiences with each of Jeremy's leavings inflicts repeated trauma upon her—she expresses helplessness and hopelessness, because her dad, like the children for whom this book is written, never stays.

Jeremy Mathews has a high level of recidivism. It is likely that Jeremy is the product of poor family support, and is in and out of prison for theft, described as property offenses.[7] Indeed, the vast number of repeat offenders are incarcerated for property offenses. "Within 5 years of release, 82.1% of property offenders were arrested for a new crime, compared to 76.9% of drug offenders, 73.6% of public order offenders, and 71.3% of violent offenders"[8]

Berg and Huebner confirmed that offenders with strong family and social support are likely to seek and find employment, as strong social support encourages men to want to rejoin society through conventional lifestyles associated with employment.[9] Formerly incarcerated men are more stable fathers and spouses when they have strong social support of family and friends.

However, according to Couloute and Daniel,[10] formerly incarcerated people are employed in the most insecure jobs, and when compared to the general population are five times more likely to be unemployed. The formerly incarcerated are also more likely to struggle to find housing, exist below the poverty line, die at higher rates from illnesses, and are usually underemployed. In addition, formerly incarcerated Black men and women "face the worst labor market disadvantages despite being more likely to be looking for jobs."[11]

With America's high rate of incarceration and the poor resources available to support fathers who return to their families, it is not surprising that fathers are unable to provide adequately for their families. Edin and Nelson[12] found that when fathers are unable to provide financial support, romantic relationships sour, and fathers—unable to cope with the stress of failure and being berated by the disappointed mothers of their children—leave home, inadvertently abandoning their children. Children like Amaya, referenced in the interview above, yearn to be with their fathers; imprisonment causes deep sadness and disappointment. In addition, while children may on one level understand the difficulties their formerly incarcerated dads face as they try to provide basic needs for themselves and their families, that knowledge cannot and does not ease the grief from loss and abandonment when dad is rearrested, in effect abandoning his children again to return to prison.[13]

Trevor: Seeds of Adult Recidivism Planted

Conversations with young men who were repeat offenders at the Youth Detention Center (YDC) give insight into the seeds of adult recidivism. I met Trevor when I was counselor for an alternate school program that gave students a chance to complete their middle school curriculum in one year. Trevor had recently returned from the city's Youth Detention Centers (YDC) to the school program, and had been in and out of YDC since the sixth grade. His offenses at that time were taking food items from convenience stores, breaking into cars, and possession of and selling marijuana.

When I asked about his going in and out of youth detention, he admitted that he disliked being behind bars, but much to my surprise Trevor stated that while the first time going in to YDC "was scary, it's not so bad now . . . it's alright." He further stated that whenever he arrives at YDC, he is known and acknowledged. "The guys know my name—I have friends in there." He explained that he had a bed, predictable food, entertainment, and an exercise routine. "I can shoot hoops."

Trevor's words may be mere bravado, but it caused me to wonder if imprisonment somehow represented a "comforting space" in its order and structure for young men who are without the protective supports that prevent risky behaviors. Sadly, Trevor's risky behaviors and familiarity with the juvenile justice system sow the seeds of adult incarceration and recidivism. Jail or prison or Youth Detention Center provide strict "parenting"—predictable rules and harsh socialization, but basic needs are assured. As Trevor's counselor, I knew that he was a frequent runaway from his mother's two-bedroom apartment because of conflicts with mother's live-in boyfriend. There is often little food in the apartment he shares with his mother, her boyfriend, and his two sisters. Trevor's father has not been active in his life since his parents separated when he was ten years old. Trevor told me he wanted to live with his father but explained that his father said he's "not straight right now. [But] I told him I don't care, I will be alright. I just need to be with him. I know he will come get me soon."

I referred Trevor to a mentoring program that has a high success rate with young men. I also referred both families to the school social worker who worked hard to provide resources for Trevor's family. I met with Trevor's mother to discuss the increasingly volatile situation at home between Trevor and her boyfriend, and with her permission, I also reached out to Trevor's father, who lived in another state. He promised to arrange his life so that his son could join him. Whether this came to pass is unknown to me since Trevor moved on to high school.

Unfortunately, if there is no change in behavior or an increase in the social and emotional support, the patterns of behavior in Trevor's life portend a dim future as he enters adulthood. The mitigating factor is the quality of family and social support. Trevor has a weak family support system and appears to have found alternate social and economic connections both inside and outside of detention.

HISTORICAL RESIDUES OF FATHERING

Black Fathers of the African Diaspora

According to Edin and Nelson, young disadvantaged men initially embrace parenting their children and maintaining a romantic relationship with their children's mother with enthusiasm. However, over time, for many, the stability of these relationships is shaken by economic pressures, mistrust, conflict, and incarceration.[14] The challenges Black fathers face are unique among fathers. In addition to higher rates of incarceration than other racial groups,[15] Black fathers are alternately vilified for their deficits and failings or praised for their resilience, resourcefulness, and their tenacity in parenting their children and relating to their intimate partners.[16]

Black fatherhood is, however, shadowed by the vestiges of the patterns of fathering that existed during the centuries of Black enslavement.

Examination of the legacy of slavery and its impact on the lives of descendants of enslaved Africans throughout the diaspora is voluminous and ongoing. Some scholars argue that centuries of enslavement have little to do with the current reality of Black lives.[17] But the fact remains that the daily lives of Black men in America are impacted by events of the past—rooted in slavery.[18] One troubling fact is that the majority of children who live without their fathers are Black.[19] Black fathers are the descendants of those who suffered the holocaust of centuries of slavery, under the brutality of captors who purposely targeted natural familial relationships through practices that made mothers, fathers, and children commodities. The residual effects of slavery remain to the present day. Studies of the impact of slavery have been numerous, including the recent re-remembering of enslaved Africans arriving in America through the *1619 Project*, which "aims to re-frame the country's history by placing the consequences of slavery and the contributions of black Americans at the center of our national narrative."[20]

Eminent writer and activist W. E. B. Du Bois cautioned scholars who sought to get a clear picture of "the family relations of slaves," reminding that "between the Southern apologist and his picture of cabin life with idyllic devotion and careless toil, and that of the abolitionist with his tale of family disruption, and cruelty; adultery, and illegitimate mulattoes, [between] these pictures the student must steer carefully to find a reasonable statement of the average truth."[21]

Du Bois further argues that slavery sought to destroy any "vestiges of a family system in America as the enslaved Black population had (1) no legal marriage, (2) no legal family, (3) no legal control over [their] children. [Indeed] a necessary consequence of slavery is the absence of marriage relations." Du Bois continues, "this is what slavery meant, and no amount of kindness in individual owners could save the system from its deadly work of disintegrating the ancient Negro home and putting a poor substitute in its place.[22]

Forty-three years after the abolition of slavery in America, Du Bois lamented that there were troubling behaviors among Black people, especially the alarming number of children born out of wedlock to single mothers and the disrespectful manner that men treated women.[23]

Given this historical context, the residual effects of centuries of enslavement and institutional and systemic racism on Black fatherhood must be explored. Orlando Patterson supports Du Bois's position, noting that one of the devastating consequences of slavery was the destruction of the roles of husband and father.[24] Patterson further argued that fatherhood meant having leadership, authority, and power over their children and families.

During enslavement, the role of father was meaningless in that enslaved Black men had no control over the lives of their children, and had no way of providing for or protecting them and their mothers.[25]

Slavery denied men the agency of managing the obligations of fatherhood. Patterson added, "fatherhood could not exist, since this meant owning one's children, having parental power and authority over them." He describes the "holocaust of slavery and what was its most devastating impact: the ethnocidal assault on gender roles, especially those of father and husband, leaving deep scars in the relation between Afro-American men and women."[26] Both Du Bois and Patterson identified the devastating effect that enslavement had on men's relationship with their children, with mothers of their children, and indeed on their own sense of personal worth.

TYPES OF FATHERING DURING THE TIME OF BLACK ENSLAVEMENT

Slavery created distinct types of fathering, patterns that I believe are residual in the behaviors of some men in the present day. Du Bois identified the deep love and attachment boys, girls, women, and men had for their families and the extreme suffering they endured to be reunited when separated. Listed advertisements from captors hunting their enslaved runaways testify to the passion and determination that enslaved fathers had to reunite with their children. For example, an advertisement from J. G. Owens of South Carolina offers: "$20 reward for my negro man Jim—Jim is about 50 to 55 years of age. It is probable he will aim for Savannah, as he said he had children in that vicinity."[27] Miraculously, despite the terrible toll slavery exacted on Black families, Black fathers engaged in responsible parenthood, evidenced by close family bonds with the extended family, mental toughness, and resilience embedded in coping strategies.[28]

However, the pernicious vestiges of the slavery past cannot be ignored. Slavery was an assault on the Black family as it systematically weakened family bonds and created distinct types of fathering. The vestiges of the fathering during the time of slavery make it difficult for some present-day men to emotionally connect to and remain with their children, thus, in effect, these vestiges encourage abandonment.

LOVING POWERLESS: BLACK ENSLAVED FATHER

The first type of fathering, a residue of slavery, experienced today is the loving but powerless father. The father who loves his children but is powerless to fully exercise his fathering role because of powerful forces working against his authority. For example, the U.S. prison system, previously discussed, was created during slavery to control Black people, particularly Black men.[29] High incarceration rates keep Black men away from their children[30] while microaggressions in the workplace emasculate and interfere with their psychological well-being and career success.[31]

The behaviors of present-day Black fathers who are loving but powerless have roots in one type of Black fathering derived from centuries of enslavement. Abolitionist, freedom fighter, and formerly enslaved Harriet Jacobs records her experiences in *Incidents in the Life of a Slave Girl.*[32] Jacobs describes her father as a strong, caring, independent-minded, and skilled mechanic. She details an interaction between her brother William and their father:

> [more] than is common among slaves [my] brother was a spirited boy; [one] day, when his father and his [slave] mistress both happened to call him at the same time, he hesitated between the two; being perplexed to know which had the [stronger] claim upon his obedience. He finally concluded to go to his mistress. When my father reproved him for it, he said, "You both called me, and I didn't know which I ought to go to first."
>
> "You are *my* child," replied our father, "and when I call you, you should come immediately, if you have to pass through fire and water."[33]

What were the feelings of this father who sought to exert paternal responsibility over his child although he himself was owned by another human being? How did the son understand his father's authority over him? It is obvious that William did understand that the slave owner had the ultimate power over both himself and his father, which was why he responded to her first. No doubt if the son had responded to his father before responding to his owner, the consequences for both father and son would have been retribution.

The power and authority of the mistress over both father and son, no doubt, motivated Jacob's father's outburst of frustration and anger at William. Not only did the son disobey the father, but by responding to the mistress first, William confirmed his father's powerlessness and weakened authority. This was a shaming experience for a good and respected father, who had no control over his child, as in that moment it was clear that both he and his child were owned by the mistress, who had the power over their lives. Jacobs's brother learned lessons of fathering from his own father. He saw his father's attempts to assert authority and control over him and indeed the situation, but his father was powerless. As an enslaved boy, his understanding then was that fathers could be kind and good, but they had no real power over their sons or even their own lives because both father and son had to submit to the will of their owners.

Given our understanding of the life of the enslaved during the centuries of slavery, it is well documented that the daily lives of enslaved Black people was shadowed by the experiences of family members being killed, traded, or sold.[34] It is likely that some men in the harsh circumstances of enslavement may have developed learned helplessness[35] feelings linked to depression, hopelessness, and detachment or a lack of attachment to children or partners.

Seligman describes specific learned helplessness and generalized learned helplessness as distinct responses to bad events. Men who respond with specific learned helplessness "may feel helpless in the one part of their lives, yet march stalwartly on in [other areas][36] with the internal understanding and acceptance of their inability or powerlessness to affect change or to solve problems in one specific area of their lives, while having agency over other areas. A man with specific learned helplessness may say to himself, "I have no power over my son's life, but I do have agency and esteem in other areas." In this instance, there is still optimism and hope. The case is similar for the enslaved man, who would have recognized his humanity and self-worth—in being a skilled mechanic, for example, like Jacobs's father cited above.

In contrast, a man with generalized learned helplessness feels powerless in all areas of his life and views himself as generally ineffective, with the voice in his head saying, "I am worthless. I am powerless." For this man, feelings of hopelessness, depression, anger, and frustration prevail. He explains his inability by blaming the "system"[37] for holding him back, which, during the cruel circumstances of enslavement, was in fact the case.

The institution of slavery robbed men of their agency over their own lives and that of their children and families, yet there are countless accounts of Black men who risked their lives and died cruel deaths to free themselves and their families from bondage. But for some there were circumstances of internalized powerlessness and a lack of competence in the eyes of their children. Some withdrew from their children; they could not fight. The father left them because he could not help or free them; to them, fighting back was useless. The father lost face, his self-efficacy, and his self-esteem.[38] This response to "the system" remains today.

The owner and master of the Black father is, in fact, the *Father*, with power and authority over life and death, over keeping families together or tearing them away from each other despite pleas and cries for mercy. The

Black father was unable to prevent or protect. Generalized learned helplessness is linked to a negative explanatory style of making sense of bad events. The meaning given to bad events is passed from generation to generation. Children—future mothers and fathers—learn to explain events that go wrong as being caused by external forces. Or they learn to view events that go wrong as their own personal internal failings, innate weaknesses, or flaws that cannot be fixed. This is the essence of internalized powerlessness. Historian Patterson argues that the "conclusion children drew would not have been that their fathers did not love or care for them, for there is evidence that fathers did what they could for their children in the little time they were permitted with them; nor was it that they themselves did not love the man that had so little power to protect them. Rather, the conclusion drawn was that fatherhood was a marginal role among Afro-Americans."[39]

Enslaved children learned that their father—in the role of protector and figure of authority—had little power over the events of their lives. But many remained optimistic despite helplessness in the face of the power of the slave master. These children saw their fathers assert agency in the obvious acts of insurrection such as fighting back, slowing down work, self-injury with maiming, and escape[40]

Other enslaved children saw their fathers, in the face of overwhelmingly dehumanizing conditions, succumb to generalized helplessness and frustration and withdrawal from them.[41] In effect, enslaved children saw their fathers either give into or put up resistance to the harsh forces of slavery.

UNLOVING POWERFUL: WHITE ENSLAVER FATHER

White fathers in former slave societies such as the United States and the Caribbean were not untouched by the "unnaturalness" of family relationships. The slave master owned the bodies of those he enslaved and used men's[42] and women's[43] bodies for profit and for pleasure. The dehumanization of the Black woman's body fostered another kind of fathering style that persists in present-day fathers. With the Black woman's body being used for pleasure, for punishment, for the master's economic gain, the children resulting from this sexual violence were considered commodities. Frederick Douglass argued that "to blunt and destroy" feelings of affection between children and parents,[44] slave masters purposefully separated them by selling, bartering, or bequeathing them in wills.

However, the purposeful disconnecting or blunting of any feeling of connection between enslaved parents and children also affected the slave master. The slave master's feelings were also purposefully blunted by the pernicious and pathological practice of treating enslaved people as less than human.[45] The master's connections to his own enslaved children and their mothers lacked the genuine connections of relationships. This hardening of the heart made it possible for the *MasterFather* to enslave, sell, or distribute his children as he would any other livestock.[46] This type of father was cruel, cold, and pathologically able to separate from his children, viewing them only as a commodity—a means of power and wealth—to be bought and sold. In his autobiography, former enslaved abolitionist Moses Roper talks about his father and slave master:[47]

> But as well as I can recollect from what my mother told me, my father sold her and myself soon after her confinement. . . . I have mentioned before of my father disposing of me, I am not sure whether he exchanged me and my mother for another slave or not, but I think it very likely he did exchange me with one of his wife's brothers' or sisters'. . . . The way they divide their slaves is this: they write the names of different slaves on a small piece of paper, and put it into a box and let them all draw. I think that Mr. Durham drew my mother, and Mr. Fowler drew me, so we were separated a considerable distance. . . . . My resembling my father so very much, and being whiter than the other slaves, caused me to be soon sold to what they call a negro trader, who took me to the Southern States of America, several hundred miles from my mother. As well as I can recollect, I was then about six years old.[48]

Roper resembled his father and knew that his father was also his master. His father had no care or interest in him as a human being, nor as a son. Roper used the word "father," yet the relationship was devoid of any of the feelings the word connotes as he described no expectation of, nor received any loving tenderness from, his father. Roper and his mother were separated in a random distribution game of "chance." He does not elaborate on his feelings about this most painful and traumatic moment in his life, but moves on with his narrative.

Roper's observations and experiences of his powerful and unloving father would likely influence his own fathering style. Records of Moses Roper's life[49] indicate that he fathered daughters, whom he abandoned in Wales, as he did not return to his family after a trip to the United States. Although he was alive and living in the United States, Roper's youngest daughter, when she married in 1883, listed him as "deceased" on her marriage certificate.[50] It is possible that she did not know he was alive and may have interpreted his abandonment as Roper having "died" to her and her siblings. A restless man, Roper moved from place to place lecturing and working any odd jobs his could find. While working as a field hand he fell ill and died in Boston, Massachusetts, in 1891.

Roper's sad outcome reflects the toll that the actions of the powerful, unloving slave master–father exacted on his child and on subsequent generations of his slave-son's children. The slave master–father was common practice. Slave masters reaped perverse pleasure from the sexual violence on enslaved women[51] and enjoyed financial profit from their offspring as valuable commodities. In this context, boys learned about fatherhood from cold, cruel exemplars whose behaviors of detachment influenced their own fathering. Slaveholders fathered children with the women they enslaved. Thomas Jefferson's fathering of six children with enslaved Sally Hemmings[52,53] indicates the prevalence of slave women bearing children for their slave masters at all levels of society. Jefferson did not free his "children-slaves" until after his death. Notes from Monticello[54] indicate that "Sally Hemmings was never officially freed. However, after Jefferson's death, she was allowed to live in Charlottesville in unofficial freedom with her two sons, Madison and Eston, who were granted freedom in Jefferson's will."

In addition, eyewitness accounts in slave narratives document these practices, such as this one from William Johnson: "I knew a man at the South who had six children by a colored slave. Then there was a fuss between him and his wife, and he sold all the children but the oldest slave daughter. Afterward, he had a child by this daughter, and sold mother and child before the birth. This was nearly forty years ago. Such things are done frequently in the South. One brother sells the other: I have seen that done."[55] These are the vestiges of detached, disconnected fathering that has its roots in the slave economy system of both the United States and the Caribbean. The pattern was repeated and passed down through generations.

De Facto Master: Overseer, Powerful and Unloving Father

During the centuries of slavery, slave owners hired overseers who were the de facto plantation masters. Many plantation owners were absentees, living away from their plantations, or some plantations were large, requiring that "eye servants" or overseers be hired to watch and control the enslaved workers. In *Masters of Violence*, Tristan Stubbs[56] noted that on the slave plantation, the overseer wielded extreme power as he ensured the profits of the plantation by deciding when enslaved people would rise, eat, work, rest, when they could talk, or even entertain themselves.

He purchased food for the enslaved people and bought and distributed materials for work. He "could disrupt family relationships, decide or suggest who should be bought or sold."

Enslaved women lived in fear of his sexual attacks. Men and women endured the lash or worse, as the overseer had absolute power over them: they were the managers of slavery. As such, they were involved in the buying and selling and subjugation of the enslaved people under their power. Under conditions of slavery, then, the enslaved were treated as chattel, had "no independent social existence [except in relation to the master, and] hence no public worth."[57] It was not necessary for the master–overseer to foster relationships or recognize feelings with nonpersons who were only necessary for pleasure, status, and profit.

BACKGROUND TO MY OWN JAMAICAN STORY

The Stipendiary Magistrate Father, Enforcer of Slavery Apprenticeship Laws

Abolition of slavery in the Caribbean did not mean the former enslaved could leave the plantations. After the abolition, a period of apprenticeship was created. Presumably to teach the enslaved to manage freedom, apprenticeship in fact give slave owners time to get the last bit of work out of the former slaves. Former slaves were required to work for over forty hours weekly on the plantation for a period of six years for field-workers and four years for domestic slaves. During this period, slaveholders also had the chance to use the forty million pounds compensation from the British government to set up alternate systems of labor and production.[58]

Stipendiary magistrates were "introduced in the British Caribbean to oversee the Apprenticeship System."[59] Supposedly impartial, stipendiary magistrates, appointed from Britain, were accustomed to rough conditions and used to enforcing discipline. Many of them, however, were bribed by the planters to use their power to enforce cruel and harsh punishment on the former slaves, especially those who resisted apprenticeship. Planters were angry and bitter about emancipation, so there was "planter coercion and exploitation [during] the apprenticeship period."[60] Sherlock and Bennett report on the cruelty of the magistrates during the apprenticeship period, with an example from an account of an apprentice in Jamaica, who, while hiding, was captured by the police:

> [The magistrate] had me handcuffed and sent me to Penshurst, and put me in dungeon for ten days before he try me. . . . Then he sentenced me to St Ann's Bay Workhouse, for nine days, to get fifteen lashes in going in; to

> dance the treadmill morning and evening, and work in the penal gang; and after I come back from punishment, I must lock up every night in dungeon till he visit the property again, and I have to pay fifty days out of my own time for the time I been runaway.[61]

At the workhouse the apprentice was given fifteen lashes with the cat-o-nine tails and chained to the neck of another man.

The description of the overseer stipendiary magistrate is not an unrelated fact of history for me. My own story includes fathers who were cruel, detached, and unloving. I am descended from an overseer or stipendiary magistrate who, according to family legend, came to Jamaica from Scotland at the behest of Queen Victoria. Memory of the elders of my family diverge as to what my great-great-grandfather arrived from Scotland to do in Jamaica. One account is that my he was an overseer, another that he was a stipendiary magistrate. In fact, historical records[62] indicate that he was a magistrate. Perhaps during colonial Jamaica, it was possible to have both roles. The behaviors of men who were overseers and magistrates demonstrate the actions of men who were driven by cruelty and control. Their mindset and behaviors impacted my life four generations later.

My Own Story: The Legacy of a Powerful, Unloving Father and Overseer/Magistrate Great-Great-Grandfather

The vestiges of the powerful unloving father–master or overseer or magistrate are seen in the current behaviors of some fathers who abandon their children. This type of fathering is rooted in the emotionally blunted, detached, unfeeling, and uncaring father who sells his children for profit, or who exercises laws that are cruel and unjust. The descendants of the powerful unloving father are alive today. Cause and effect is difficult to prove, but this type of fathering behavior may explain the behavior of my own father. My experience with my own emotionally detached father is the main reason I am writing this book. All my life I struggled to understand my father's emotional aloofness and lack of empathetic fathering toward my siblings and me.

One of my elder uncles reported that my great-great-grandfather was an overseer on a sugar estate in Jamaica, arriving from Scotland with his English wife immediately after the abolition of slavery. He and his wife had to contend with the harsh, unfamiliar conditions of Jamaica. As overseer, my great-great-grandfather had to get reluctant, underpaid, hostile workers in the part slavery–part freedom period, to produce on the sugar plantation.[63]

My great-great-grandfather stepped into the role of overseer/magistrate making sure that the profits of the still owners of the plantations were guaranteed.

Stories of my great-great-grandfather who arrived from the United Kingdom with his wife were not discussed in my family. My father has no memories of him or stories about him, and my oldest uncle (eighty-seven) with the clearest memory of his great-grandfather repeats that he was an "overseer for the sugar plantation in St. Thomas [Jamaica]." They called him "busha," the Jamaican term for overseer.[64] My eighty-seven-year-old uncle repeats this as though in and of themselves the terms "overseer" and "busha" explain everything.

Another telling of my paternal ancestry is from a cousin who researched documents and interviewed a ninety-eight-year-old distant cousin, who reported that my grandfather's grandfather was in fact a stipendiary magistrate who arrived in Jamaica to oversee apprenticeship. He at some point fathered three children with a formerly enslaved woman (both my uncle and my distant cousin agree on this), and that grandfather's father repeatedly stated that his mother was a "Black slave woman."

I believe my great-great-grandfather's attitude toward the newly emancipated Black people impacted his relationship with his own children. In addition, he abandoned his three children born to the slave woman and returned to Scotland, where he later died. The life of the three children born to my single great-great-grandmother in 1800s Jamaica is unknown to me. However, accounts of her son, father to my grandfather, are that he was a bitter, unhappy, and unloving man who did not demonstrate love for his five children. He was very focused on money and owned large tracts of land in Jamaica.

I recall my grandfather, his son, as impatient, detached, and uninvolved with his own children and certainly uninvolved with us, his grandchildren. I believe he learned this detachment and "lovelessness" from his own bitter father. My grandfather grew up with a father who inherited the legacy of pain of abandonment and an attitude of cold detachment toward enslaved Black people from his own "busha/magistrate" father—my great-great-grandfather

I recall my siblings' and my visits to our grandfather's house, visits that were orchestrated by my mother as she attempted to force our father to see us, connect with us, and provide for us. Our father stayed away and remained physically and emotionally distant from my siblings and me all our lives. As adults, and now responsible for his care, we have asked him why he abandoned us, causing us to suffer as our single mother struggled to feed, clothe, and send us to school. He has no clear answer; his responses are vague, unsatisfying. But he is adamant, stating repeatedly, "I never meant to hurt you children." Still, there is nothing he can say to erase the pain of abandonment my siblings felt over the years.

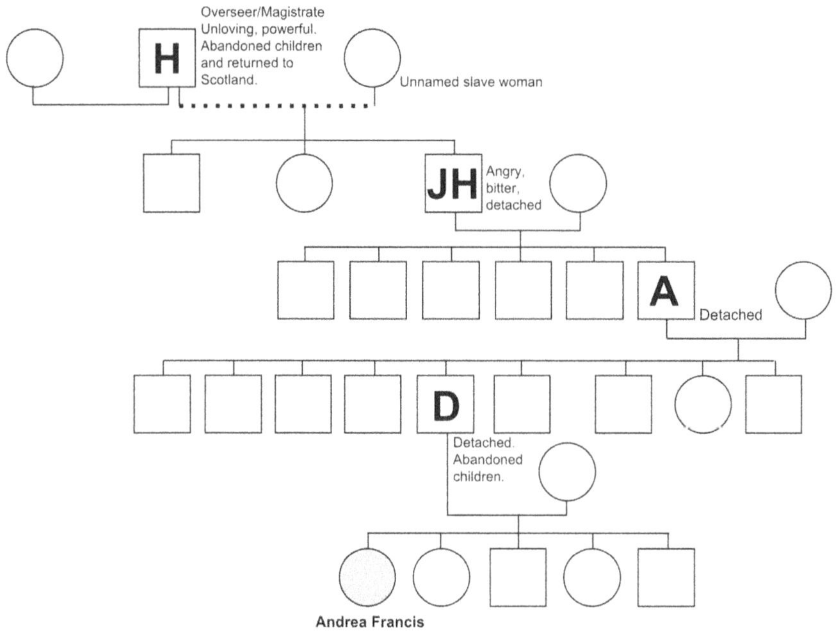

Figure 6.1 Author's paternal genogram.

Figure 6.1 is a genogram that diagrams the relationships in my family on my father's side. The 1839 Jamaica Almanac[65] records Henry Laidlaw—my great-great-grandfather (H) on the genogram—listed under Assistant Judges and Magistrates in the parish of St. Mary, Jamaica. The genogram begins with Henry (H) and wife arrived from Scotland. It shows Henry fathering two sons and a daughter with an unnamed enslaved woman. So far, family legend has not revealed a name for my great-great-grandmother. The third child (JH), described as angry and mean, married a white woman and fathered six sons from whom he was reported to have been aloof and detached. The last of JH's children is my grandfather (A), who subsequently married a Black woman and fathered nine children—eight boys and one girl. My father is identified on the genogram as middle child (D). He married my mother, a Black woman. I am the eldest of the five children of their union.

ANOTHER TYPE OF FATHERING ROOTED IN SLAVERY: BLACK MAN AS BREEDER

Another form of fathering prevalent during the time of slavery was the practice of forced reproduction or "breeding." In fact, "she a breed"[66] is a derogatory term still used in Jamaica to describe a woman who is pregnant by an unknown or absent man. The Black man's role as "breeder" has had significant impact on current fathering. During enslavement, some men were set apart from their families and communities because they possessed desirable attributes[67] that they would pass to the children they fathered. Former enslaved man Willie Williams remembered a man who was put with five women after being checked by the doctor. The man did no work but was "the husban' for dem all . . . cause the marster anxious to raise good, big niggers, de kind what am able to do lots of work and able to sell for heaps of money."[68]

Men were also "abroad" fathers living on other plantations, sold away from their families because of their ability to impregnate. Other men were rented out and used to father children with women living on other plantations as well. Foster notes, "[forced] reproduction divided men along lines of fertility and virility, isolated men who were prolific, and fractured families and communities."[69] In addition, smaller men who were deemed less virile were shamed by the slave master in the presence of the women and the community. Foster noted that "men who were undesirable were prevented from fathering children. Smaller men [were] devalued. One Tennessee slave woman remarked that a 'scrubby' would not be permitted to father children."[70]

The high value placed on prolific men is remarked on by former enslaved woman Ida Blackshear Hutchinson. Hutchinson notes, my "Grandfather on my father's side, Luke Blackshear, was a stock Negro. Luke was the father of fifty-six children and was known as the GIANT BREEDER (sic). He was bought and given to his young mistress in the same way you would give a mule or colt to a child."[71]

The stories of enslaved Black people in the United States testify time and time again that not only was the practice of forcing couples together common, but men and women who did not choose each other were forced to have intercourse to reproduce. If they refused, they were forced to do so in the presence of their owner under the punishment of the lash or worse.

> On this plantation were more than 100 slaves who were mated indiscriminately and without any regard for family unions. If their master thought that a certain man and woman might have strong, healthy offspring, he forced them to have sexual relation, even though they were married to other slaves. If there seemed to be any slight reluctance on the part of either of the unfortunate ones, "Big Jim" would make them consummate this relationship in his presence. He used the same procedure if he thought a certain couple was not producing children fast enough.[72]

Frederick Douglass, famed abolitionist and former enslaved, recalled that his overseer Covey purchased a woman "breeder and [after] buying her, he hired a married man of Mr. Samuel Harrison, to live with [her only]; and him, he used to fasten up with her every night! . . . The result was, that, at the end of the year, the miserable woman gave birth to twins." Covey, he explains, was highly pleased both with the man and the wretched woman."[73]

This practice of forced reproduction was common business practice and is recorded in narratives of enslaved Black people, in wills of slave owners, and in other documents. Some owners of enslaved Black people forced not only couples but groups of young people to reproduce. Ida Blackshear Hutchinson recalled: "Once on the Blackshear place, they took all the fine looking boys and girls that was thirteen years old or older and put them in a big barn after they had stripped them naked. They used to strip them naked and put them in a big barn every Sunday and leave them there until Monday morning. Out of that came sixty babies."[74]

We can well imagine that young adolescents coming to an understanding of their own bodies and sexuality would experience a range of complicated emotions as they engaged in forced couplings. The hedonistic nature of this forced weekly event violated the experiences of intimacy and bonding, especially since the known expectation was for reproduction; the intimate act of sexual connection reduced to forced orgy, and one that must produce results. Young people in this forced debasement learned to detach from connecting with each other in affection. Girls learned that ultimately the resulting pregnancy pleased the master. Boys in particular learned to enjoy the pleasures of copulation without the expectation of real responsibility for their partners or offspring—learning instead to be proud of a sexual prowess that generated children and ultimately pleased the slave master. Sex was a means to producing valuable property for the master. Indeed, Ida Blackshear Hutchinson reports the yield, "out of that came sixty babies."[75]

The human need to attach and form bonds of relationships through trust, affection, and love were undermined by the brutality of the dehumanizing forced breeding. When girls became impregnated, there was a limit to their involvement in forced breeding—they were now carrying profit in their bodies; boys however, were forced to continue coupling. Boys learned the value of their sexual prowess and fertility. They were trained, expected and rewarded from an early age to couple with and impregnate as many girls as possible. Forced coupling made it extraordinarily difficult for boys as they matured into manhood—and still prized for their sexual prowess to make profit—to manage and sustain stable intimate relationships. For the boys—their natural human need to connect and attach to form bonds of kinship and love would conflict with their learned and rewarded behavior of moving on to the next partner. Children born of forced couplings would also learn about relationships and what to expect from the opposite sex. In this type of slave environment, girls learned about serial partners, while boys learned about serial fathering. This type of complex male–female relationship is evident in the present-day pattern of serial fathering in some families of descendants of enslaved people.

RESIDUAL HISTORICAL LINKAGES EXPLAIN WHY SOME FATHERS LEAVE

Edin and Nelson's study on fathers identifies a pattern of "serial fatherhood where a man's children are spread across multiple partners."[76] Present-day men in this situation wrestle with modern expectations of fatherhood—that children should be cared for by their fathers. As a result, a father today "hopes he will manage, through . . . pricey trial and error, to finally father at least one child well."[77] Under pressure, the father fights to connect with his children and to parent according to the expected norms of contemporary society. However, he struggles against his own experiences, patterns of bonding with intimate partners, and others behaviors inculcated by family and tradition.

It is important to note that modern-day serial fathering described by Edin and Nelson describes one pattern of fathering prevalent today that was also prevalent during slavery in the United States and in the African diaspora. Caribbean fathers, as the descendants of enslaved Black men, also experienced the assault on their stable family relations. During slavery, historian Orlando Patterson notes, "the role of father and husband and indeed all other significant males roles [were destroyed]; this was even true of the slave gulags of the Caribbean archipelago."[78] Patterson further adds that while this male emasculation did not lead to "matriarchy," it did change the position of women in relation to men, a change already set in motion by the particular circumstances of socialization on the plantation."[79]

Enslaved girls grew up believing they were equal to boys. The same was true for the enslaved in both America and the Caribbean with kinship connections through the female line "because paternal kin lines were weak under slavery. [Slavery] bred distrust in gender relations, especially on the part of men."[80] Men could not be sure their offspring was theirs, since women could be impregnated by other men including their captors. Patterson further says that "the male slave was placed in an impossible situation, one bound to reduce him to a state of chronic jealousy and insecurity about women."[81]

Arguably, then, significant patterns of fathering inculcated during the centuries of enslavement laid the foundation for some present-day fathers leaving their children. The first, the powerless Black father, was broken under the pressures of slavery that directly attacked and erased his fatherhood, forcing him to a state of learned helplessness. The second, the white father who disconnected and detached from his children because of emotional blunting, saw his children in economic terms, as a return on investment. The third, the "serial father," was valued for his ability to father children and had little connection to them. The vestiges of these patterns of fathering manifest themselves in the behaviors of men who abandon their children today. For example, the intersection of residual effects of the problematic serial fathering and modern-day expectations of fatherhood could explain the behavior of entertainer Rapper Future, who is the father of several children with different women. Future has been sued by at least three of the mothers of his children for failure to pay child support and for emotional stress. His behavior has been the subject of intense scrutiny in the current "callout culture" as he is being pressured to "man up" in popular media.[82]

The vignette below describes my interaction with middle schooler Tyon. His father Tyronne is a serial father.

Figure 6.2 following is Tyon's genogram. It shows the complex web of Tyronne's intimate relationships with women identified as #1 - #5 and the 7 children that resulted from these intimacies.

Tyon: A Middle School Youth Learning the Game

Tyon is the seventh child of father Tyronne. Tyronne's other six children are with four other women all of whom live away from him. Tyronne tries to see Tyon as often as he can. Recently, their contact is by telephone as Tyon lives in another state. Tyon's mother is very hostile toward Tyronne for unresolved hurts in their relationship and for inconsistent child support payments. Tyon struggles academically but is very popular with students and staff as he is attractive, outgoing, charming, and athletic. He recently came to my attention because of altercations between female students for his affections. As Tyon sat with me, he was charming. He expressed concern about the disruption the recent fights between girls has caused the school community, but shrugged as he explained that it's not really his fault that girls fight over him—and in reality he had broken off the relationship with J a long time ago, but because she is jealous when she sees him with D, she starts drama. He was matter-of-fact when he decided that he was over D too and was moving on. Tyon said he was close to his dad, who talks with him almost every day. He said he is also close to his fifteen-year-old brother because they are so close in age. When he is able, Tyronne spends time with both sons going to ball games. He encourages the relationship between them and teaches him and his brother how to handle girls.

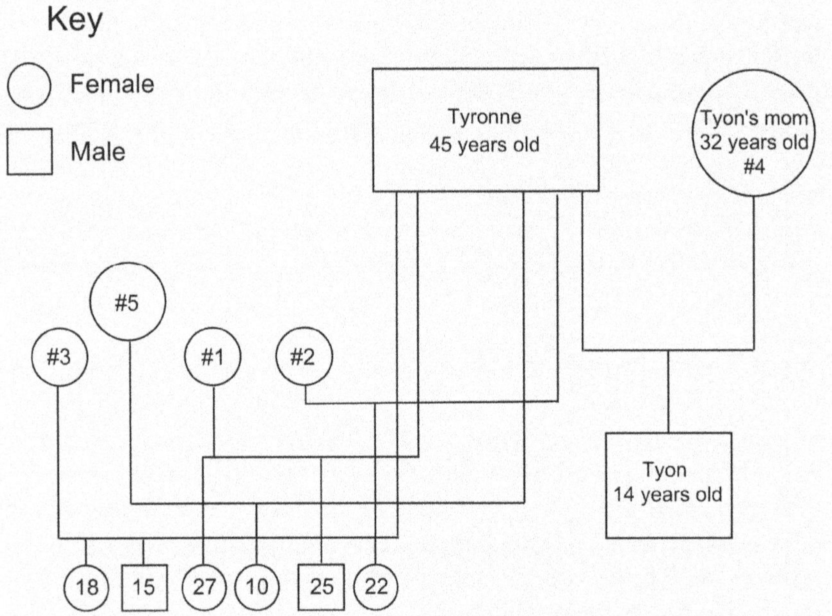

Figure 6.2 Tyon's genogram of half-siblings on his father's side.

DISCUSSION OF TYON AND THE CONCEPT OF SERIAL FATHERING

Tyon's genogram or basic family tree shows that his father could be described as a serial father. The pattern of fathering children and the resulting dissatisfaction of the mothers and their pressure for more than Tyronne was able to give forced him to leave. In addition, Tyronne started on the path to fatherhood at a young age, fathering his first child at eighteen. The stress of young fatherhood without the maturity to manage the responsibilities of parenthood inevitably leads to unhappiness.

Tyronne's serial fathering behaviors echo those of men described by Edin and Nelson.[83] This pattern also echoes the behavior of men centuries before, discussed above, who were valued for their virility, and bought and sold to father as many children as possible. In addition, Tyronne's fourteen-year-old son Tyon appears to have the attractiveness that makes him interesting to teenage girls. Whether he will develop empathy and learn responsible behavior toward women remains to be seen. As a teenage boy, the power of his charm is heady as he is well aware that he is popular and desirable, so much so that young teenage girls fight each other for his attention and affections.

The legacy of slavery means that men who are present-day descendants of slaves must work hard to overcome vestiges of mistrust and lack of connection to their partners, behaviors rooted in enslavement. As previously discussed, relationships were contrived by the master, with the slaves' role of father attacked and erased. Sex and intimacy were transactions. Present-day fathers grapple with maintaining norms of loving, stable parenting, in contrast to the predecessor stud father who was not needed for any emotional and functional support, but for his prolific virility.

Responsible fatherhood today is mitigated by centuries of enslavement that had an immensely damaging impact on families. Marriage between Black couples was illegal, and bonds between children and their parents were brutally, routinely, and systematically severed, with children and parents sold to other masters. Fathers and mothers struggled to maintain the close bonds with their children, often to their peril. Husbands lived on other plantations and in many cases needed permission to visit their wives. Fathers were barred from having any custodial claim on their children, who like them, were property, nonpersons, bred, bought, and sold at the whim of their owners.[84]

Slavery has been long past, and relations between Black men and women are measured by the white-standard societal ideal of the nuclear family. However, the Black family cannot simply shake off the vestiges of slavery as though the systematic assault on Black families did not occur. For some Black men, disconnecting from past patterns of fathering is not easy. They abandon their children, unconsciously repeating behaviors rooted in slavery.

However, the psychological impact of slavery did not only take its toll on the enslaved Black community. The toll on the slave-master owner–father, white men who practiced contradictory fathering behaviors, also would be immense. One set of children, the Black, were unloved nonpersons, dispensable commodities—bought, sold, bartered away. The other children, the white, were seen as persons worthy of attachment and care. The psychological repercussions of the slave-master father's dichotomous responses to his two sets of children not only impacted the children but his society for generations to come. Study of the psychological impact on the descendants of men who enslaved their children would shed further light on attachment-detachment behaviors of enslaver-fathers toward both their enslaved Black and their free white children.

Domestic Hostilities Keep Dads Away

Domestic tensions and hostilities between fathers and mothers of their children are another factor that keeps fathers away. Edin and Nelson assessed the behavior of the deadbeat dad as a man who is trying to parent his children but is faced with challenges both within himself and from a society that despises him.[85] These fathers separate themselves from their children's mothers and try to focus on parenting their children despite her hostility and a disapproving society. Edin and Nelson's interviews with unwed fathers in Camden, New Jersey, and Philadelphia, found that some men are initially not fully committed to their sexual partners. The relationship is casual, tenuously held together by romance with no firm commitment on the man's part.

When pregnancy results from the relationship, men are excited at the idea of fatherhood and dream of an idyllic "nuclear" family, the ideal. The men imagine themselves spending time with their child, as a "time for redemption, and a chance to nurture a better image of themselves."[86] This "accidental" fatherhood causes an urgent need for the men try to care for and support their children. However, they lack mature emotional connection to the mothers, and possess limited economic and psychological preparation for the fathering role. Viable fatherhood in these conditions is unsustainable.

For instance, a man will quickly find that his pregnant girlfriend is very practical in her expectations of financial and emotional obligations. Romance is soon replaced by the drudgery of day-to-day pre- and postnatal child care needs. Edin and Nelson report that the demands of the child's mother become increasingly unbearable and therefore unattainable, shattering the man's fantasy of the perfect family.[87] "The sudden change in a woman's expectations may, in fact, be read as a betrayal, conclusive evidence that she is lacking in commitment, willing to throw him over as soon as he fails to meet her mounting demands. Men often counter with the charge that their new baby's mother is an overbearing know-it-all."[88]

Unable to meet the demands, feeling like nothing more than a paycheck,[89] men leave mothers while still craving a connection with their children. They drift from one relationship to the next, leaving children behind. With each new relationship they begin the cycle of fantasy—of the perfect family. With each new relationship and the subsequent demands from their child's mother, the man's disappointment continues. Based on the fathers' stories, it may be inferred that the motives behind men leaving their children is rooted in their immaturity and unpreparedness for the realities of fatherhood and lack of commitment to a strong partnership with the mothers. In addition, current pastime activities such as online video gaming keep young fathers in an immature state of distraction that reduces the time they work and spend time on family obligations.[90]

Edin and Nelson argue that some fathers, with limited education and subsequently limited earnings, struggle with feelings of inadequacy, being unable to provide for their family. It is also true that most of these men's familial and economic resources are also poor. They struggle with their own pasts, which are "often sources of continued trauma, rather than emotional sustenance. . . . [Their histories are] punctuated by a series of failures—at school, at the workplace, [and] in relationships."[91] The fathers' internal conflicts are the inevitable consequence of fathering patterns discussed earlier. The pattern of helplessness, rootlessness, and disconnection are results of the perfect storm of social and economic forces colluding against their ability to father their children positively.

Baumeister[92] asserts that although men desire closeness to their children, they struggle against societal pressures that depict them as useless and unnecessary for children's well-being.[93] In addition, when fathers have low levels of parenting self-efficacy, they tend to allow mothers to manage parenting.[94] Single mothers are depicted as strong and capable of managing without the help of the father. Popular media reinforces the biased notion of the useless father with images of the hapless comedic dad, in contrast to the wise, stable, capable mother. Not only does the hapless dad reinforce gender stereotypes of women being better at raising children, but also it alienates men who want to be involved with their children. Recently, there has been pushback against this image. Chad Prevost argues in the *Washington Post* that the image of the bumbling dad is passe and not in keeping with current trends of the rising numbers of stay-at-home fathers who positively parent their children.[95]

Gatekeeper Mother

It is no wonder that domestic hostilities result from the disappointment both fathers and mothers feel about the father's inability to meet expectations. Mothers take charge of the children and feel justified in managing the "trifling" father's connection with their children.[96] Recognition of and demands for dad's involvement in their children's lives are increasing. Organizations such as the National Fatherhood Initiative have identified how mothers' gate-keep, in effect, blocking father's access to their children. Mothers who are gatekeepers usually have perfectionist expectations of the father's ability to parent children,[97] and in effect block fathers and any possibility of a good relationship. Gatekeeping mothers believe that as mothers, they innately possess higher levels of parenting skills than their children's fathers. The mothers also deeply distrust the fathers' ability to manage childcare, and are especially restrictive of the fathers if they demonstrate low self-efficacy or low self-confidence with regard to childcare. Gatekeeper mothers have poor psychological functioning and are anxiously wedded to traditional gender roles of parenting. Such mothers are also likely to block fathers if they feel insecure romantically about their relationship with the father.[98] In an attempt to avoid conflicted feelings, whether romantic or sexual, mothers exert power and control by managing fathers' access to their children. Therefore, if a mother feels confident in her childcare abilities but lacks confidence in her relationship with the child's father, she asserts power by managing his access to their child.[99] This mother in effect uses her child as a buffer between herself and her emotional–romantic insecurities with the father.

Melissa Steward of the National Fatherhood Initiative[100] explains that gatekeeping mothers control the relationship by making negative comments directly to or in front of the children. The comments foster emotions that encourage the children to distance themselves from dads. Mothers also deliberately withhold, purge, manipulate school records and information about school activities, health records, extracurricular activities, and social life events to prevent fathers from participating in the lives of their children. Mothers further gate-keep by criticizing dad's ability to parent effectively. Custodial mothers often feel they are closer to their children than the fathers, and therefore know what's best for the children, while the father does not. Mothers with strong negative feelings toward their children's father also engage in power struggles with him, unfortunately increasing parental conflict and their children's suffering.

The powerful blocking role of the gatekeeping mother is so concerning that the National Fatherhood Initiative *Mother as Gateway* project devoted workshops with full curriculum to encourage mothers to allow safe, nonviolent fathers into the lives of their children. The "Understanding Dad" curriculum encourages mothers to explore their own lived experiences as daughters, and their relationship with their own fathers. Mothers are also trained to manage their own strong feelings about the separation from children's fathers. They learn skills to actively co-parent and are taught to recognize ways they can help fathers engage positively with their children.[101]

SOCIAL SERVICES BLOCK DADS, TOO

Social services were created to support families in ensuring the best interests of the children. However, experiences with social services leave fathers feeling sidelined and powerless in major areas of their children's lives including child support and parenting decisions.[102] Black and Latinx fathers have also experienced a lower rate of connection with their children as social workers were unlikely to seek them out in family reunification processes.[103] In addition, men reported that they desired respectful and fair treatment by caseworkers, but many fathers felt judged and felt that caseworkers took the mother's side before meeting them.[104] Social service gatekeeping only served to keep fathers away from their children and increased hostilities between them and their children's mother.[105]

The marginalization of nonresident fathers was confirmed by caseworkers who admitted that such fathers were given scant regard by the social service system, which reinforced their position on the periphery of their children's lives. Most services were directed to supporting mothers, while nonresident fathers were treated with suspicion and received severe consequences for dereliction of duty.[106] Further, because fathers felt unfairly treated, they did not seek services and avoided the social service system altogether. Frustrated by the system, fathers had low tolerance for the obstacles to services. Social service caseworkers confirmed that they recognized that mothers were often gatekeepers who frustrated nonresident fathers and interfered with their attempts to access services for their children.[107] Despite this admission, they did little to disrupt the negative dynamics.

In addition, caseworkers were also less likely to locate and unite Black and Latinx fathers with their children.[108] Social workers' own gendered attitudes toward fathers also blocked men from their children. Female social workers often see fathers as hostile, threatening, and detached, and may relate to these men based on experiences with their own fathers.[109] As a result, female social workers inadvertently side with and, in effect, support mothers' blocking behaviors, keeping men away from their children.

As an extension of the family support social system, family courts also push fathers out of their children's lives. Kamala Harris's father Professor Emeritus Donald Harris, recalls his own experiences with the family court system:

> The early phase of interaction with my children came to an abrupt halt in 1972 when, after a hard-fought battle in the family court of Oakland, California, the context of the relationship was placed within arbitrary limits imposed by a court-ordered divorce settlement based on the false assumption by the State of California that fathers cannot handle parenting (especially in the case of this father, "a neegroe of da eyelans" was the Yankee stereotype, who might just end up eating his children for breakfast!). Nevertheless, I persisted, never giving up on my love for my children or reneging on my responsibilities as their father.[110]

Yet, despite gains in equality in childcare, years after Donald Harris's painful separation from his daughters, research by Miller found that judges still make decisions in favor of the mother even if the father is equally or more suited to provide care for his children.[111] Thus, both the judicial and social services, designed to "help" families, operate from a gender-biased view of parenting and, in effect, reinforce the mother's role as gatekeeper by becoming the state gatekeeper and block well-meaning fathers from their children.

Economic Reasons—Dads Need to Work

Economic factors are another reason men leave their children. Men work to provide for their own needs and the needs of their families, and some must leave their children and families to find work. For these men, the need to find the means for paying bills and fulfilling the basic needs of family are powerful motivators. For "adult men (twenty years and older) the employment [to] population ratios for Asian men and White men were approximately seventy-three percent and seventy percent, respectively. [While] Hispanic men (seventy-seven percent) continued to have the highest employment–population ratio. Black men (sixty-four percent) had the lowest [employment to population ratio], continuing a longstanding pattern."[112]

That Black men have the lowest employment of all men in the United States is troubling; however, an alternate reading of this figure could be that Black men participate more in the informal sector than other groups. The informal sector—off-the-books work provides ease of entry and flexible hours, making multiple jobs or the "hustle" possible. Work in the informal sector also allows for more disposable income since workers there do not report their earnings and avoid paying taxes[113] and child support.

While leaving is difficult, men in relationships are more willing to move to find work than women who live with a male partner.[114] Even if a man is in a satisfying domestic living situation, he is likely to move for better job opportunities, so strong is his desire to be a good provider. Women demonstrate more unwillingness to move, and actually "reject profitable moves more than men."[115] Perhaps women bear more of the burdens of the domestic responsibilities and are constrained by their attitudes toward traditional gendered roles in relation to family. Women appear to be more aware of the costs of moving than men.[116] According to *Glassdoor*, "men are also more likely to move metros. After controlling for job titles, education and age, men are three percentage points more likely to apply to jobs in another metro than women."[117]

Further, men move to different countries to find work. In 2020, 77 percent of foreign-born men were sixteen years and older and participated in the labor force at a considerably higher rate than their native-born counterparts, who made up 67 percent of the labor force.[118] Fifty-three percent of foreign-born women worked this way at a lower rate versus native-born women, who made up 57 percent of the labor force. Importantly, 93 percent of the foreign-born men who made up the labor force in 2020 were fathers with children under eighteen years of age.[119]

Millie: Dad Left to Find Work

When fathers leave their children to find work, their leaving is mourned, especially if the mother becomes involved in a new relationship. Middle schooler Millie expressed her strong feelings to me as she sat in my office. She came to see me to get away from class, where she felt she was about to explode from anger and frustration. Her anger, directed at her mother, made it hard for her to focus on school. Millie described her mother as a hypocrite who insisted that Millie remain involved in faith-based activities, stay away from boys, and come straight home. Yet her mother did not wait to get involved with another man as soon as her father left the state to find work. Visibly upset, Millie explained how she feels physically sick when through the shared wall, she hears her mother and her boyfriend being intimate at night. Millie admits that her mother's boyfriend helps with the bills and the groceries; however, while she grieves for her absent dad, she also grieves the lost closeness between her mother and herself.

Millie's father had to go, as employment prospects meant leaving his daughter and her mother to find the means to pay the bills. His leaving to find work came at the high price of not only physical separation from his family, but the loss of emotional connection to his grieving daughter. Millie at an intellectual level understands that dad had to go find work, and understands mom's need for companionship and perhaps immediate help with the bills—filling gaps left behind. Millie nonetheless deeply mourns her father, feeling abandoned by him. She must cope with dad's absence and the intrusive presence of mother's new man. Dad's absence not only creates an emotional void in Millie's life, but means he is not able to effectively partner her mother either.

DONOR FOR CONCEPTION

Since most donors do not think of themselves as parents to their donor offspring,[120] how can a man who donated his sperm for conception be accused of abandoning his child? The argument of this book is that it is the experience or *feelings* of the child in response to the action of the parent that determines abandonment. So while the adult may not understand their behavior as abandonment, their offspring *experience* that behavior as making them feel forgotten, left behind, and not mattering.[121]

When single mother Janis brought her eleven-year-old daughter Lainey to see me, it was for the very reason of giving Lainey a space to voice her hurt, disappointment, and confusion about being donor conceived. Janis decided to tell Lainey about her conception before she entered middle school. The outcome was that in the summer Janis noticed Lainey becoming restless and moody. Lainey expressed her "understanding" with a barrage of questions including, "Am I normal? How much did I cost? He did not care, he just gave his sperm?" Janis struggled to explain how much *she* loved Lainey and how badly she wanted a child; but this failed to assuage Lainey's feelings of confusion and abandonment by her donor father.

Although children respond in different ways when they understand that they were donor conceived, experts advise that it is best that children are informed early in life, at least before age seven.[122] The earlier children are told about the circumstances of their conception, the more positive their well-being at adolescence and the closer their family relationships.[123] Children view their donor as a whole person rather than a sperm donor. He is seen as an "imagined father" who can teach the child about his or her identity and ancestry.[124]

Donor fathers, on the other hand, have mixed views on wanting to connect with their "children." Their expectations range from not wanting a close personal relationship with their offspring to being curious about or wanting one.[125] Men, after all, donated their sperm for a variety of reasons, the most common of which is wanting to help others and having the desire to procreate without wanting their own children.[126] Some men who were already parents wanted others to experience and enjoy parenting but did not want the responsibility of being an active parent.[127] In the past, donors expected anonymity, but with the increase in DNA family search and family find sources such as 23andMe, children who were donor conceived are locating their donor fathers, with mixed results.[128]

How can a donor father be said to have abandoned his child? The words of Alana Newman[129] explain. At age five her mother told her about her conception, and that she would never be able to locate her donor father. Newman spent years reconciling her life history, one filled with shame and anger. She comments:

> In my view, third-party reproduction is not a new way to create families; it's a new way to rip them apart. Like slavery, there are many profiteers in the infertility business making large sums of cash taking children away from their natural parents. The problems of toxic shame, anger, and poverty will compound. The fertility community will be perplexed. "Why are these kids so angry?" they will ask. My answer, born from my own experience and the experiences of other donor-conceived children, is simple: "Because you obliterated our fathers."

Children suffer because they feel a piece of who they are is missing or erased. Even with loving mothers, donor-conceived children experience curiosity about their fathers and grapple with the fact that they came to be because of the anonymity of donor conception. It is a very painful conversation that a mother has with her adolescent child who, in attempts at finding self, must accept the donor status of "dad." Children feel that they do not matter to the donor father. He abandoned them when he decided to become a donor. Again, this is a complicated issue and is tied to a woman's choice to mother a child through a donor. The reasons, of course, vary as to why a woman chooses this path, but the consequence is that the child, if not informed early, will suffer profound feelings of shame and loss.

As donor-conceived children mature, they want to know who their fathers are.[130] They seek them out, hunt them down, and create social groups with half-siblings, seeking connection to him. Ravelingien, Provoost, and Pennings found that donor-conceived children had

> at least 7 different objectives [that] can underlie the wish to know [their] donor: to avoid medical risks and consanguineous relationships; to connect with one's roots; to complete one's life (hi-)story; to understand where one's traits come from; to discover or assess one's defining characteristics and capabilities; to rectify a wrong-doing, and to map out one's ancestral history.[131]

Simply put, some children felt they began to know themselves through knowing the other half of themselves. Children's knowledge of their father has significant impact on their achieving self-knowledge. Knowing who their fathers were helped them understand their worth within the context of familial relationships. Even where children have a loving, caring mother and/or other caregiver(s), they want to know, even if father turns out to be a disappointment, or a less than ideal man.

Pappas reported[132] that the United States has no regulation outlawing anonymous donation, while in the United Kingdom, the practice was outlawed in 2005. Advocates for donor-conceived children are adamant that the right to know their donor identity "can be identity-confirming in its own right."[133] Knowing who their donor father is helps children know themselves. Further, "searching for one's biological origins is a typical urge, and a deep desire to know about genetic history does not indicate that a person is rejecting the family that raised him or her. Second, the earlier families are open about origins the healthier they seem to be."[134] Mothers utilize donor conception to help her or herself and her partner conceive a baby.[135] But babies grow up and as they mature will be naturally curious and ask questions about their ancestry. The questions are really a search to be anchored or grounded in their ancestral history, and often satisfy the desire to know "who am I?" Donor fathers are uniquely invisible and nonexistent; and because they seem to be abstract constructs, not real, their absence is keenly felt and mourned by their children.

WHY FATHERS ABANDON THEIR CHILDREN

Men abandon their children to heartbreak for historical, social, and economic reasons. Fathers make up a large percentage of men in prison.[136] Many are repeat offenders; and when they leave and return to prison, their children learn with each return home that dad really cannot be trusted, he never keeps his word. In addition, incarcerated men are harshly judged by social services. They feel disrespected and mistrusted.[137] Their time in prison also negatively impacts their relationship with their children's mother.[138]

When the romantic relationship sours, men become disillusioned with the domestic burdens of parenthood. Over time, their children's mother becomes unsympathetic as she is practical in her expectations of material support for their children.[139] Working-class men are particularly vulnerable to feelings of being burdened when they are unable to meet financial needs. While the men separate their financial responsibilities from their relationship with their children, the mothers connect the relationship with the material support. Some fathers would be content to be a presence in their children lives despite not being a strong source of financial support.

Mothers gate-keep or block the relationship between fathers and their children.[140] Even married women who feel they are better able to parent their children block or prevent fathers from parenting their children.[141] Men who doubt their ability to parent are most often blocked by the more confident mother, who is often committed to gender-specific roles. Even when men try to connect with their children, once the legal system is involved, they find themselves blocked and frustrated by social services and a judicial system that most often rule in favor of the mother when there are cases before the courts. Because of prevailing gender role expectations, mothers are routinely awarded custody and fathers are viewed with suspicion and hostility. Men are often misunderstood in their attempts to gain access to their children and are blocked. As the men leave their problems behind, they also leave their children.

Patterns of fathering steeped in historical practices still have influence today.[142] Patterns of the loving but powerless father are evident in fathers who are ineffective but involved in their children's lives. Perhaps the psychological construct of learned helplessness is at play, and result in the systematic stripping of the father of his agency to parent his children during centuries of enslavement. The detached powerful father is another pattern that has its roots in centuries of enslavement. This father is cold, uncaring, and unloving. His relationship with his children is motivated by the philosophy of the return on investment. He remains away from his children because he is unable to foster attachment as he is emotionally and psychologically disconnected from them.

Another fathering pattern nurtured during the centuries of enslavement is the "serial father" created from the practice of breeding,[143] whereby men were forced to propagate to enrich the finances of their owners. A man's worth and indeed ability to remain alive depended on his submitting to being hired out or put with women with the sole purpose to impregnate them. Foster reminds that the "practice of forcing enslaved men to reproduce thus influenced Black manhood during slavery and beyond."[144]

Some men abandon their families to find work. More than women, men are willing to and do leave their homes for this purpose. Men will move across states and across countries to find work either in the formal or informal sector, leaving their children behind. Donors for conception are often not seen as fathers, but their offspring, their children, view them as being integral to their lives and to understanding themselves. Donor dad is the absent missing link. Their offspring children feel abandoned, shamed, and unimportant to their donor father. They go in search of him to connect with him as their father and in so doing attempt to connect with themselves.

The factors that keep fathers away from their children are powerful, pervasive, and complicated. Regardless of the reasons, their children feel abandoned and yearn for connection with them. Abandoned children experience deep emotional struggles that impede their ability to thrive, stunting their capacity to joyfully mature into emotionally balanced individuals. Abandoned children are angry, bitter, confused, frustrated, sad, and in doubting their worth exhibit antisocial behaviors that portend the recurring cycle of grief as they mature, form their own relationships, and become parents themselves.

Therefore, the fact that children yearn for both their parents is natural. Parents and their children are connected from before birth, conceptualized in the "theory of prenatal attachment [that] posits that a unique relationship develops between parents and fetus long before a child is born."[145] Prenatal maternal and paternal attachment to the unborn child is important. To the children I work with, it does not matter if they were abandoned before birth; they feel alone, hurt, shaky, unsafe, and incomplete. Children create responses to the memory gap because they are connected to their parents before birth and feel their absence after.

As Pappas[146] explained, the search for self is a normal process, driven not only by the need to know but by biological attachment to parents. The not knowing and absence of the parent regardless of circumstances of conception are keenly felt by the child, who experiences a lack of completion like a story with missing elements. This missing, not knowing is traumatic—because at its core is the psychological chasm of parental absence, the missing psycho-emotional gap. To fill in the gaps and have the questions answered about a missing parent, children respond with "twoness," a coping mechanism for being left behind. Abandoned children seek connection, feeling like they matter, that they are worthy of love, that they were wanted, that their abandoning parent will turn back and see them, and cherish them as their own.

Figure 6.3 below depicts the reasons fathers abandoned the children and families I interact with in my role as school counselor and in private practice.

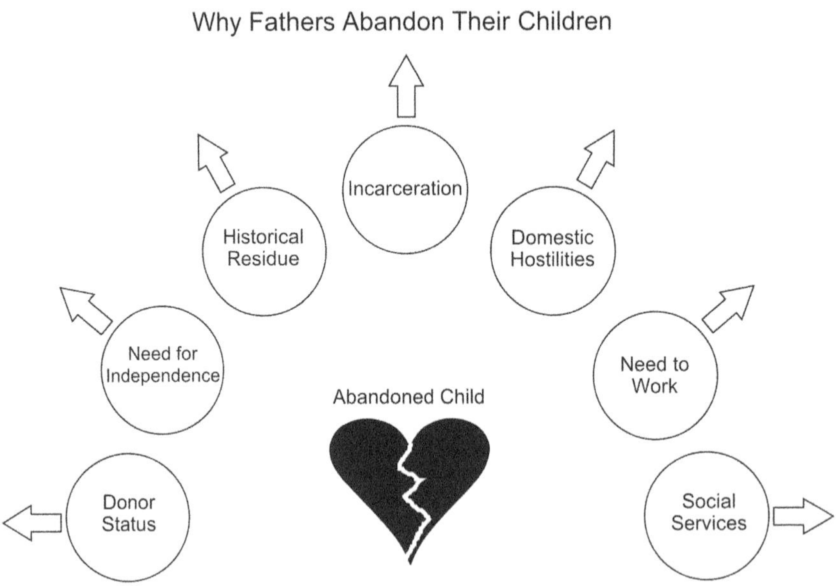

Figure 6.3 Main factors that keep fathers away from their children.

7

Why Both Parents Leave

The attacks on the Twin Towers on September 11, 2001, changed the lives of Americans and indeed people of all parts of the globe forever. The reverberations of that national trauma still have devastating effects even to this day. Siblings Eric, sixteen, and Callie, thirteen, experienced the devastating impact of 9/11 in the most personal way imaginable. Both lived with their mother and father in a comfortable middle-class home when the planes destroyed the Twin Towers. One of those Towers housed the headquarters of the company where their father had been branch manager for over fifteen years. His job was destroyed in an instant, and he never recovered. The children learned to remain quiet as their father raged about the house. Frustrated by yet another resume rejected, a job interview not panning out, or having to work below his expertise and experience, unable to regain his former status at the workplace, with friends, and from his perspective, at home, Eric and Callie's father began to stay out later and later. Always a social drinker, their dad began to drink heavily and indeed became an "ugly, frightening drunk." Callie commented in a sad, low voice, "I don't know my daddy anymore. He is always angry now."

Originally a stay-at-home mom, their mother was able to find work at a department store, but her income was not enough to meet expenses, and their dad was unable to find his way back to his confident, provider self. Eric and Callie witnessed their father, in a fit of frustration and rage, strike their mother as they argued about their mounting debts. The police intervened. Released on bail, Eric and Callie's father walked out of jail and out of their lives. The children watched helplessly as their mother tried to make ends meet by juggling two low-paying jobs while her health deteriorated.

"Mom has a new friend that she stays with sometimes," Callie said. "Eric just stays in his room. He has a lot of friends online. We used to have fun, before. . . ." Her voice trailed off. "I think I am going to have to leave this school. I think soon. I'm going to miss my friends. Mom said something about us living with grandma and grandpa."

Eric and Callie's maternal grandparents did intervene. The children withdrew from the school and went to live with their grandparents, who had the financial stability the children needed. "This was temporary." their children's mother told me. Their house was in foreclosure, and with her juggling two jobs, she decided stay with a male friend until things settled down for her. "I just need a minute when I am not worrying about the children. They'll be fine with my parents."

The destruction of Twin Towers in New York had enormous repercussions at the macro level—impacting economies and global markets. However, at the micro level, the tremendous devastation was felt on one family that deteriorated over time. The deterioration was expressed in the grief and loss of Callie's and Eric's stable family. Both father and mother were unable to withstand the pressures of economic ruin; both eventually walked away from each other and from their children. When the planes destroyed the Twin Towers, their lives started to unravel, and soon the grief of losing both parents would began for Callie and Eric.

PANDEMIC COVID-19 KEEPS MOM AND DAD AWAY

The coronavirus COVID-19 entered our world and changed relationships on a scale unimagined. Children are among the most severely impacted because their parents, caregivers, and close family members were suddenly snatched away by unexplained disappearance or emotional and physical distance and death. Further, the grieving process was disrupted as opportunities to mourn and comfort—rituals of repast, remembrances, or family gatherings—were severely limited and constricted by social distancing rules. Children struggle to make sense of parents who are now detached in quarantine or communicating via technology only—no longer holding or hugging them or actually suddenly completely absent from their lives, taken to the hospital and barred from seeing them because of fears of infection. Many children despite the information overload regarding the coronavirus do not fully grasp what their parents' sudden and harrowing disappearance means. Children are frightened and anxious, uncertain if they will ever return. For some children, the parents never will, snatched away by COVID-19-related deaths.[1]

Similarly, children who spend time in shared custody with one parent who is an essential worker also suffer. Driven by fears of infection, ex-spouses have petitioned courts to be granted sole custody from parents who are firefighters, doctors, nurses, and other essential workers on the front lines. The responses of the courts have varied with the states, with some parents losing custody or having their custodial rights temporarily suspended until stay-at-home orders are lifted in their states[2] or some change occurs in their job placement.[3] Dr. Bertha Mayorquin, a New Jersey physician, for example, lost custody of her eleven- and eight-year-old daughters, regaining rights only after the hospital—her employer—agreed to remove her from direct treatment of COVID-19 patients and allowed her to practice telemedicine. Firefighter Steven Biakanja could not realistically provide the negative coronavirus test results before each scheduled visit to his children. Despite assurances, his worried ex-wife was not convinced that their three children, eleven-year-old twins and a nine-year-old son—would be safe from contracting the virus. After stressful court petitioning, the courts in this instance denied mom Ms. Chu temporary full custody unless Mr. Biakanja exhibited signs of COVID-19.[4] One can imagine the anxiety the twins felt torn between both parents' desires to keep them safe, their parents' inability to agree on what safety looks like, and the ultimate need for an external entity, the court, to make the decision for their parents.

COVID-19 Interrupts Attachment and Child–Parent Bonding

Essential workers who are nursing mothers fear infecting their babies with the coronavirus. Many stayed away from their babies, interrupting critical bonding and attachment. The *New York Times* reported on the agony of essential workers and doctors in daily direct contact with infected COVID-19 patients. Dr. Bhardwaj, a gastroenterology fellow at Lenox Hill Hospital in Manhattan, describes her grief at being unable to physically hold or nurse her child.

"I haven't seen my baby since yesterday," she said. She wondered if the baby would be safer living somewhere else. "I'm so conflicted," she said. She's pumping milk so her in-laws can feed the baby, but she's terrified of getting her child or her in-laws sick.[5] Her husband, also a doctor, tested positive for the virus and lived away from her and the baby, describing another unfortunate effect of the current pandemic on parent–child bonding.

While this family may reunite in the future and the baby will recover from the forced abandonment of its parent—with perhaps little memory of the separation—what is the feeling experienced by older children of other essential workers? Weiss[6] documented that some hospital workers have sent their children to live away from them and voiced the fears of frightened doctors who are writing their wills—leaving the care of their children to family and friends with the provision of moving to the next level of carers in the event of death of the original carers identified in the will.

The experiences of children traumatized by dramatic unexplained separation either by quarantine or death during the Ebola outbreak in 2014 help us understand the fright children faced during the coronavirus pandemic. On comforting children after the Ebola outbreak, a World Bank paper described the negative impact on children's mental health such as sadness, worry, and fear when protective factors such as a nurturing family, the dependable extended family, and stable supports from school and other social organizations like church or sports clubs are destroyed or unavailable.[7] Mercy Corps[8] workers noted that children who faced the trauma of losing loved ones were at risk of depression and anxiety, prolonged worry, not feeling safe, and in danger of fatal self-harm. These children required intense interventions to help them cope with the grief of separation and the feelings of abandonment.

Arlene: She Wants to Go Back Home

Arlene's mother Janice's voice sounded raspy and exhausted. Janice works in a nursing home where several residents came down with COVID-19. A single mom, she must work to pay her bills and to keep everyone safe. Janice sent Arlene and four-year-old Austin to stay with her sister. Arlene has been very upset and angry with her and wants to go back home. However, because the four-year-old is sickly, Janice is refusing to allow him and Arlene back home; she believes it is too risky.

I called to check up on thirteen-year-old Arlene because she had not been attending her virtual classes. Her mother gave me permission to call the aunt's house. The aunt, another kind of essential worker, goes every day to work at the local supermarket. I told Arlene I was just checking in with her and that her teachers and I missed her presence in virtual classes. Arlene explained that she was tired from babysitting her very active brother, but more so, she was upset with not being with her mother. While she understood the worry her mother felt about her and Austin being exposed to the virus, Arlene insisted that she would have helped her mother self-quarantine in their own space. Arlene explained that she loved her aunt but wanted to be home with her mother. Austin also constantly asks about going back home and cries for their mother. He has lately started to kick and throw things around. "I have a hard time controlling him when he gets like that. He never used to do that when we lived with Mommy. Why can't we just go back home?"

Arlene is suddenly thrust into the role of mother for her little brother. Although her aunt is her current carer, Arlene feels the burden of her mother's dependence on her to manage—not only manage Austin but to also manage her changed world. This new world where her mother is staying away from her and Austin because of fears of infection and also her new world of attending school online, where she can't interact with friends, other students, and teachers. Arlene is required to manage her little brother's misbehavior, his own acting out when he cannot verbalize his own fears, worry, and frustration. At thirteen, Arlene lacks the maturity to manage online school, manage her little brother, manage missing her mother, manage the absence of her aunt whose own work as an essential worker causes anxiety as well.

Figure 7.1 indicates that mothers and fathers share common factors that push/pull them away from their children. Shared factors are incarceration and the high rates of recidivism resulting in diminished opportunities for work. Both fathers and mothers suffer mental illnesses, which is often compounded by alcoholism and/or substance abuse. Both leave to find work, and both mothers and fathers suffer the stressors of being too young to parent their children or navigating unforeseen events such as natural or human-made disasters. Interestingly, there is the recent trend of women leaving their children to pursue personal goals. This quest to seek adventure and to "find self" is not new to men and in fact is so embedded in culture and folklore for men that it is taken for granted. Consider folktales and legends of the cowboy riding off into the sunset, the adventurer or swashbuckling pirate on the high seas all seeking fame and fortune. Surely these men left spouses and children behind, but their wanderlust was understood and supported by gendered expectations that women stay and take care of the children, freeing the men to roam.

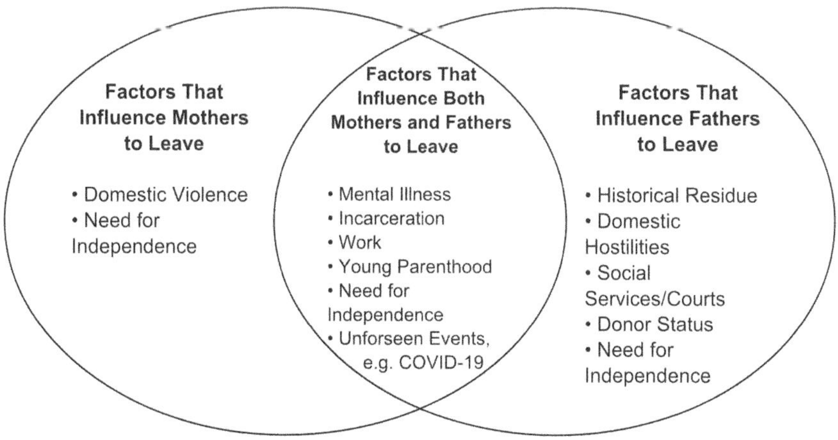

Figure 7.1 Factors that influence parents to abandon their children.

Fathers however, still make up the majority of parents who abandon their children. Fathers do face more factors that encourage abandonment of their children. As discussed, several of the factors are rooted in gendered notions of the role of men in their children's lives, most significantly, the role that social services and the court system play in placing obstacles in the way of men to easily participate in their children's lives. Mothers have high expectations of the fathers of their children and block fathers' access to their children if these expectations are not met. Finally, a detailed assessment of the impact of slavery was discussed and proved to be a significant factor that influences fathers to abandon their children. Patterns of fathering inculcated over generations of enslavement cause some men to disconnect from their children and abandon them even in the present day. The one factor that is unique to women is their fleeing their homes and inadvertently abandoning their children because of domestic violence.

8

Parental Abandonment: Traumatic for Children

Since the 1998 publication of the Centers for Disease Control-Kaiser Permanente Study on Adverse Childhood Experiences (ACE),[1] much more has been understood about the negative impacts of childhood trauma on adult well-being. ACEs are traumatic events that children experience before their eighteenth birthday. These events are personal stressors on a child directly such as physical, verbal, or sexual abuse; physical neglect; and emotional neglect. Other ACEs involve family members whose behavior negatively impacts children such as divorce, abandonment by a parent, mental illness, alcoholism, incarceration, and when a child witnesses domestic violence.

There are many other traumatic events that children face that were not included in the original study,[2] the most recent of which is the COVID-19 pandemic and the subsequent stresses associated with the loss and grief that have resulted from this virus. The ACEs model is a valuable framework for assessing the needs of children traumatized by parental abandonment. Without interventions, children are likely to mature into adulthood impaired by physical and emotional illnesses that lead to early death.[3]

What are the yearnings of children as they try to make sense of being left by their father or mother? A child grieves the severing of attachment to a parent they have never met. Attachment to both parents begins before birth, and children inherit not only physical attributes from their parents and grandparents but emotional and psychological inclinations as well. For instance, the concept that "an individual's experience might alter the cells and behavior of their children and grandchildren"[4] was explored in a study on fathers who were prisoners of war (POWs) during the American Civil War.[5] The impact on the men's descendants provides insight into the connections between ancestors and their children. When the men returned home, "They returned to society with impaired health, worse job prospects and shorter life expectancy. But the impact of these hardships did not stop with those who experienced it. It also had an effect on the prisoners' children and grandchildren, which appeared to be passed down the male line of families."

Thus, even though their sons and grandsons did not experience the hardships of the POW camps, the trauma of the experience impacted the physical and psychological health of other sons and grandsons. Sons and grandsons suffered higher rates of death from cancer and cerebral hemorrhage than their daughters and granddaughters. Sons of the Civil War POWs "were 1.11 times more likely to die than sons of non-POWS."[6] It is important to note that the sons of POWs who fared better than their peers had mothers who had had good nutrition and likely healthier well-being.[7] Costa notes, "There is an awful lot of research about what happens to the mother when a child is in utero, but there's been very little looking at the father's contribution. One of the nice things about this paper is that it shows, yes, both the father and the mother do matter."[8]

The resulting impact on the sons and grandsons of the POWs and subsequent generations have implications for their family relationships. The nuances of how children responded to a father who was ill and would die early is unexplored. However, one can imagine the anxiety, and perhaps feelings of fatalism, that children experience if the known family history is that fathers die early. Since, according to studies, traumatic responses are passed through the male line in families, there is an inkling of insight into understanding fathers who face the additional stress of coping with the perceived inevitability of cancer and death. The stress of this generational predisposition to cancer and death could lead to maladaptive coping strategies such as addictions and frustrations that could lead some men to violent behaviors. The impact of these behaviors was previously discussed as some of the reasons fathers leave their children.

By extension, then, from the Civil War example, the trauma response is passed from great-grandfather, to grandfather, to grandson, to father, to son of formerly enslaved Black people. DeGruy explains that post traumatic slave syndrome[9] is the devastating impact of racism on the Black community in general and on families and individuals in particular. Black people and their descendants suffer disproportionately[10] from chronic diseases such as cancer, high blood pressure, and diabetes. Black people also have a higher mortality rate. "The death rate for African Americans is generally higher than whites for heart diseases, stroke, cancer, asthma, influenza and pneumonia, diabetes, HIV/AIDS, and homicide."[11]

Economic historian Sir Hilary Beckles argues the Caribbean's current public health crisis of high incidence of hypertension and diabetes in its population is the direct result of slavery.[12] An examination of the stress profile of Caribbean people indicates that 60 percent suffer from high incidences of hypertension and diabetes.[13] Research shows that the chronic diseases are directly inherited from the their enslaved ancestors, who over generations endured a life of extreme stress, mental terror, overwork, and a forced diet of heavily salted meats and sugar. The bodies of the descendants of enslaved people in the Caribbean have difficulty metabolizing salt or sugar, and high blood pressure and diabetic drugs that work in Caucasian and African populations have limited effect. In addition, Yehuda et al. found that the adult children of Holocaust survivors were a high-risk group vulnerable to post-traumatic stress and psychiatric disorders, supporting the argument that debilitating trauma responses are inherited.[14]

Animal studies further inform our understanding of the impact of generational trauma. Through conditioning, cherry blossom fragrances were used to induce fear in rats.[15] Later, second- and third-generation mice were "jumpy and nervous," displaying extreme sensitivity to the smell of cherry blossoms. The great-grand-descendant mice still reacted to the smell of cherry blossoms; although not fearing the smell, they were still sensitive to it.

In another study somewhat reminiscent of the classic Harlow studies[16] on young monkeys deprived of their caring mothers, researchers examined the behavior of young mouse pups. Right after birth, young mice were taken away from their mothers. The young mouse pups, traumatized by the separations, exhibited risky behaviors; they impulsively overate and became more and more antisocial as they matured.[17] These behaviors are seen in children who are traumatized at an early age, deprived of loving caregivers, especially their mothers, previously discussed as Adverse Childhood Experience (ACES).[18] Epigenetics identifies how trauma responses are passed down through the generations; how a child responds to stress and anxiety is related to their ancestors' experiences. According to Lacal and Ventura, "Parents' stressful experiences can influence an offspring's vulnerability to many pathological conditions, including psychopathologies, and their effects may even endure for several generations. Nevertheless, the cause of this phenomenon has not been determined, and only recently have scientists turned to epigenetics to answer this question."[19]

However, the over-focus on the negative impact of ACES and the retelling of traumatic events often overlook the "strengths and competencies"[20] of children and how they cope with loss and abandonment. Consequently, the following chapters describe the ways children cope with the trauma of being abandoned by one or both parents and explains how we can help these suffering children cope with loss and feelings of not mattering to those who should love them most.

PART III

Strategies for Healing

9

Twoness Contextualizes How Children Cope

Regardless of the reason, when parents leave, children suffer. They feel their mother's or father's absence keenly. In my experience, children exhibit a common response to being abandoned. As they yearn for connection to their absent parent, many children and adolescents escape to a state of "twoness," or dual reality. Twoness is a unique behavior that helps children cope with the trauma of being left by one or both biological parents. In a state of twoness, children voluntarily exist in two worlds—the present realities and an imaginary world, a mental space they create and manipulate at will. This is a magical place of escape and self-soothing, where they feel safe, loved, valued, and in control. The theory of twoness[1] describes how children fill the gap of feeling unloved and unwanted. This concept of twoness as a mental means of coping is influenced by the teachings of preeminent scholar W. E. B. Du Bois.[2] Du Bois used the term to describe the unique experience of Black people in America. He argued that Black people experience a peculiar "sense of always looking at themselves through the eyes of others, of measuring [their] soul by the tape of the world. One ever feels his two-ness, an American, a Negro; two thoughts, two unreconciled strivings; two warring ideals in one dark body, whose dogged strength alone keeps it from being torn asunder. The history of the American Negro is the history of this strife—the longing to attain self-conscious manhood, to merge his double self into a better and truer self."

Du Bois's description of the split awareness of Black people and the simultaneous awareness of self in two states inspired my reading of the behaviors of parent-abandoned traumatized children. Both theories, mine and Du Bois's of twoness, recognize twoness as a response to trauma. While Du Bois focuses on the response to being Black in America, I use Du Bois's twoness concept to focus on the trauma experiences of children whose lives are interrupted by their parent's walking away from them. I recognize the twoness state of coping from the stories children tell me about how they experience their parent's leaving. For Du Bois, "double consciousness" is being at once in two realities, in response to the pernicious trauma experienced by Black people in America—in particular, the awareness of being the "other" not really belonging but at the same time being part of the very fabric of America.

The twoness or double consciousness Du Bois described is the perpetual state of living two identities both as a Black person and as a Black person in America. The twoness or double consciousness is the Black person's "striving to merge [their] double self into a better and truer self."[3] However, for abandoned children, twoness is a coping strategy used to reconcile the feelings of loss and of being unlovable and unworthy, while having to function effectively in their world. Regardless of race or ethnicity, children who use twoness to cope describe it in several ways. Some describe that they are at once present going through their day while at the same time reliving the time they were abandoned in an almost seamless movement between reality and memory. For others, twoness is living their day-to-day reality and at will moving seamlessly to fixed imagined scenarios where they experience a loving, public interaction with the parent who left. The third manifestation of twoness is the creation of a new powerful self who is utilized in secret. This secret self has the ability to manage and manipulate, in effect controlling their environment and the people in it.

My theory of twoness extrapolates from the double consciousness postulated by Du Bois, and identifies the two selves of the abandoned child. One self is sad, hurt, rejected, the one who did not matter to their abandoning parent. The other self is the ideal, better, more desirable, and powerful self who gives them control over their world. Abandoned children create this latter self to escape. Because abandoned children experience profound loss at their parent's leaving, they strive for control over their parent's behavior, the circumstance of the parent's leaving, and their parent's interaction with them. The alternative reality they have created is particular to the child's abandonment experience.

The twoness that abandoned children experience is different from the dissociative disorders. The American Psychiatric Association (APA) identifies three types of dissociative disorders[4]—dissociative identity disorder, dissociative amnesia, and depersonalization/derealization disorder. The APA notes that "both acute stress disorder and post-traumatic stress disorder (PTSD) may involve dissociative symptoms."[5] The APA descriptors further note that dissociative identity disorder is marked by the existence of two distinct personalities or identities with changes in memory, thinking, and behavior. People notice the difference, and there is often a shift back and forth with distinct change in attitude, choice of clothing, or food preferences. People with this disorder report that their bodies feel different, and they feel that they are outside their bodies looking on. Another significant feature of depersonalization is the "experiences of unreality or detachment from one's mind self and body—as with dissociative identity disorder, having the feeling of being outside their bodies and watching events happening to them [feelings that] things and people in the world around them are not real"[6]

Abandoned children in the state of twoness do not report having the shift of self or a different personality, out-of-body experiences, or changes in their understanding of space, time, or who they are. The twoness children describe is not the feeling of un-realness of the world around them—but instead the awareness of and conscious participation in their real and current world while still in their other imaginary world. They shift seamlessly between both mental states. They keep in check the profound sadness they feel as they go through their day. However, their ideal-self fantasy is fixed, ever present, and easily retrieved.

For children who witness violence—who have not reconciled the shock of seeing pain inflicted on their mother, for example—their fantasy–memory is stuck in that dark place. They experience twoness as being at once here and at the same time reliving the trauma experience of the parent leaving. They experience the post-traumatic stress of being stuck in the memory of the moment of shock, having witnessed violence between parents and then with the parent abandoning the family. The child easily recalls this moment, as it is ever present in their minds, just below the surface of memory. The memories are frightening and shocking, being the critical moment when after violence, attachment bonds were cruelly severed by the abandoning parent. So while in a state of twoness. the child lives the traumatic memory while at the same time appearing to be going on with their normal day. This state of twoness is unique in that it is often connected to a memory of witnessed violence or frightening aggression between parents. In recalling the searing memory of her five-year-old self, the experience of fifteen-year-old Nandi illustrates this.

Nandi: I'm in Two Places

I remember this all the time. I am between them both, looking up. They were kind of wrestling.

Mom is crying. She is holding her hand. There is blood.

The door opens, and he runs away. I am looking through the window and I see him in the distance. I see the back of dad's shirt. He is running up the street.

That was the night my dad left us, left me for good. He never came back to our house.

I stay at that night most times, even when I am at school. It's just always there. I'm in two places.

Nandi voices experiences of many traumatized children who are frozen in that moment of the painful witness-experience. The shock of being a helpless witness to parental aggression, violence, and abandonment is an emotional disaster that forever alters the child's emotional and psychological state.[7] Children report that they live in two realities—the re-experiencing of the traumatic moments and the experiencing of everyday life. Moments are easy to recall in mental flights, reliving the moments of helplessness, hopelessness, fright, and grief. While they go through the motions of everyday life, children's hearts, minds, and feelings are divided between their present state and the moment they were abandoned. The child lives in an "automaton-like" state as they move through their day-to-day lives. I call this living in a state of twoness.

The second manifestation of twoness is when children escape to another mental state to cope with deep unhappiness or grief associated with parental abandonment. Children in this state of twoness fantasize, daydream,[8] and create alternate lives that they access as they go through their daily lives. It is a happy place that they consciously choose as they detach from their day-to-day reality. Children live in both the real world and their world of imagination, and move easily between the two. Allie describes living in a state of twoness as she copes with the loss of her missing father.

Allie: Dreaming of Dad

I dream about my dad all the time.

Sometimes at school, I would just imagine that he would come to school and get me. All the kids would see me run into his arms and he would lift me up and take me away. Because I am kind of short for my age, kids bother me a lot. When my dad comes for me, they would see how he loves me and they leave me alone.

Mom said my dad was dead. But I found him on *Facebook*. He has a new family. His daughter is pretty. She looks so happy. It makes me sad.

Allie has no memory of interaction with her father. He left her when she was an infant, yet there was attachment—I believe forged at conception—severed when he left her as an infant. She dreams of his reattaching to her. Her other self is publicly and lovingly acknowledged in front of all her peers. Dad is her rescuer, saving her from bullies who see that she is loved and protected. His public show of love and attention assures her and those who see that she matters to her dad.

It is interesting that abandoned, traumatized, children who have no memory of a father in their lives create a happy memory through twoness. They imagine that they are with him in a state of acceptance for who they are; they are loved, safe, and protected. Allie goes through her day to day, in another kind of twoness as well, this time the duplicity of pretending to accept her mother's excuse that her father is dead while knowing he is alive. She plays along with the story her mother tells, while in secret Allie joins her father in her dreams as he demonstrates that he loves her for everyone to see.

In Shawn's vignette, the third type of twoness I identified is demonstrated.

Shawn: Invisible and in Control

Middle schooler Shawn purposefully escapes to his state of twoness to cope with the disappointment of his father's imprisonment. Shawn described his longing for his incarcerated father; he told me that he misses him so much. Shawn says his father is in jail now, but he gets out soon—Shawn thinks he drove without a license. He doesn't want to go to the jail with his grandmother, so he rarely gets to see his father now. He's decided he can see him when he wants to. He told me he becomes like thin invisible smoke that can just slide in and out of spaces, so that he can see his father when he wants to and make sure he's okay.

Shawn's custodial parent is his paternal grandmother. She confirmed the closeness between Shawn and his father when they are together. She expressed dismay, however, that over time Shawn has become more and more detached each time his father returns to prison. She explained that when Shawn was younger he would go with her to visit his father, but lately he has refused to visit him.

To manage his grief at his father's abandoning him to return to prison, Shawn creates an alternate self. At will, he slips in and out of prison to see his dad. Shawn becomes *in*-visible, powerful and in control of his movements, in contrast to his father, who is visible to the judicial system, being in and out of prison; incarcerated, and therefore powerless, with no control. Shawn has the power to move at will, between his everyday world and the one where he becomes smoke and is in control of where and when he visits his father. Shawn creates an alternate self and watches over his father in his imagination. He worries about his father's safety, while at the same time grieving his father's frequent returns to prison, and repeated abandonment.

Lele: Online with Power

Twoness is also apparent in the behavior of middle schooler Lele, who uses the internet to create an alternate self. Lele's voice was matter-of-fact as she told me that her biological parents divorced several years ago. She said that over time, her father stopped calling to talk with her, and that they only talk if she calls him. She doesn't think he cares about her anymore because he has a new family, and she says he loves her two stepsisters more.

In addition, Lele is infuriated by her mother's recent marriage to a long-time boyfriend. Lele insists that he will never be her father; she doesn't care how hard he tries.

Lele escapes to online fantasy and joined an online fan-fiction community. She says the members are from all over the world and have become her friends. She stated that most are her age and like her, enjoy "shipping"[9] (friend-shipping or relation-shipping) their favorite characters. As Lele explained, when "shipping," she puts characters from different genres and different stories together to create new relationships, changing the narrative. She said she is happy and powerful in her online world, often creating scenarios with characters having romantic fun or engaging in sex. In addition, Lele created a persona for herself, Eden, and puts that character in her favorite stories either as a supportive friend to one of the main characters or as a successful rival for a relationship with either a male or female protagonist. Lele also shared with me that some of the online members of her fan-fiction group were more extreme in their stories than she, depicting graphic sexual acts between characters that made her uncomfortable. However, as persona Eden, Lele is able to handle the discomfort, as her character is older, mature, sophisticated, and desirable. She says sometimes her online persona emerges when she has arguments with her mother.

In addition, Lele also began to engage in self-injury and said she would cut herself when she felt anxious and sad. With Lele's knowledge, I shared this information with her mother. Her mother is well aware of her daughter's sadness about being abandoned by her biological father and that Lele has always wanted her and Lele's dad to get back together. Lele was very angry when her mom married her stepfather. Simone expressed her own sadness at her daughter's hostility and refusal to accept her new husband.

We also discussed Lele's self-injurious behaviors and some root causes, especially that the girl felt abandoned by her father. His abandonment plays a major role in her anxiety, sadness, and feelings of having no control. In addition, she struggles with her mom's moving on to a romantic committed relationship with her new husband. I asked about Lele's online behaviors. Her mom explained that because Lele was an avid reader and writes her own stories, she did not see harm in her fan-fiction activities. I cautioned about

Lele's access to mature sexual content and to persons who are really unknown, who could be older adults trolling websites where young people like Lele gather. Her mom appeared interested and promised to pay closer attention. I also recommended family therapy to help with the family dynamics, and a therapist for Lele, to help her cope with the pain of loss and loneliness. Lele also needed to explore her online alter ego and how positive characteristics in her character can help her cope with loss and lack of control in her day-to-day life with her mom, stepfather, and absent father.

Lele lives the twoness—in one life as an unhappy fourteen-year-old who feels abandoned by both her father and her remarried mother; and in her other life as the online in-control persona Eden. Lele escapes to the online world as Eden, who she creates as desirable and in control of her world. Particularly telling is that as creator, Lele manipulates stories—fashioning endings and beginnings at her whim. Lele grieves that her father does not seem to care for her. She also grieves the death of her hope that her parents would reconcile. Her second self is the powerful creator, a master controller who can manipulate the behaviors of well-known characters and celebrities. Lele has found a tribe, a place to belong in the supportive online community who appreciate her.

Talia: Half My Heart Left with Him

I met middle schooler Talia in the school hallway crying. As she sat in my office, she explained that she was worried about her father. Talia had a shy but open and friendly manner as she explained that she had been thinking about her father for a long time. She even tried to run away to find him. My interview with Talia was particularly heartbreaking because she was deeply sad and puzzled about her mother's silence about her father. She feared that he might be dead or homeless. An academically struggling student, Talia told me that she would be stronger than she was now if her father were in her life. She said she could do more things.

While talking with me, Talia would occasionally drift off in deep thought. When I asked her father's name, she was silent for a long time, and when she finally spoke her voice was soft and wistful. She said she never knew his name although her mother thinks she does; she said she would only call him "Daddy."

Talia explained that her father separated from her when she was young. He just did not return home one day. Talia recalls spending a lot of time with him when he lived with her and her mother. Her face lit with joy as she recalled him picking her up from school and carrying her in his arms. She was unable to recall his face, though, and her mother has not permitted her to see pictures of him. Talia said she remembers a shadow or a sense of his warm presence in her life. She told me that when he left, he took half her heart.

I discussed Talia with her mother and encouraged her to help Talia manage her loss with a therapist. Her mother expressed surprise. She said that Talia's father left the family when Talia was an infant, long before she started school. She was confused as to why Talia would imagine a dad who took her to school. Talia's twoness emerges as she tries to reconcile her infant memories of a warm caring father. Her infant memories are feelings of being safe and loved, by a caring presence that she identifies as her father. Talia misses and worries about a father who physically left her when she was an infant, yet she imagines him taking her to school and being in his arms, being safe and loved. She created a happy, safe memory that she can access at will. This created memory provides her with heart ease.

Windrush Baby Speaks

At age sixty-eight, Claire remembers her mother leaving her to be part of the Windrush generation[10] and the feelings of abandonment that persist even to this day. As a mature woman with grown children, Claire understands her mother's need to have an adventure, to be a part of something big, the drive to have a new start in the colonial "motherland." Claire writes her feelings as follows:

> I never got over my feelings of being abandoned. These feelings have been persistent all my life. Even though I was left in the care of loving, caring great grandparents, I could not shake the feeling of being left behind by my mother.
>
> I resented her and the adults in my family who I felt allowed her leave me. All my life I was guarded with people, unable to trust. How can I be sure that a loved one won't leave me? I had the deep feeling of being unworthy, of being unlovable. I carried deep in my heart the longing for my mother. . . .
>
> Visits to my father's family exposed me to a caring extended family. I remember sitting at dinner when I was three years old with aunts and uncles and receiving the same sized serving as the adults. I recall my paternal grandmother asking about my day at school and what I learned. I remember her praising me for being smart. My father, however, while present when I visited his family, remained aloof.
>
> My grief at the loss of my mother's presence and the pain of her lack of concern for me was sometimes unbearable. My great-grandmother would read aloud her very infrequent letters from England. I was painfully aware that my mother never once asked how I was doing.

I know this longing and feelings of being forgotten modified my personality. I am convinced that these feelings are carried over to the next generation. My children tell me that I vacillate between smothering and doing too much for them and then on the other hand taking—what they describe as a hard-line approach, for them unreasonable and inconsistent. From my point of view, I was giving them tough love and it was necessary at that time.

But how do I know my mother abandoning me for England changed me? From a young age I was guarded, afraid to be spontaneous, I was obsessed with being good and wanted to please adults. I was all the things adults said "good" little girls were. I was obedient, respectful, quiet, deeply anxious of the outcome of not being liked by adults. I was reluctant to give authentic opinions and was afraid to articulate my deep-rooted feelings.

I was deeply insecure, lacked confidence, although on the surface I was academically and later as an adult professionally successful. I became a perfectionist. I had to get it right all the time. I could not express my fears or worry to anyone.

I did not want to cause trouble. As a result, I was excessively tolerant of emotional abuse by other people. This excessive tolerance manifested in physical and medical conditions. I kept everything inside. I would boil up inside—furious.

And then would come the contradictions. I would rebel . . . do something that did not conform, something that was puzzling or forbidden. Something that did not match their perception and expectation of me. Then would come the panic attacks, ulcers, anxiety, depression, the feelings of being a misfit, being outside of myself, of not being good enough.

I made up for the rejection by working harder, doing more, always achieving, always striving for more to prove my worth. Always with the feelings of not belonging, where do I fit in? What was wrong with me? Why wasn't I invited to join my mother and her new family abroad?

As an adult I had a chance to talk with my mother before she died. Over a series of visits to England I tried to connect with her. To understand her, to get her to know me, and maybe love me. I reconciled myself to the hurt and humiliation of being introduced as her niece.

I raged inside and did not talk to her for a long time. When I was finally able to talk to her again, I listened to her [my mother] explain her reasons for not looking back and for starting an entirely new family that did not know of my existence. Her reasons made no sense to me at the time, and they still are unfathomable to me now. I am a mother and her behavior and explanations make her leaving even more painful.

I had to work hard to come to understand my own worth and my own purpose. I had to seek my own redemption and healing and had to find my way to forgive my mother for abandoning me.

Children who are abandoned by a parent suffer. They try to make sense of the abandonment and the feelings of not being good enough for the parent to stay with them. The feeling that they did not matter to their parent forces abandoned children to create a secret world where they do matter. Interestingly, some purposefully created alternate scenarios in their twoness state. Often the created situations are where the abandoned child has status. For example, Lele is powerful as she manipulates relationships in her online persona. Another common theme is where the abandoning parent displays how much their child matters to them. Allie's father sweeps her up in his arms, while Talia has a memory of being taken to school by a father who left her as an infant. Philosopher Rebecca Goldstein explains that "the notion of mattering is intimately linked with the notion of attention. To say that something matters is to assert that attention is due it, the kind of attention that both [recognizes] and reveals its reality . . . that demands to be known. If something doesn't matter, I'm saying that it's not worth paying attention to."[11]

So Mom and Dad are at war. The relationship did not work out. They are disappointed in each other. They may use tactics to hurt and injure each other, like social media to malign or prove one or the other is unfit to parent. They may even despise each other. With the help of attorneys, they face off in court battling over the children. Meanwhile, children like six-year-old Lily imagine a different scenario. In dreaming, she goes into a state of twoness to quiet her anxieties and her emotional earthquake. Lily draws pictures of her mommy and daddy holding hands. She also draws pictures of her and her little brother with mom and dad in a happy family circle. Lily tells her baffled and heartbroken mother, "I can't wait for daddy to get home again." And although a witness to violence between mom and dad, Lily stated, "I don't know why you won't let him back into the house. Daddy loved you so much." I tried to explain trauma to Lily's mother and Lily's attempts to quiet her anxieties and emotional earthquake by her creating a world that she controls—a happy, hopeful world where both her parents get along.

Children use fantasy to create a world of escape. They use twoness to make themselves lovable, cared for, publicly acknowledged as important to their mom or dad who walked away from them. In their imaginary world, their parent stays with them because they have worth, value, and they matter; there is harmony and love in their home. Children seek attention from and connection to the abandoning parent even though that parent may have caused hurt and pain. They demand control and affirmation of their agency on their world. Abandoned children use their state of twoness to manage their grief and powerlessness.

Twoness helps children connect with the abandoning parent by changing the narrative from being unloved and unnoticed to being loved and recognized. In their imagination, abandoned children have the power to manipulate the relationship with their abandoning parent to reflect the outcome they desire. Indeed, those who dream, or daydream, are in fact engaging in healthy coping and problem solving. Day dreams are healthy[12] and indicate creative and critical thinking. Thinking for pleasure increases happiness and feelings of well-being.[13]

It is easy to "pathologize" children's experience of twoness. However, I see twoness as a necessary response to coping with the severing of attachment bonds between themselves and a parent. Western psychology has been criticized for its emphasis on pathology and the "what is wrong"[14] approach to the human experience. Firestone,[15] for example, argues that dreaming and imagining a connection with an abandoning parent is a form of defense mechanism, an "illusion of fusion." This illusion helps children's cope with the anxiety and distress of separation. This "fantasy bond," while helpful in childhood, is really a "primary defense mechanism in neurosis" and sets the child up for troubled romantic relationships in adulthood.[16]

While Firestone offers strategies for couples to overcome the challenges caused by childhood fantasy bonds, there is little offered to the child who needs to create a relationship with the abandoning parent. The internal connections they create to their absent parent help children deal with the grief of being left behind. Dreaming of a loving connection helps children self-soothe and fosters feelings of mattering. Therefore, if we "un-pathologize" twoness, we see that children living in two worlds, living twoness, is their response to and attempt to make sense of and manage broken attachment bonds.

10

What Children Need

Trauma expert Bessel van der Kolk explains that the brain matures in the context of attachment to caregivers, and if a caregiver causes trauma, the child's brain is severely impacted. The trauma caused by a caregiver is an adversity that disrupts the attachment bond. Caregiver trauma separates the child not only from the caregiver, but from their internal selves. Van der Kolk argues that the task of healing children traumatized by their caregiver—the primary attachment figures in a child's life—is to restore and strengthen connections to the child's internal self and to others.[1]

RESTORING CONNECTIONS

Above all, then, children need to feel loved and connected. How does a child begin to heal when abandoned by either mom or dad, or worse, both parents? What do children need? They need to know that they matter. Mattering means that children feel they "make a difference in the lives of others,"[2] and they are missed by others. Children want to feel that they matter to their missing parent, the way their missing parent matters to them. Mattering keeps away sadness and dark thoughts of self-destruction[3] and thoughts that their lives have no value. These thoughts are especially prevalent at adolescence when children are searching for meaning and identity.[4]

Where do parents begin? They begin by focusing on the children. Agree to be mature and allow the other parent to thrive. Let the children know that although mom and dad cannot be together, they will always love them and miss them terribly when they are not around. It means making every effort to connect with their children as often as possible and being honest when it is not possible to communicate. Do not go absent or disappear. Explain to the child in as caring and loving a way as possible why mom or dad is not/was not able to make contact. Be adult enough to swallow the pain of the series of events that led to the eventual separation. In spite of justified hostilities, try to part on civil terms.

Civility between parents is critical to the success of co-parenting. Find a good and kind therapist to help with unpacking the pain of separation. Children need to know that *they* are loved *even if their parents stop loving each other.* Therefore, parents, though separated, should try as best they can to co-parent for the sake of their child.

Divorced Co-Parenting Mother Sharee: "The kids need their dad and he needs them"

"Everybody is better," Sharee stated. She was responding to my question about how her children were doing after divorce from her children's very involved and loving father, James. Sharee is a thirty-four-year-old teacher and recent divorcée. "I get along better now with my ex than when we were married," she laughed. Why is that, I asked? Sharee explained that she had to give up all unreasonable expectations of James. She had to come to see him as a person with flaws, not the prince who would rescue her, not "Mr. Right," nor the "perfect" man. Sharee, with the help of a therapist, came to recognize her role in the breakup of her marriage and to accept that she herself was not perfect.

Sharee also had to reconcile her own grief and disappointment before she was able to work with James in parenting their three children. "My eldest child [daughter] is the angriest with both of us. She feels he let us down, let her down and she blames me for not forgiving him and staying in the marriage. I had no models of forgiveness or co-parenting. All the women in my family are angry or estranged from their children's fathers," Sharee reflected. She went on to say that she had to create a new path and a new set of norms. "I wanted my marriage to work and did not want my children to go through the grief and pain I experienced growing up with an angry mother and missing father."

She continued, "I had unreasonable expectations of my ex. And when mistakes were made, I could not forgive. But now that we are co-parenting, I feel that the children know they are loved by both of us." Sharee also noted that since she is now involved in a loving relationship, her own emotional needs are being met. She explained that her feeling loved has been an important component of her own self-care and healing. "Although sometimes when he calls I get so angry, and when I see him, all the memories come rushing back. But it's not about me. It's for the kids. They need their dad and he needs them."

WHAT IS CO-PARENTING?

Co-parenting is both parents working it out together, and not withholding information or access to the children. It means being in constant communication and abiding by the clear guidelines of custody agreements. Advice abounds as to the importance of co-parenting to the well-being of children of separated parents. Co-parenting protects children from suffering long-term emotional damage because of parent separation and hostility. This requires both parents taking the high road, ending the relationship with compassion, peace, and if not forgiveness then understanding, and most importantly, finding ways to share the responsibilities of raising the children.[5] Co-parenting asks that both parents work actively on their own healing for their own sake and that of their children.

Author and columnist "Mr. Dad" Armin Brott[6] admits that co-parenting is asking parents to be superhuman. For separated parents to share in raising the children, it takes huge effort, determination, maturity, and putting the children first. Brott advises getting a mediator or collaborative lawyer who will help with drafting clear rules of custody and interaction with the children. Most importantly, he emphasized, avoid being nosy and asking the children information about the other parent's life. Take the high road, be a grown-up, follow the Golden Rule—that is, treat the other parent the way you want to be treated.[7] It seems a difficult task for warring parents, especially when there is unforgiveness for past hurts.

CO-PARENTING IN THE TIME OF COVID-19

How does co-parenting work during very stressful times of sadness, fear, and anxiety, especially with parents worrying about the safety of their children. Previously held ideas that children were immune to the COVID-19 virus has been debunked by alarming child infections just as deadly as adult infections. News reports worry parents, and the baffling nature of how the virus has affected children fuel fear and panic in already stressed parents.[8] NBC News reported on the creative approaches parents are taking to resolve custody arrangements during sheltering-in-place orders.

Parents who separated amicably appeared able to resolve shared custody arrangements with the least disruption to the agreements. In one instance described, ex-husband Henry temporarily moved back in with ex-wife Lisa during the pandemic to give their nine-year-old son stability, and so they both could see him. Other parents made the pact to follow guidelines of social distancing, to meet each other halfway, or to have the children spend a longer time at one parent's home to avoid unnecessary movement.[9] Ultimately, the best interest of the children guided parents' behavior and interactions, always being mindful that ex-spouses who co-parent were helping their children cope with the anxieties they may be feeling. Above all else, it was critical that children feel loved, securely connected to their parents, and not abandoned at that very challenging time. In addition, it was important to note that when mothers and fathers separated on amicable terms, children exhibited less acting out and depressed behaviors, as mothers allowed nonresident fathers to nurture meaningful bonds with their children.[10]

Use Technology to Bond

It is important to note that the presence of a caregiver does not guarantee care for traumatized children. In addition to self-care, it is critical that caregivers pay attention to the time they spend distracted or online. Recent studies[11] indicate the concerns of health care professionals over caregivers' use of cell phones, their distraction, focus on their device, and harsh responses to children who were unsupervised and emotionally abandoned.[12] Their advice: "Turn off the smartphones."[13] Further research shows that parents on their devices spend less time connected to their children. Parents are distracted, disengaged from their children, and while absorbed in the activity on their device are often harsh in responding to their children's needs.[14] With parents on their devices, there is less time to bond with their already rejected and hurting child. McDaniel argues, however, that rather than focusing on the intrusive and exclusionary nature of electronic devices, emphasis should be on parents using technology to bond with their children. Since our use of technology will only increase, it is wise not to resist but to incorporate technology into parenting strategies. Technological devices can "further strengthen family relationships," and parents can use technology to "teach the various skills needed in an ever connected world. Including teaching children how to deal with distractions and to delay gratification."[15] Opinion writer Caspian Kang explained that he played video games with his four-year-old daughter, simply to have fun and. most importantly. to spend time with her.[16]

OTHER CONSIDERATIONS

What if Dad Was a Bad Man?

How does a mother tell her child that dad was abusive? That they were conceived from a violent act such as rape or incest? How the mother healed and reconciled her own feelings of violation and trauma will facilitate the conversation with the child. Is it hard to say with as much love and empathy as possible, "Your father and I were not friends. You were a surprise. I am glad you are with me now. I love you"? Can there be a purpose in the conception of a child born from such circumstances? If we believe that life is sacred and that it has meaning, then a child who came into the world under these harsh conditions must be here for a purpose. One mother pregnant from rape told me, "I know why she is here now [ten years later], to bring joy. She makes me happy." This mother said she was only able to work through the horrific experience with the help of her family and therapeutic support. The burden of the hard, painful conversation does not have fall on the mother only. Leaning heavily on sources of resilience—family and friends, spirituality, self-awareness, and optimism—focuses the child on life having a purpose and that the child is valued, loved, and matters to the mother and the family.[17]

Why This Difficult Conversation?

This conversation is inevitable. It is implicit in the "who am I?" question asked most pointedly at the adolescent stage of child development. It is normal for children at that time to question the way things are. It is a normal stage of adolescence to search for identity, asking "who am I?" and "Where do I fit in?" This search naturally begins at home (ideally with both parents). "Do I look like dad or mom?" "What did my parents do when they were growing up?" These are a few of the questions asked when seeking self-knowledge and purpose. They are the child's attempts to please themselves in the context of family history, expected behaviors, hoping to gain a sense of connection to the past, positioning themselves in the present and future.

Through this quest, adolescents gain resilience and hope, knowing other family members on mom's and dad's side have overcome challenges, made mistakes, made amends, and whose actions have brought the child to where they are. If dad is missing, unavailable, referred to in disparaging terms, when an adolescent child says, "I don't have a dad," the child is in fact saying "I don't know or acknowledge or understand that part of me. That part of me is a dark, shameful, a mystery, best left unexplored. That part of me does not matter." Research has proven this to be untrue. It does matter.

11

Grandparents Help to Heal

The extended family provides a naturally important safety net for children traumatized by parental abandonment. Ideally, close relatives who remain neutral, and understand the nuances of the parents' separation, help grieving children understand and accept their parent's absence from their lives. It is ideal if the relatives do not take sides nor fan the flames of hostility and unforgiveness. Grandparents are often the caregivers of abandoned children and are critical in helping them heal from abandonment trauma. However, because grandparents are human and are often enmeshed in the drama of separated parents, by taking sides they foster hostility and unforgiveness. Grandparents may also be victims of their own life traumas that interfere with the children's healing.

Grandparenthood is universally understood as the involvement of the parents of father and mother in the lives of their grandchildren. Yet significant gaps remain in understanding the role and meaning of "grandparenting" nuanced across cultures and contexts.[1] In many societies, grandparents provide care to their grandchildren, especially in cultures that encourage multigenerational involvement. Schwab and Ziarat[2] noted that in general, grandparents are living longer and are able to spend more of their active years with their grandchildren. The researchers recognize, however, that grandparenting tends to focus on the caretaking role of the grandmother—the assumption is that this focus on the grandmother is based on the traditional roles of women as maternal caretakers of children. For this reason, grandmothers are very important in facilitating or blocking healing in children dealing with parental abandonment. Not only do grandmothers help heal, they can often hinder.

ROLE OF GRANDFATHERS IN HEALING

Like fathers, involved grandfathers play a unique role in the lives of their grandchildren.[3] Grandfathers grandparent differently from grandmothers. There has been an increase of interest in the role of grandfathers. Reported in the *Deseret News*,[4] psychologist Lynn Johnson and his son Chris constructed a zip line and helped his granddaughters conquer their fears. As the girls zipped across his backyard, Johnson reported that he believed Chris and his other children's resilience and optimism were nurtured by his teaching them to face their fears and overcome challenges. He further noted that his children grew into stable, successful adults because he encouraged them to take "chances—not foolish ones, but still real ones—[actions that] enhance a child's problem-solving skills, builds resilience and boosts psychological and physical well-being."

In supporting son Chris's fathering, Johnson played the time-honored role of sage and role model. Perhaps, then, this is the role of the grandfather who, from experience, understands with his longitudinal perspective and wisdom how to demonstrate the skills necessary for survival outside the home. In our discussion of the role of father in this book, we noted that the father's skills are both different from and complementary to the mother's—in the same way the skills taught by the grandfather differ from and complement the grandmother's. It is important to note that the roles and responsibilities of grandfathers have changed over time and are tied to men's changing roles in society.[5]

STEPS TO FORGIVENESS

To help parents who struggle with unforgiveness for past hurts, Luskin advises that the first step to healing is to fully acknowledge that harm was done, that something was lost. The second step is to accept the strong feelings that come with this negative experience. The third step is to choose to share the difficulty of the grieving/forgiving with a few caring, trusted people, because being connected to others during this painful process is critical. The support and love of others heal and encourage self-compassion and acceptance.

For women who are gatekeepers, forgiving is essential to changing the patterns of unforgiveness. Forgiveness changes the patterns of unhappiness that lack of forgiveness spawns in relationships between men and women, even onto their descendants. The process of forgiveness asks a great deal of women and men who have suffered abandonment as children or later when romantic partners walk away and leave them to care for brokenhearted children.

Grandmother Gatekeeper: Meeting Grandfather Heals

"I really should have paid more attention to your father while he was growing up," my father said, as he looked up at my niece Ash. She assessed his situation. My twenty-eight-year-old niece, a critical care nurse, accompanied me on a visit to my father, her grandfather. He lives in an assisted-living home. "Don't worry about that now," Ash responded. "What I need you to do is to practice sitting up on your own." She guided him with professional expertise.

As I watched her take my father through the steps of independent movement, I wondered what she was feeling and thinking about his statement. My father did not give my brother (her father) and indeed any of us, my four siblings and I, the attention and care we needed.

We lived being parented by our single mother. She demonstrated her love by hard work to provide for us. However, she did not let us forget our father's abandonment. Each day our mother reminded us of his present or past behaviors that contributed to our current hardships. The stories were painful to hear because they were real, since we were experiencing the evidence of his neglect. We felt the lean doing-without days, including the often meager pantry, no fees paid for school, no school supplies, and the waiting for my mother's payday when there was brief abundance. My father was absent from our social, school, and church events and never inquired about our progress. Sadly, we knew he was magnanimous when spending on friends and in his many social activities.

When my siblings and I became parents, we informed our own children about our father from each of our own perspectives. Our mother—a very active grandmother—made sure the grandchildren knew the many instances of their grandfather's dereliction of duties and the rationale for her hostility toward him. However, as is normal with maturation and the search for identity, the grandchildren wanted to know more about him. Grandchildren's queries were often met with the brick wall of silence from our mother or a terse response such as, "Why are you asking me that? Why do you want to know about him? Just understand that he was careless and irresponsible. He did zero to help me raise your [parent]. I had a very difficult time, while he was living the good life."

However, in stark contradiction to her words, our mother taught us to be kind and forgiving. So, despite our own ambivalence, my siblings and I agreed that we would allow our children to meet their grandfather at least once. Of her own choice, my niece Ash met her grandfather for the first time in his assisted-living home. He was eighty-four years old. We did not tell my mother prior to the visit because over the many years we have often heard her say, "He does not deserve to know any of the grandchildren. He wants to show off. Look at how I suffered and struggled to raise you all. Leave him to his loneliness. I predicted this would happen. Now, at this late stage of life, he is interested in all of you and your children."

But when we reminded her that she taught us to forgive, she added, "Look, I don't hate him, I just don't like him. And I don't see why he gets to feel proud and show off about the things you and your children all achieved."

> But when my niece met her grandfather, she showed him kindness and care.
>
> Later, I asked her how she felt about seeing her grandfather and hearing his seeming regret about not paying attention to her father. I joked that she had her "professional nurse" face on and that I could not get a read on her feelings. Ash considered for a while, then said, "I had to focus on what grandpa needed for his care. He is frail and he needs to practice moving and not just laying in bed. I just put my feelings aside and focused on him. But now, on reflection, I feel like grandpa has some regrets in his old age. And I feel really protective about my dad. He is such a great dad to me. But I see how grandpa's neglect affected my father's self-esteem. Still, I am glad I met grandpa. I feel like I understand the family, myself and my dad a whole lot more."

My father missed out on the wonderful years of being part of his grandchildren's lives. He was absent as they matured from childhood into adulthood, missing their challenges and joys. He missed out on partnering with our mother to co-grandparent. Indeed, he kept away because of his lifestyle choices. My mother's "grandparent gatekeeping" also blocked his connection to his grandchildren, even if he wanted to create bonds of attachment.

CO-GRANDPARENTING

The story just told shows that even divorced or separated grandparents benefit from forgiveness and from co-grandparenting. In "He's No Longer My Ex-Husband, He's My Co-Grandparent," psychiatrist and *New York Times* columnist Jennifer Taitz[6] describes her and her husband's relief when her parents finally decided to forgive each and co-grandparent her children. Their children benefit from valuable grandparent relationships and understand their identity within the context of family history and tradition. As mother Sharee stated earlier in this section about co-parenting, "Everyone is better [now.]" Sadly, the COVID-19 pandemic was particularly devastating to our elders,[7] complicating interactions between surviving grandparents and their grandchildren.

12

Self-Care for Carers

Single mothers,[1] single fathers,[2] and grandparents—especially grandmothers[3]—experience a myriad of psychological stresses as they attempt to care for abandoned children. To adequately care for suffering children, parents and caregivers need to ensure that they are themselves flourishing even while meeting the challenges of helping their suffering children heal. Eminent psychologist Martin Seligman created a framework for assessing important elements of well-being. The framework consisted of five "building blocks that enables flourishing"[4] of positive emotions, engagement in fulfilling tasks, being connected to others in positive and supportive relationships, having meaning or purpose for their lives, and recognizing their accomplishments or successes. Collectively, these measures are summed up by the acronym PERMA.[5]

PERMA is one of the tenets of positive psychology and is grounded in the optimistic mindset that while there are problems and challenges in life—such as those faced by caregivers to traumatized children—the converse is also true, that there are aspects of life that if nurtured will provide the means of flourishing and contentment with life.

I use the five building blocks of well-being to help parents and caregivers frame how they take care of themselves and the brokenhearted children under their watch. For example, I encourage caregivers to pay attention to creating opportunities for positive emotions. What are positive emotions? Consider sweet memories, the pleasurable feeling after a workout, feelings of awe looking at the moon or walking outside, basking in the sunlight.

Carers nurturing children abandoned by a parent must themselves seek well-being in order to fully manage the challenges they will face. In practical terms, this means, as divorced mother Sharee stated earlier in this book, when she was in a positive relationship of her own and experiencing the positive emotions of love and affection, she was able to parent her children more effectively. Positive emotions, however, do not only refer to romantic relationships but include a range of positive feelings such as gratitude, joy, peace, delight, contentment, satisfaction, hope, and excitement.[6]

Research has shown that the positive emotion of gratitude in particular facilitates an abundance of outcomes that increase overall well-being.[7] Emmons and McCullough[8] argue that gratitude increases pro-social attitudes such as the appreciation of friends and loved ones. Gratitude also encourages spiritual connections through reflection and supports altruism by focusing us on life experiences. Being grateful increases humility and builds resilience to manage challenges and adversity. Most importantly, gratitude cements bonds as it promotes feelings of love and being loved.

Thankfulness can be increased by the nightly reflection on the day and recalling the good events. This is not to disregard negative events that occur, but nightly reflection encourages a mindset of optimism "by approaching life in a more reflective detail," as Seligman notes. This exercise increases life satisfaction and sweetens memories of the past. Seligman continues that nightly reflection on *three good things* will, over time, reduce anxiety and depression, making us more deliberately conscious of good events and so to count our blessings.[9]

Another step caregivers can take to nurture positive emotions and so increase their well-being and the well-being of their children is to practice the simple act of savoring[10]—that is, paying attention to and lingering over the small things of the day, for example, slowly sipping a cup of coffee or stopping to listen to birdsong. It could also be stopping to listen and enjoy small talk with their child. Another important self-care activity is for caregivers to engage in activities that are healthy, energizing, and that maximize positive feelings. Exercise and healthy diet cannot be ignored. Raising broken children requires physical, mental, and emotional stamina that begins with caregivers' own self-care.

Mindfulness has gained popularity for fostering inner calm, self-awareness, and several other benefits. Van Dam et al.,[11] however, argue that the tenets of mindfulness are so wide-ranging it is difficult to capture all of its meaning. As a result, it is best, then, to simply encourage parents and caregivers to practice setting aside time to take deep breaths, to quiet their thoughts, to meditate,[12] pray, and to make spiritual connections. Research confirms the connection between well-being and spirituality.[13] Caregivers should try to model spiritual awareness for children to make connections to a force beyond themselves in ways that are meaningful to them. Children who have spiritual awareness demonstrate robust resilience in the face of challenges.[14]

So far in our discussion, encouraging caregivers to pay attention to their well-being has focused on increasing positive emotions—the P in

PERMA. The second building block of the PERMA model is Engagement. Engagement is being absorbed in activities that one is passionate about, such as reading, drawing, or cooking. Children will notice the full concentration and what Csikzentmihalyi describes as "flow."[15] When children notice, they learn about passion and the joy of flow, the focus on one thing, getting lost in it, and gaining mastery over that activity. For parents and caregivers to manage the stress of the responsibility to care for a grieving child, it is important to have their own source of encouragement and love.

The third building block of the PERMA theory of well-being is Relationships, or positive social connections. Toxic relationships are unhealthy and work against the well-being of both parents and their grieving child. The current excessive online use by both parents and children often causes stress, anxiety, and depression. A single parents may, for example, be tempted to use social media to peek into the life of the abandoning parent. Muise et al. argue: "Facebook may expose an individual to potentially jealousy-provoking information about their partner, which creates a feedback loop whereby heightened jealousy leads to increased surveillance of a partner's Facebook page. Persistent surveillance results in further exposure to jealousy-provoking information"[16]

The desire to follow the life of a former lover can become an obsession—the incessant need to know becoming an addiction. The parent may become a voyeur, living vicariously through the posted images.[17] For children abandoned by a parent, the trauma they experienced is linked to the disconnect between themselves and the abandoning parent. As previously discussed, these children withdraw, and although appearing to be engaged, struggle with connecting or bonding with others. Children put up a wall of mistrust, they are hurt. When caregivers model positive connections to others, children learn the importance of trusting others because they see their parent or caregiver doing so. It is therefore important that parents and caregivers cultivate close bonds of trust and mutual support with close family friends and members of the extended family, not only for themselves but for the children in their care.

To continue our understanding of well-being, using PERMA as our guide, we recognize that the Meaning or the purpose caregivers give their lives will determine how they spend their time and what drives their behaviors. Proponents of positive psychology describe meaning and purpose as being involved in, "belonging to and serving something bigger than the self."[18] This awareness of service is grounded in the understanding that we have gifts and talents to share for the greater good. Perhaps a parent is part of a community organization concerned with social issues or involved in a religious group. When parents find time to give back, children learn that we all something to share no matter how small. Parents may, for example, give items regularly to a shelter for the homeless. Children learn compassion, kindness, and gratitude when they witness these acts of service.

The last component of the PERMA well-being model is Accomplishment. What has the parent or caregiver accomplished? What can they be proud of? Small things are worthy of acknowledgment such as completing a task well—succeeding in a new recipe or learning a new skill. Children watch and learn as their parent or caregiver balances difficult tasks of day-to-day life. They see how small goals are met and how these bring satisfaction. Children also learn about delayed gratification if, for example, they notice their parent persevere in mastering a new skill.

USE WOOP TO TEACH CHILDREN HOW TO SET AND ACHIEVE GOALS

Gabriele Oettingen's WOOP[19] exercise is an effective method of helping children set and achieve goals. The four-step approach begins with first identifying the goal to be achieved—the dearest Wish. Secondly, think and dream about what would happen if the dearest wish came true—the positive Outcome. Third, identify the Obstacles in the way of achieving the dearest wish, the goal. Lastly, Plan a strategy to overcome the obstacle. The plan must be achievable and practical, and should include a *when then* component—that is, when an obstacle blocks me from achieving my goal, then I will take action. The WOOP exercise is simple and effective and manageable. I have taught it to my children and adults clients, and taught the WOOP goal setting to my students and indeed shared it with my entire school.

The five building blocks of well-being summed up by PERMA—positive emotions, engagement, healthy supportive relationships, having a life meaning and purpose, and celebrating small achievement—are valuable in helping frame caregivers' healthful behaviors that will also benefit the children they care for. The value of high well-being cannot be overstated, with some of the advantages being an optimistic outlook, satisfying relationships, and high coping skills. In order to help abandoned children heal, their parents and caregivers will need to take care of themselves so that the children in their care see how to manage life.

PART IV

Taking Care of the Children

13

Positive Psychology Interventions for Well-Being

Love. The term is so overused, but it is really all abandoned children need to feel safe, whole, and worthy. Children damaged by abandonment need consistent love. As described in their own voices, they believe they are unworthy of love, having been rejected—unwanted by either mother or father. Caretakers must be mindful that the traumatized children in their care have learned not to believe their need for connection or attachment will ever be met. This need, unreciprocated, causes pain—it hurts badly. In my theory of twoness, I describe how traumatized children often appear to be coping, but the surface masks deep anxiety and grief. When caregivers show traumatized children signs of love and affection, the effect is huge in the child's experience. Loving words, hugs, and touch foster many positive emotions, especially feelings of worthiness and of being lovable. Emotion scientist Barbara Frederickson[1] explains how love is different from other positive emotions such as joy or gratitude. Although supporting our growth to our best selves, joy and gratitude are fleeting. Love lasts a lifetime.

Frederickson further notes that love is "especially beneficial for our health and growth. Apart from slowing down aging, love broadens our awareness of others' needs and increases our feelings of social connections and oneness with others."[2] Love increases compassion and empathy, fosters forgiveness and hope. In addition, Frederickson references current research that shows the connection between caregivers and child that fosters oxytocin, the social bonding hormone.[3] Intangible but powerful, love shows itself when a caregiver spends time with their child, demonstrates interest in the child's daily life, gives compliments, encouragement, and remains a consistent source of warm, nurturing protection.

Cassie and Lucas: Love Heals Traumatized Children

"Why didn't she love me?" eight-year-old Lucas asked me. His nine-year-old sister Cassie squeezed his small hand. 'It's okay," she assured him. Lucas shook his head, "I will never forgive her."

Abandoned by their mentally ill mother, Lucas and Cassie were placed in the care of their father and stepmother by Child Protective Services. Both children suffered the traumatic effects of being left alone for days at a time by their unstable mother. Their toddler half-sister lived with them.

When the children's father and stepmother brought Cassie and Lucas to see me, they wanted help with the children's transition to living with them—in a new state, in a home with new rules. Cassie constantly worried about being safe, while Lucas had recurring dreams of monsters with sharp teeth looking down at him. Both needed constant assurance that they would not go back to the frightening time of being left alone by their mother and having no food. Cassie bit her nails constantly, while Lucas pulled at his hair. The children wet their beds and were assessed by their school psychologist as having learning difficulties. The children's parents immediately partnered with their teachers to help navigate school and to overcome challenges of the new environment. After four years of stable, loving parenting and consistent psychotherapy, the children are thriving. Cassie and Lucas made the honor roll three years in a row, and Lucas was identified as gifted.

What Worked

Caregiver mindset: Both caregivers had an early game plan as to how to integrate the children into their home. They agreed at the outset that consistent love and patience would be the core of all interaction with the children and indeed with each other as they were now responsible for two traumatized children. When the children arrived, they quickly sought professional help with me early, and participated fully in family therapy. Both parents worked hard to understand trauma and educated themselves on the signs of trauma the children would likely display. They were aware that the children would struggle with trusting them and would likely revert to behaviors that show that they are afraid, worried, or experiencing flashbacks. As the family's therapist, I partnered with the family on their journey to help the children heal.

Cassie and Lucas's father and stepmother provided a safe, structured, and playful environment for the children to communicate their fears and worry about the past, the present, and the future. I was immediately informed of any changes and causes for concern. Therapy sessions always had an element of play and targeted specific areas of concern. I used role-play, storytelling, puppets, drawing, and songs to explore the difficult topics of grief, abandonment, and forgiveness as well as to teach strategies to cope with anxiety and feelings of inadequacy. We discussed dreams and what they could mean, and explored their ambivalent feelings toward their biological mother. Cassie worried about her health, while Lucas worried he would be sent back to live with his biological mother. Both were adamant that they wanted her to be safe but that they did not want to ever live with her and repeatedly expressed their love, gratitude, and attachment to their father and stepmom.

In one session, we looked at Lucas's recurring dream of the monster at his bed while he hid under the sheets. He explained that he would often awake frightened. Lucas drew a picture of the monster, and we discussed who it might be and what it was trying to do. It was fear. We decided to use comic strip art to design a frame-by-frame neutralizing of Fear. First, we had to identify what Lucas was afraid of and how that fear made him feel—helpless in bed cowering under the sheets. We discussed where he would get his powers to overcome fear. How will he fight back? He used his voice. Lucas drew a picture of himself shouting "Go Away!" He used his karate moves, learned in a real class he attended, "Take that!" Lucas drew himself, taking a deep breath and blowing out his birthday candles. "Outta here, Fear!" He also drew himself turning to love in a picture of himself hugging and being hugged by his dad. The cartoon balloon read, "Dad, I am afraid." His dad's balloon read, "I am with you, son. I won't leave you"

Cassie and Lucas thrived because events and outcomes were explained and discussed with them with age-appropriate openness and transparency. Their father and stepmother gave constant assurances of how much they are loved, cherished, and wanted. They thrived in the role of big brother and sister to their toddler sibling. Cassie and Lucas's caregivers tried hard to avoid negative talk about their biological mother, putting her behavior in the context of mental illness.

I believe that because of the intensity of the hurt the children experienced being abandoned by their biological mother, anxiety personified will always be their "frenemy." Anxiety will suddenly cause worry, signaling that there has been a triggering thought or event in their lives. However, the children are now trained to and do believe that they can talk about their feelings with their dad and stepmom without judgment. They know these feelings are normal. They can talk with me in ongoing sessions.

After four years of stable, loving parenting and consistent psychotherapy, the children are thriving. They are creative, happy, and optimistic. Cassie and Lucas have many friends.

Any intervention strategy we use to help abandoned children heal should be based on love. First, we must love the hurting, fragile child as they are now and also love what we see the child will become in the future. For Cassie and Lucas, their parents (father and stepmother's) steadfast commitment to loving and being always there made the children secure and resilient. They were able to manage the difficulty of traumatic memories of being abandoned by their mother and at the same time make sense of her mental illness. Cassie's stepmother and father were optimistic and believed that in the future, the children will be adults who are balanced, productive, resilient, and hopeful, and further along the healing continuum. Healing from childhood abandonment is a lifelong process.

LOVE FOUNDATION, PERMA FRAMEWORK FOR CHILDREN'S WELL-BEING

In the previous chapter, I described PERMA, a theory of well-being, as one technique that helps parents and caregivers manage their own well-being. The five building blocks are positive emotions, engagement, relationships, meaning, and accomplishment (PERMA).[4] PERMA can be used to enable flourishing in suffering abandoned children as well. Children traumatized by parental abandonment are disconnected and deeply wounded. Many brood, act out, and create alternate realities, experience "twoness" to attach to the missing parent and or to connect with, and heal, their inner hurt selves. Loving parents and caregivers understand and see the children's deep hurts.

THE FIRST BUILDING BLOCK OF PERMA—(P) POSITIVE EMOTIONS

PERMA provides a framework to help children heal. Let's explore a few interventions that foster the five building blocks of the PERMA well-being model. The first is increasing a child's positive emotions by play. Play is that critical and pleasurable feature of childhood that fosters positive emotions.[5] Many abandoned children are often self-conscious, insecure, afraid to be themselves because they are unsure of their worthiness. In particular, those abandoned by dad miss out on the benefits of the rough-and-tumble play associated with fathers' style of interacting with their children. Marc Bekoff, professor emeritus of ecology and evolutionary biology, explains that play is "a banquet for the brain, a smorgasbord for the senses, providing nourishment for the body and spirit."[6] Researchers on play further explain that children who play feel connected, safe, and that they belong. Play transforms aggression and builds attachment.[7] If we keep the needs of the abandoned child in mind, we realize the value of healthy play that helps a child relax with wild abandon, get lost in flow,[8] and/or bond with others. Play, of course, involves the wide range of activities that children engage in individually or with others including imaginative play, activities with or without rules, and activities that require movement. It is important to note that positive emotions are more than happiness. Positive emotions include feeling at peace, hopeful, content, and grateful. The positive emotions of feeling calm or soothed, safe and comforted are particularly important for the abandoned child and may be fostered by specific activities such as the contact-comfort activity described below.

TO HAVE AND TO HOLD (CONTACT-COMFORT OBJECT)

Abandoned children self-soothe, that is, they engage in activities that calm their fears and anxieties, and help them connect to the missing parent. In the late 1950s, Harry Harlow[9] demonstrated how important holding, touching, and snuggling with a caregiver is to an infant and young offspring. The loss of this opportunity is keenly felt by children missing the contact-comfort of either mother or father. Creating an object to represent the missing parent is a very powerful activity that allows a child to connect with the missing parent.

To restore feelings of connection to others, we start with a child's primal attachment at birth first to the mother, then to the father. I have argued that with either parent absent, a child suffers psychological pain and in fact grieves. An aware caregiver can begin connecting the child to their feelings of loss with the contact-comfort attachment exercise first introduced to me by psychologist Judy Kuriansky.[10]

The contact-comfort exercise requires simple, plain felt fabric cut into the size of a small pillow. Markers are used to draw a bird on one side of the felt representing freedom, hope, promise, dreams, and then any other design or words the child chooses. The sides are closed with colored thread (embroidery) after soft batting is inserted to make the pillow soft and tactile. Children enjoy creating their own contact-comfort object; holding and touching it help channel their strong feelings like anger and insecurity. Decorating the sides of the felt pillow is especially healing as children may write messages to their absent fathers or mothers, as well as their own hopes, dreams, and wishes. It is also small enough to sleep with at night or to carry around to have and to hold, especially in moments when they feel anxious or need to connect with their missing dad or mom. This is a bonding exercise that connects the child to the missing parent. It could also be an attachment activity as the remaining parent or caregiver guides the child through the process of creating the comfort-contact item. A psychotherapist could also use the exercise to help a child process and reconcile their feelings about being left behind by a parent.

When I met Allie[11] in the office of my private practice, I invited her to create a contact- comfort of her own. I encouraged her to be as creative as she wanted to be in decorating her pillow and to think of dad. Allie chose pale blue fabric and set to the task of drawing and sewing with quiet concentration. One side of her small pillow was covered with a nightscape of muted pastel shades. I asked about the many stars that covered the night sky on her pillow. Allie smiled and touched the pillow to her cheek. "Those aren't stars," she explained, eyes shining as she looked up at me. "They are messages to my dad."

THE SECOND BUILDING BLOCK OF PERMA—(E) ENGAGEMENT

I will continue to use the PERMA theory of well-being to frame the activities I discuss in this chapter, having described how we may increase positive emotions in abandoned children. The second building block of the PERMA well-being model is engagement. How do we encourage abandoned children to become enraptured in a task that increases their well-being? Give them opportunities to engage in tasks so absorbing and pleasurable—such as reading a good book, dancing, playing a musical instrument—that it produces what Csikszentmihalyi[12] described as "flow."

THE THIRD BUILDING BLOCK OF PERMA—(R) POSITIVE RELATIONSHIPS

The internal pain that abandoned children feel is rooted in the primal relationship severed when their mother or father left them. The fostering of the third building block in PERMA, strong positive relationships, is critical to helping abandoned children heal. Children left behind suffer the trauma of severed attachment so are deficient in how they connect to others. Parents and caregivers should restore well-being by helping children understand that they are worthy and that they matter. Children over time will begin to trust others and to open their hearts to connections to caring adults and with positive peer relationships. Research has shown that social media is excellent for helping young people to thrive as they connect with others and build strong social bonds. For some, however, social media opens up dark spaces that exacerbate their vulnerabilities, loneliness, and despair.[13]

I believe the positive relationships identified in PERMA extend to helping the child not only connect to others outside themselves but also to make connections within themselves—to discover who they are. One impactful way to self-discovery is identification of personal character strengths. Psychologist Chris Peterson[14] introduced the idea of character strengths and virtues, which if understood, nurtured, and used in a balanced way, help us understand ourselves, be our best selves, and help us thrive. Internal connections, self-integration, grows through self-knowledge. This shift is a way of thinking about the children's strengths rather than deficiencies, to focus on what *is* working rather than what is not working.[15]

Peterson identified six core virtues[16] recognized as universally morally good.[17] These virtues—wisdom, courage, humanity, justice, temperance, and transcendence—are the basis from which twenty-four character strengths are derived. The character strengths include humor, forgiveness, hopefulness, creativity, zest, and bravery. What are the gifts and talents that are natural but may show themselves in excessive ways because of the pain of abandonment? The example of Dominik illustrates further.

Dominik: Class Clown

Dominik was sent to my office after upsetting his teacher. He caused quite a ruckus with his outrageous jokes and mockery of his exasperated teacher. I was curious about Dominik's persistence in disrupting his classes despite repeated concessions from teachers and administrators and many chances to start anew. When I asked Dominik about his behavior in the class, he shrugged, "Mom says I am crazy just like my daddy." I quickly realized I had to find a way to change the narrative that Dominik had heard all his life.

I called Dominik's single mother, who, despite her best efforts, was overwhelmed by raising four children, with Dominik being the eldest. My call was yet another from the school. My contact, however, was different. I was not calling to complain about Dominik; instead, after explaining why Dominik was with me, I asked her permission for her son to take the Values in Action (VIA) survey[18] Dominik was excited and curious, relieved not to have to endure another lecture about his inappropriate behaviors. For my part, I was genuinely interested in his strengths.

The results indicated that Dominik's top strength is humor—playfulness, bringing smiles to others, lightheartedness, seeing the lighter side—from the virtue of transcendence.[19] I asked him his thoughts about humor as his top strength. He said, "I love to make people laugh." Now Dominik's behavior made sense. Motivated by his desire to fit in and to feel worthy and valued, he overused his core strength good humor by becoming the class clown. The VIA survey gave me an answer to help fill the space of Dominik's feeling of unworthiness.

I praised him for having such a powerful gift. I told him that we needed laughter and joy. We needed him to help us to have fun, to play, and to gladden our hearts. "But," he reflected, "I don't know when to stop." The excess of humor is "buffoonery,"[20] becoming the class clown. Now that I knew what motivated Dominik, I was able to share my knowledge of his strength with his teachers. With his mother's permission and to Dominik's delight, we arranged his class schedule to include drama class. He thrived in this class and became a favorite.

Through the VIA survey we were able to channel Dominik's talent and energies, provided affirmation of his talents, supported his needs, and increased his positive emotions. This positive change helped us provide other school-based interventions including more project-based work to increase his engagement, positive relationships, and encourage his feelings of accomplishment. These positive changes are tenets of PERMA, the theory of well-being.

Abandoned children, suffering broken bonds between themselves and their absent parent, may gain some understanding of that parent from the extended family. As previously discussed, some mothers are gatekeepers who block their children's access to their fathers. However, a child will experience a greater sense of self, personal identity, and feel connected, when they know both paternal and maternal family members. Family stories also help the child become connected to their extended family and the family in the larger social context.

FAMILY STORIES, STORY WRITING, AND STORYTELLING

Family narratives, whether personal tales of challenges, joy, and pain, if contextualized as part of life's journey, help bolster children's understanding of their own life's journey. In addition, by learning family stories, children come to understand that complexity and richness of life, that narratives can be changed, and that one decision over another has implications—such as those made by family members or characters in stories.

Rico: Determined to Provide Better Options

Rico told me he had to work to help his single mom and older brother make ends meet. He remembers talking with his father, who told Rico that he regretted not completing high school and dropping out at the eleventh grade. His father explained how at first the freedom of not attending school was wonderful, and he enjoyed the independence of earning his own money and spending time with like-minded friends. However, over time, with the birth of his two sons, he became frustrated at the challenges of not having a high school diploma and as a result being stuck in backbreaking low-paying jobs.

When Rico was in middle school, his father left the state to find work, returning home sporadically. Heartbroken and helpless, Rico watched his parents drift apart as his father visited the family less and less while his financial support decreased as well. Rico's older brother also eventually dropped out of high school to work. In high school, Rico worked part-time at the neighborhood supermarket. He was accepted to college, and because of dual enrollment already had some college credits. Rico told me he chose not to make the mistakes his father and brother made by dropping out of school. He was determined to provide better options for his own future family. Despite the challenges, this was a promise he made to himself and planned on keeping.

Young people like Rico have the opportunity to learn from the behaviors and decisions made by family members. Through stories told, children learn that they can make different choices. They do not have to repeat the missteps or mistakes made by family members, especially those painful ones made by parents.

Family stories may be told through oral traditions and/or through art and diagrams such as genograms. Genograms are an exciting and fun tool to facilitate children's exploration of their family story. Using chart paper or any other means of documenting, children can learn about their ancestors and other family members. They learn and can explore the behaviors and life histories of estranged members caused by mother–father separation, or mom's or dads' absence. Children learn about family strengths and weaknesses by connecting to family members and close friends. This is an opportunity to learn how members on both sides overcame challenges. When children make family connections, it helps them to understand themselves within the family, and that they too will overcome challenges. They learn about family hardiness, inherent biological strength, and resilience.

I created the *Story Tellers* club for a group of students who were without one or both parents. The main objective of the group was to "give back" and provide a service by writing stories to share with elementary students. I wanted to shift my students' attention from the ever-present internal focus of loss and grief to one of giving themselves to others. I partnered with a colleague counselor in an elementary school who arranged for my students to read to a kindergarten class. I reasoned that young children were nonthreatening as middle "schoolers" will always be "big kids" to seven-year-olds.

When *The Storytellers* group met, I outlined the group's objective: write a story that they will read to a class of kindergartners. I asked the group to describe the types of stories they enjoyed. We then focused on stories they enjoyed when they were very young. I modeled oral storytelling by telling the well-known classic "Three Little Pigs," and from my Caribbean heritage, Louise Bennett's poem-story "New Scholar,"[21] about the introduction of a new student to his teacher. I invited students to tell a story using the oral tradition and from their cultural heritage, and was thrilled when some of my Latino students shared "La Llorana," about a beautiful woman who cries at night looking for her children. I also read several children's stories to the group, such as, Beatrix Potter's *Peter Rabbit*[22] and *Tales of an Ashanti Father,*[23] about the spider character Anansi of West African/Caribbean folklore; and watched episodes of *Happily Ever After: Fairy Tales for Every Child.*[24] Students were able to identify the different mediums of storytelling. We discussed themes and the structure of stories for young children. Common ideas were that the stories had simple story lines, were fun, had interesting characters (human or animal). The stories also taught lessons in values that made us better world citizens and increased our feeling of well-being—these included the values of kindness, hope, forgiveness, and courage. It is important to note that these values were previously discussed embedded in the Values in Action character strengths.[25] The *Storytellers* were then tasked with working alone or in a team using guidelines discussed and with the help of the software *StoryJumper,*[26] to write a simple story that teaches a lesson. In addition, before writing their story, each student completed the Values in Action survey to discover their unique strengths. I believe that if each student knew their signature character strengths, it would help them frame the story they planned to share with the kindergartners.

Alex: Finding His Pack

One of my favorite stories was "The Lone Wolf," written by thirteen-year-old Alex. Alex lived with his single mother, after his parents separated. His father returned to South America, where all of Alex's family lived. Alex rarely saw his mother, who worked two jobs. He recalled that she was either working, sleeping, or going out with friends. His father spoke with him by phone on special occasions, such as his birthday or at Christmastime. At school, Alex was often seen walking alone, with his head down, appearing lost in thought. In the *Storytellers* group, he often sat alone and even while involved in group activities remained reserved. Alex's signature character strength was bravery.

When Alex read his story to the kindergarten class, his voice wavered as he began. In his story, the "lone wolf" had no pack to call his own. He had no family or friends. The pack did not include the lone wolf in wolf community events, because he just did not fit in. They shunned him. He was different. The lone wolf roamed the forest alone and ate his meals alone. Each night he howled sadly at the moon. Alex continued his story, "One day all the wolves had a meeting. The lone wolf hid behind a tree. He listened and watched." The wolves met to discuss the lone wolf, whose howling at night made them sad. What could they do? "Let's invite him to join us," one wolf suggested. "Maybe he is lonely," another added. The pack invited the lone wolf to come into the meeting. He was afraid. He was not sure they really wanted him. Were they joking? "We are not joking, please come and join our pack," they said. The lone wolf joined in and felt at home. Now he travels with the pack; he is no longer alone.

The children applauded when Alex finished reading his story. One student asked Alex where the lone wolf's family was, another asked if it took a long time to learn to read. My heart was full and happy for Alex as the children surrounded him to ask more questions and to look at the pictures of lone wolf and the pack. I noticed a marked change in Alex after his interaction with the kindergarteners. He told me the experience was one of the best in his life. But although still quiet, I noticed he started to talk with and walk with his peers at school.

In my discussion on twoness, I described how children create another self, an alternate version of how their lives could be. The story they create is a better version of themselves and replaces the sad, the frightening, and the void caused by the missing parent. Journaling, one of the tried-and-true means of documenting intense feelings,[27] can be taken further with the use of technology. Children can use technology to make their stories come to life. The internet provides opportunities for dreaming, imagining, creating, and exploring—all avenues that facilitate healing. Creating fan fiction is one narrative approach to change the present and imagine a new and better reality. Through fan fiction, young people can enter an online space as a new character with a new imagined better life. This activity must, however, be carefully supervised by caregivers as children in these online spaces are vulnerable to predators and to other negative influences.[28]

There are other narratives that children can learn from as they use their imagination to dream of happy endings. Fantasy, yes, but their imagination allows for a time to hope and think of things in a different way. Stories often concern the unlikely hero who must conquer their fears and complete a challenge, with the help of a few steady companions, each with his or her own gifts abound.[29] This kind of story is called a *bildungsroman*. The popularity of this trope means that a child can relate to stories about finding their identity. This quest for self must be completed with the help of others. The journey to healing cannot be achieved alone.

Other stories besides the *bildungsroman* connect children to themselves. Folktales teach simple virtues and also connect children to their ancestry. For example, stories of cunning and resilience is embodied in the Caribbean stories of Anansi,[30] the small spider-man who uses charm and wit to conquer larger, more powerful animals. This could be a guided activity with the help of a therapist trained in narrative therapy or who one who understands the power of stories and storytelling. In addition, when parents or caregivers tell stories, they bond with their children and teach how to draw strength and learn life lessons from folktales and legends. Stories help parents and children bond and help children connect with their cultural identity.

FOURTH BUILDING BLOCK OF PERMA—(M) MEANING AND PURPOSE

I continue with my use of the PERMA theory of well-being to frame interventions for abandoned children. The fourth building block signifies the importance of meaning and purpose to well-being. As children mature, the sense of meaning or purpose they give their lives is nurtured by their connections to and service to others. Parents and caregivers are critically important in providing opportunities for children to become involved in "societal organizations that enable a sense of meaning, such as religion, family, science, politics, work organizations, justice, the community, social causes (e.g., being green), among others."[31]

Abandoned children need to see themselves as worthy and capable of giving to others, and being agents of change. Serving others provides a myriad of benefits that will help children. These benefits include increases in positive emotions of belongingness, of making a difference, all derived from the satisfaction of connection to others—turning the child's focus outward, not the inward pining for the missing parent. Conversely, connecting to a spiritual source turns the child inward to reflect, meditate. and in wonder and awe. In my interaction with children traumatized by abandonment, I often hear the heartbroken question, "Why did my parent leave me?" The child tries to understand and cope with being unworthy of the parent's love and attention. Activities that inspire purpose such as doing work for others is healing as the child learns that they are important, and when they serve in the smallest capacity, they make a difference. The reason for their abandonment may never be clear to the questioning child, but the traumatic experience in the context of service to others helps to ease the pain.

FIFTH BUILDING BLOCK OF PERMA—(A) ACCOMPLISHMENT

The final building block of PERMA is accomplishment. Since abandoned children often have thoughts of unworthiness, parents and caregivers should provide those under their care with opportunities to set and meet goals, to achieve mastery, and experience success. Academic and social skills goals come quickly to mind, but abandoned children are often risk averse. Girls who did not have their fathers in their lives report that they often feel nervous and insecure.[32] Teaching children to take risks—to a try a challenging task—promotes resilience.

Risk-Taking Promotes Resilience, Healing, and Hope

The impact of risk-taking is also embedded in the narratives children learn about their family members. Risk-taking is an important part of a child's healthy growth. When mothers allow dads to engage in rough-and-tumble play and later organized sports with their children, they encourage goal setting, resilience, courage, persistence, and grit. Celebrity dads interviewed by *People Magazine*[33] shared their joy in fostering courage in their children, especially encouraging their daughters to be brave. One father built an obstacle course in his backyard, another encouraged his daughter's feelings of power and control by superhero play, another by daily words of affirmation. Risky behavior in play has many benefits for children, as it allows them to set the goal to conquer their fears as they role-play in a safe environment. Using tools and instruments, exploring and constructing, teaches children how to regulate their emotions and to experience the accomplishment of managing fear, anger, and pushing through pain. "Risky play teaches emotional resilience, and not to mention, it's fun!"[34]

Schools also provide the opportunity for development of mastery and self-efficacy in academic and extracurricular pursuits through risk-taking. A child trying out for the school's soccer or debate teams, for example, and with the help of patient and compassionate teachers, helps them discover a love for science and join the school's science club.

Interestingly, schools in Britain[35] are taking encouraging risk-taking beyond the norm of our risk-averse schools. British educators, after decades of creating risk-free school campuses including playgrounds and classrooms, are cautiously reintroducing risk to bolster children's resilience and grit. Playgrounds have discontinued plastic playhouses, and under the watchful eyes of adult supervisors, children now play with loose bricks, crates, two-by-fours, mud pits, tire swings, and workbenches with hammers. Classrooms now have sharp scissors.

TRAUMA INTERVENTION FOCUSED ON BUILDING TRUST

Another trust-building exercise is based on the work of Karen Purvis's Trust-Based Relational Intervention (TBRI).[36] TBRI is grounded in attachment theory and emerged from work with adopted children and children in foster care. The three main tenets of TBRI are empowering principles, connecting principles, and correcting principles, and are intended to help traumatized children feel safe, to self-regulate, and to connect to others. The heart of this intervention is trust. Abandoned children are traumatized because bonds of connection were broken when their parent left them. Abandoned child struggle to trust others, knowing firsthand that parents and caregivers do leave. The task of the loving, consistent parent or caregiver is to become worthy of the child's trust by keeping promises, demonstrating that the child matters and deserves full attention and care.

CONNECT THE CHILD TO NATURE

One thing experts agree on is that being outdoors is excellent for mental health. As carers try to balance their own mental health and foster the same in the children they care for, one simple and very cheap way is to enjoy the outdoors. One recent study identified feelings of satisfaction, reflection, a sense of "connectedness," and wonder at nature with being outdoors.[37] Indeed, being outdoors is one way to detach from social media and model for children respect and appreciation of nature and things transcendental, like hope, gratitude, and awe. As a spin-off on time outdoors, a growing pastime for many now is bird-watching.[38] Parents have started to use bird-watching as a way to reduce children's screen time and to help themselves and their children experience the wonder and delight of nature. Advice abounds as to how to start,[39] as well as advice about bird-watching in both urban and suburban spaces.[40] And even with weather changes, children can learn to delight in the magic of nature,[41] as they connect by walking barefooted.[42]

NEGATIVE THOUGHTS: THINKING TRAPS BLOCK WELL-BEING

The children I see in my private practice and in the school setting, who are grieving a missing parent, often ruminate, reporting that they have the same thoughts of past events over and over again. For example, the persistent thoughts may be fixed on a parent's chance word that deeply hurt, a broken promise, or a moment of rejection. Rumination is the thinking loop of the same thought over and over. Thoughts are usually sad or distressing, and often lead to depression and questioning self-worth. Holdaway et al. found that rumination was associated with suicide risk, ideation, and attempts.[43]

Resilience expert Karen Reivich[44] describes ruminations as a "thinking trap," thoughts or beliefs that after a triggering event keep recurring, causing negative feelings especially that of having no control. This "internal thought process convinces us of something, when in reality it is completely untrue."[45] Thinking traps convince us of our helplessness and block coping and resilience. Reivich describes four common thinking traps: mind reading, me or them, helplessness, and catastrophizing.

"Mind reading" is assuming we know what another person is thinking and expecting the other person to know what we are thinking. An example is a child believing that their abandoning parent was thinking that the child was unlovable and not worth staying with. The "me or them" thinking trap is when we believe that setbacks or problems *are all* our fault or *the sole* fault of another person. I recall my own thoughts when our father left us, that as the eldest child, it was *my* fault that he left; maybe if I had been a better daughter, he would have stayed with us. The "helplessness" thinking trap is believing that the negative event will forever impact our lives and we will never have control. As a result, we become passive, abandoning motivation and giving up—behaviors akin to the learned helplessness previously discussed. An example from my previous discussion of twoness, Talia, an academically struggling student, stated, "I would be stronger than I am now. If he were in my life, I could do more things." The thinking trap "catastrophizing" is ruminating on "the irrational worst case outcomes of a situation,"[46] This thinking leads to the inability to take action, anxiety, and physical ailments such as stomach pain and headaches. An example is Grace, who, abandoned by both parents, stated "I know I will never be adopted, nobody will ever want me." We will explore Grace's story at the end of this chapter.

Reivich described ways to challenge thinking traps as "mental judo."[47] Children readily relate to taking actions that challenge and do battle against the dark, negative thoughts. The first is to confront the negative thought with "Where is the evidence? Where is the truth in this thinking?" With the help of a trained professional, children learn to use evidence to "argue against themselves." The process of using this strategy is that the child's inner negative voice presents all the negative arguments or words in the child's mind, words such as "you are worthless, you will never do well, nobody cares," but the child is taught to counter the words of the negative inner voice with opposing arguments. So in this example, the child would say in internal dialogue, "No, I am loved. Grandma told me she loves, she hugs me every day. My teacher is nice to me. She says I am smart, I have an A in Science. Grandma cares about me, my teacher cares about me." When children argue against themselves, they examine the source of their negative thoughts and prove that what they are thinking is not true.

The second strategy to attack negative thinking is reframing, that is, looking at the source of the negative thought in a different way, so a parent or helping professional guides the child by stating, for example, "Another way of looking at this is that it is not your fault your father left home. He left home because he and I could not make each other happy." Reframing teaches children that there are other points of view or other perspectives on the situation. It encourages mental agility.

The third approach to battling "mental traps" caused from anxiety and worry, is the plan—"if *x* happens, then I will do *y*." For example, a child whose worst fear was their recently released mother reentering prison could be asked, "Okay, so what if mom goes back to prison, then what will you do?"

When I teach a child the three mental judo strategies, I sum up by naming the process as "coming up for AIR." I encourage children to take deep breaths before using any or all of the three—Arguing against yourself, (A), If x then y (I), and Reframing (R) as they battle anxiety-promoting, negative thoughts.

Indeed, negative thoughts reduce an abandoned child's feelings of self-efficacy, resilience, and overall well-being and blocks them from achieving PERMA. When parents and caregivers learn and use strategies to help their child challenge thinking traps, the child will thrive. But how do we manage feelings when bad things happen?

SEARCH FOR GOOD, ENCOURAGE GRATITUDE

Sadly, bad things happen to children. Sometimes children suffer, are injured, or mortally hurt at the hands of their parents or caregivers. It is difficult to find purpose and meaning in terrible, painful events, but we can train the abandoned child to think about the good things that happen daily. Hunting the good stuff (HTGS) aims to build resilience by increasing mental toughness with an effective strategy of restructuring our thinking away from dwelling on negative events. HTGS was one of the components of the Master Resilience Training, a joint initiative between the University of Pennsylvania Positive Psychology Center and the U.S. Army.[48] HTGS is embedded in the gratitude exercise described earlier in our discussion on PERMA, and increasing positive emotions. By "hunting" for good things, children actively seek out the good events that happened that day. Older children benefit from keeping a "gratitude journal," writing out the day's good events.

Research on gratitude confirms the importance of counting our blessings. Abandoned children grieving and feeling unworthy will benefit from the mind shift as they review their lives and identify good events—no matter how small or apparently insignificant. Although this may seem counterintuitive, research shows that being grateful for the little things breaks up depression and increases happiness.[49]

Therefore, each night before going to bed, caregivers should encourage their child to reflect on their day, to notice and remember three little things that sweetened the day. The child should write these down. This chronicling will become a documentation of good events. Consistent with research, clients report to me how over time they begin to notice good events—even in the smallest happening—eventually feeling grateful even for their sandwich at lunch and how their empathy for those without food increased. Gratitude also fostered a sense of awe, awareness and connection to the spiritual. Another client reported how her heart gladdened at birdsong each morning. She began paying attention and became grateful for nature. This simple exercise of noticing good things increased well-being by fostering positive emotions and building resilience.

The story of Grace illustrates how the PERMA theory of well being helps in framing interventions.

Grace: "Yeah . . . nobody can hurt me"

"I really don't get attached to anyone." Curious, I asked what being attached meant to her. "Well, that's what my last therapist said; I think it means I really don't connect with or get close to anybody." She paused here, looking down at her hands. "Why? I mean . . . um, it's better right? Nobody can hurt me if I'm not attached." Grace looked up at me, eyes sad yet defiant. "Yeah . . . nobody can hurt me."

This was my fifth meeting with fourteen-year-old Grace, who was abandoned by her mother at six years old. Her mother did not return to get her from her babysitter. The babysitter and her husband subsequently adopted her. Grace lived with her adopted parents for four years, when the adopted father was tragically killed in a road accident. Unable to manage on her own, Grace's adopted mother moved in with family. One year later, the adopted mother suffered a heart attack and died. Since that tragic event, Grace has been in number of foster homes. She had also been hospitalized for psychiatric care and took medication for mood regulation. Grace's visits to me were court mandated as part of her foster care service. She has had a series of therapists, the last refusing to continue sessions because Grace was either unresponsive, maintaining a stony silence during their meetings, or was extremely rude and aggressive.

Ms. Powell, her current foster mother, told me that records show that Grace was the second of a several siblings, all of whom were taken into care and placed in different foster homes. Ms. Powell reported that Grace had enrolled in several schools before living with her. At her current school, Grace had no friends, was extremely hostile to anyone who tried to befriend her, and spent her time drawing. She was also failing any class that required group work. Grace presented a cool detachment from all those around her. Her detachment made her appear angry, hostile, distant, and cold. Potential adoptive parents reported that her aggressive demeanor discouraged them from considering taking her into their lives.

I took Grace to lunch for our first meeting. I accepted that she saw me as yet another adult trying to control her and "get inside" her head. She would not speak up to order her own meal, and I had to coax her to project her voice so that the order could be placed. I soon realized that she was not familiar with ordering in public. After understanding what she wanted, I placed the order for her. She did not thank me but ate her chicken tenders and her favorite soda in silence, avoiding my eyes. After some time, she responded to small talk about lunch. I then decided self-disclosure was the best course. I spoke briefly about the sad days I experienced as a child when I witnessed my parents' violent arguments and my father leaving me and my siblings behind. I shared that I coped with my sad feelings by writing poems and stories and dreaming a lot.

Grace kept her head down, focused on her meal as I talked. I plunged on. I explained the positive psychology intervention called Hunting the Good Stuff (HTGS).[50] I remarked that I never guessed that those years of sadness and feeling abandoned by my father would lead me to understand the feelings of loss experienced by children I work with. I moved on and asked about her art. I told Grace her foster mother said she was a pretty good artist. Silent, Grace looked at me for a while—as though trying to make up her mind. I did a mental happy dance when she opened her bag and took out her sketch pad and showed me her drawings. I was able to genuinely praise her work, which was really quite good. Seeking to engage Grace further, I asked her, "Does drawing help you feel better? Help you deal with sad thoughts?" Grace did not respond. I moved on. I praised her capturing the form and likeness of a current pop star. I asked another safe question: "Where do you see your art taking you?" I was genuinely curious, but also wanted to assess her future thinking and gauge her level of hopefulness.

Grace told me that she wanted to be a fashion designer. Common ground! We talked about fashion and the latest trends. Before we parted from our first session, I asked her how she felt about meeting me twice per month with one session over lunch and one session at my office. I told her I needed her assessment of my office décor, and perhaps we could talk some more. Grace agreed to meet me again. I gave her homework, which was the *Gratitude Exercise*.[51] Each night, until we see each other again, before she goes to bed, she should write down three things or happenings that day that went well or that she was thankful for. She should, if possible, jot down why that event was a good thing. I encouraged her to write anything that came to mind as she reflected on her day's events—nothing was too small to acknowledge, even a chance to draw, a piece of candy, lip gloss. The idea was to help Grace focus on what was working in her life and to shift her perception to the little good things in her life.

Ms. Powell later told me that Grace said she did not mind seeing my again, not just for lunch, but because I gave her choice, that is, I gave her control over her seeing me again. I did not force, insist, or take it for granted that she wanted to meet with me again. Also, I earned points because I was interested in her art. My journey with Grace was ongoing and tested my patience and stamina. She was very careful about what she shared with me. However, over time I saw encouraging signs and understood some of her concerns. Grace told me that the *Gratitude Exercise* made her feel a little better. Her foster mother noticed that Grace was saying, "thank you" to her without being told.

One significant moment occurred, however, when I decided to discuss trauma with Grace. I felt it was risky because she may shut down and just glare at me. I learned that angry withdrawal was her way of controlling the situation and managing her anxiety when she felt threatened. But I took a chance. Probing indirectly, I asked, three questions: Has she ever heard of trauma, and what was it? What causes trauma in kids? How traumatized kids act? Grace was quiet for a while. When she spoke, her responses were insightful. She said abuse can cause trauma, like being yelled at and called names or being hit. She said that kids can react with sadness, feeling lonely, or being angry, and pulling away from everyone and not trusting people because they will hurt them. I then asked if she has ever had these feelings. I was met with a glare and stony silence. I did not probe any further but reintroduced the idea of *Hunting the Good Stuff* and resilience.[52] We mulled over how can we find good in bad events and reflected on the age-old question of why do bad things happen to good people. Grace and I agreed that life has such difficult aspects. I was not surprised when we discussed that her top strength was creativity from the Values in Action[53] survey.

We discussed the thinking traps. I explained that I am always in danger of catastrophizing and mind reading, and that I have to be mindful of where my thoughts are going when I get I anxious. I shared the "mental judo" techniques that helped me. I asked Grace which strategy she felt would work best for her. She thought for a moment and then said, "if x then y"[54] This was the plan for "if this happens, then I will do that" I was not surprised at her choice of "mental judo" since this strategy helps with thinking ahead and planning for the worst-case scenario. For action plan reflection at home, I asked Grace to practice one of the strategies of "mental judo" just to see if any of them worked. I told her I was interested in her assessment.

When we met for the subsequent session, Grace told me that "if x then y" helped her with a school problem. She was worried about not completing a reading assignment, and because she never spoke in class, she was afraid her teacher would publicly "call her out." I thanked her for sharing with me. I asked her to help me design a survivor's guide for children who have had some sadness in their lives. Grace drew a comic strip showing in one panel a female stick figure crying in a corner and a male stick figure standing yelling. The other panel showed the female stick figure surrounded by other figures consoling her.

This is the closest I have come to understanding a little of what Grace has experienced. Her foster mother told me that Grace's past has been difficult to understand but that there was definite abuse. However, Child Protective Services has been unable to ascertain what type. As previously mentioned, her adopted parents died, and since she is from out of state, her historical data is incomplete. In addition, Grace will not freely speak about her past. I have since used genograms to get a "picture" of her family. She displayed marginal interest and would not say her biological mother's name. However, she said she saw her father once at her paternal grandmother's funeral, but does not know where he is. Grace focused on the deceased adopted mother as her mother. In describing her, however, Grace said her adopted mother was usually angry, but that her husband was very nice and kind. Given the sketchy biographical history from Ms. Powell, I suspect Grace's original trauma stems from her disconnection from her biological mother—her subsequent abandonment and her father's lack of involvement. In addition, Grace has experienced repeated trauma related to abandonment, loss, and abuse. Where the abuse occurred is unknown, as Grace has been in and out of foster homes out of state, and had been institutionalized for depression. I understand her coping with her internal pain with detachment and hostility.

Well into our sixth session, I experienced Grace's wrath. I was initially taken aback by its ferocity. In a session over lunch, I asked about her plans to pursue art and fashion. I indicated the path was graduating from high school then to college—a two-year or four-year program for training. Grace completed the *WOOP* exercise[55] and identified her failing math grade as the major obstacle to her achieving her goal. Her failing grade was because she refused to ask for help and refused to participate in group work. I asked what steps she thought she could take to communicate with her teacher and peers. I assured her that together we would figure out a way to overcome her fears. I was ready to start with a plan. But I unknowingly pushed Grace too far too fast. Passing math—to graduate high school and to get to college—to get the training to pursue her dream of fashion design all hinged on her communicating with her teacher and her peers in math class. Communicating with others causes Grace a great deal of stress and anxiety.

Unable to manage these feelings, Grace angrily got up from the table. She pushed her chair, which fell with a clatter to the floor, startling other diners. She glared at me with clenched fists, her face suffused with fury. I was initially quite taken aback and could get no response out of her except a furious glare and hostile body language. She folded her arms and remained in angry silence until her foster mother came to pick her up. Grace then stomped off, jumped in the car, and slammed the door. Confused, I outlined the events to her foster mother. Ms. Powell apologized and stated that Grace gets into these rages when asked to do something she does not like, or does not want to do.

On reflection, I told Ms. Powell that I thought I understood what was going on with Grace. When she gets anxious and feels she has no control, she is unable to manage uncomfortable feelings, unable to articulate her discomfort—she rages. Her behavior certainly gives her back control of the situation as it shuts everything down, effectively blocking any stressful action. Ms. Powell said she would contact the teacher and explain the difficulties Grace was having in math, seeking support at the school level. We hoped we were not too late to salvage her grade. It was already very close to the end of the semester. I was surprised that Grace wanted to continue seeing me.

Grace's inability to regulate her emotions—her stony, tightly controlled detachment or extreme anger and aggression—remind me of those sad baby monkeys of the Harlow experiments. Deprived of a mother to cuddle with when frightened and anxious, they threw tantrums and exhibited rages and out of control behaviors. In addition, all the attachment theories previously discussed emphasize the importance of early attachment to a caring mother who nurtures and facilitates their young's exploration of the unknown, while both physically and emotionally anchored to the mother. In this way, the child experiences anxieties, fright, and worry but learns to regulate these feelings from the safe harbor of the mother. Grace did not have a close bond with her biological mother, and has experienced repeated interruptions to bonding with other maternal caregivers. She has therefore not learned how to regulate her uncomfortable feelings.

Now understanding Grace's behaviors, I noticed her helplessness and anger was obvious after "adoption parties." At these parties, Grace and other children in foster care meet with potential adopting parents. As previously stated, Grace's aggressive and noncommunicative attitude was so off putting, she was never considered for adoption. Unwanted, she repeatedly experienced rejection, and in one brief frank moment told me, "I know I will never be adopted, nobody will ever want me."

Fortunately, her foster mother, with her own successful children, provided a stable, loving home for Grace. Ms. Powell and I both believe that at fourteen, Grace will most likely remain in care until she ages out of the system at eighteen years old.

Over time, Ms. Powell has noticed that Grace has begun to show tentative affection to her. Grace would occasionally rub Ms. P's arm or touch her hair. She never verbally expresses love; the one exception is to Ms. P's bichon frise, Dotty, to whom she is devoted. Grace had his picture on her phone. Her foster mother jokes that Dotty was also devoted to Grace; she expected that when Grace leaves, she would have to take Dotty with her. I made recommendations to the Foster Parent Board that Grace remain with Ms. Powell until (if) ever) she gets adopted. Another change, another loss of a caregiver, would devastate Grace.

I continue to work with her and her foster mother. We found that Grace blossomed when she taught younger children art. In addition, when she was physically active she was in a better mood. Grace was, however, inconsistent with her dance classes, as she was self-conscious about her body and felt that she was being judged. While with Ms. Powell, Grace participated in the Outward Bound Program and thrived in the nonthreatening environment. She shared her art with compassionate and patient facilitators, and participated in the after-school program, teaching younger children to draw. Grace made slow progress because of her deep-seated trauma from abandonment, severed attachment, and abuse.

She was very anxious about the possibility of being transitioned to another foster home as has been the pattern of her life, and projected a cool, detached demeanor, understandably cautious about becoming too attached to Ms. Powell and then having to move on. Grace did transition to another foster home, back to her home state, away from Ms. Powell and me. Ms. Powell explained that Grace was in treatment with a therapist and at the time, adhering to taking her medication to manage her depression.

The PERMA theory of well-being is a powerful framework to guide interventions to help children who are sad and disconnected because their parent left them. PERMA supports activities that nurture the whole child, and places full attention on bolstering the child's potential for healing and living a good life. The building blocks of fostering—positive emotions, engagement, positive relationships, meaning, and goal achievement—are essential to human beings thriving. The theory does not in any way ignore the challenges of pain and brokenness from abandonment, but it does offers an optimistic perspective and road map to targeted interventions.

14

Butterfly Stages: Metamorphosis Model of Interventions

USING THE THEORY OF WELL-BEING (PERMA) FRAMEWORK

When I attend high school graduations, I am always delighted when I see beautiful, self-assured, funny, happy young adults walk across the stage to receive their diploma. Like butterflies, they excitedly fluttered among each other, and their family and friends. I am often thrilled when one of these beautiful creatures extracts themselves from the group, come over to me, and says, "Do you remember me?" I must confess that very often I must peer closely at the young person's face and search through my mental files. "Yes! I do." The physically mature, well-dressed, beautiful, confident young person may still have some of the facial features from middle school when we last saw each other.

But often, I do not remember and must be rescued by the young person's kind reminder of their name, and, "You were my counselor in middle school. I came to see you when I was sad about (my mother or my father)." As I am brought up to date with future plans, hopes, and dreams, I think this young person is on the path to achieving well-being. I marvel at the metamorphosis. In front of me is a wonderful creature ready to take on the world. Behind is the sad, brokenhearted, and vulnerable stage of—no longer a child but not an adult—the adolescent. Over my many years of working with vulnerable children, especially adolescents, and witnessing their transformation into young adulthood, I am reminded of the butterfly' journey to adulthood through its life cycle.

As I thought about the optimal needs of the human child to thrive into adulthood, I also considered the needs of the butterfly for optimal development from egg, caterpillar, and chrysalis to glorious transformation in adulthood. What are the optimal conditions for a butterfly egg to mature and majestically soar as an adult butterfly? The National Wildlife Federation[1] advised that the best environment is one that meets the needs of all the stages of butterfly development. "The insects need places to lay eggs, food-plants for their larvae (caterpillars), places to form a chrysalis, and nectar sources for adults."[2] The butterfly needs sunny places with colorful, nectar-filled native flowers that should be planted for continuous bloom. Caterpillars need plants with leaves that they can eat to thrive on, and butterflies need places to land, warm their wings, and places to gather to drink water and extract minerals.[3]

The main focus of this book was to examine parental behaviors that negatively impact their child achieving well-being. I also discussed actions that may be taken by caregivers to help children thrive despite the fact that they have been hurt by their parents actions. When parents abandoned their children, they created an environment of neglect that interrupted their child's healthy thriving. Similarly for the monarch butterfly, "parent" butterflies can pass the OE (Ophryocystis elektroscirrha) infection to their offspring. While there are inherent dangers in the butterfly environment, the monarch butterfly is particularly vulnerable to this protozoan parasite.

Conservation biologist and butterfly expert Karen Oberhauser explains that OE is an inactive spore that is transported by an infected butterfly and deposited on the surface of the leaf or sometimes on the egg itself. The egg matures into a larva or caterpillar. "A new cycle begins when it is eaten by the emerging larva."[4] While some monarchs with low OE infection may not show any symptoms, other individual caterpillars show evidence of infection at pupa or chrysalis stage and at adulthood. The infected pupa has dark spots that often become visible a few days before the adult emerges. At maturity, the infected adult "butterfly is weak, has difficulty emerging from the chrysalis casing, or failure to emerge from the chrysalis, failure to cling to the chrysalis upon emergence; crumpled or wrinkled wings that aren't fully expanded."[5] The negatively impacted monarch will be a weak, "deformed adult with crumpled wings, [often] unable to fly,"[6] Therefore, from its earliest developmental stages, the infected monarch was deprived of the conditions necessary to thrive.

The butterfly–human comparison is not new. However, I compared the needs of the butterfly with the needs of the human child as they mature into adulthood using the framework of optimal thriving of the PERMA theory of well-being.[7] As discussed, the PERMA theory of well-being identifies five building blocks for children to thrive (positive emotions, engagement, positive relationships, meaning, and feelings of accomplishment). PERMA helps children be the best they can be as they cope with the pain of being left behind by their parents. We encourage children to maximize positive emotions and so encourage optimism and hopefulness. We keep them engaged with activities that teach them skills to connect to their inner selves and to others. We encourage healthy relationships with others and teach them to recognize and shun toxic people in their lives. Meaning and purpose are connected to a young person's involvement in activities that are outside of themselves—activities that foster gratitude, awareness of a spiritual world, and the value of service to others. Finally, young people need to feel the sense of accomplishment, that they are worthy of setting and achieving goals.

Resilience training[8] is important for the children who must cope with sorrow and feelings of being unworthy of their parent's love. Resilience is embedded in PERMA. A child's ability to cope with adversity is linked to the child's biological makeup. Biological makeup is the inherited qualities that support a child's ability to cope. Some children are naturally more resilient than others. Many come to understand their innate resilience from stories told about family members who overcome challenges. Reivich[9] identified seven other variables that contributes to a child's resilience: optimism; self-awareness; self-regulation; mastery over self-efficacy; being connected to others and to positive institutions—such as family and caregivers who believe in their success—school, religious, and service organizations; and mental agility. They learn grit and not to give up when faced with upsetting or demoralizing challenges. An abandoned child in a nurturing environment that fosters PERMA and builds their resilience will heal, grow, and thrive, and like the healthy butterfly, soar.

The butterfly is a universal symbolism of hope. The butterfly's delicate beauty, so varied and delightful, is the result of a transformation from four completely different yet uniquely connected phases of its butterfly life. According to Kelly of Joyful Butterfly,[10] each butterfly egg or prenatal butterfly must be with the right host plant to be safe from predators. The young infant, the caterpillar, is sensitive as it molts and changes, and must have the right nurturing environment and host food or it will not thrive. The hard shell of the adolescent butterfly—the chrysalis, the hard mysterious shell that protects the soon-to-be-adult butterfly—must be safe and nurtured to emerge into its best beautiful self. The final stage, the adult butterfly, needs a sunny garden with nectar plants for them to drink, thrive, spread their wings, and fly.

The developmental stages of human beings parallel those of the butterfly. At each stage, the butterfly needs positive nurturing and protection. So, too, the human child, without positive love, support, and protection, will not thrive. The OE-infected butterfly's life is akin to the unhealed life of the child who struggles to live without the positive interventions—interventions from caring adults that foster feelings of self-efficacy, self-esteem, self-worth, purpose, of being connected to others and of mattering.

The two key elements identified in the butterfly-stages model[11] are that the interventions using PERMA are (a) needed at all stages of the child's life including adulthood and that (b) the interventions should be developmentally appropriate. Activities that foster the positive emotions of joy and excitement, for example, in an elementary school–aged child and an adolescent will most likely be different. At all stages, the human child needs consistent love throughout their lives. Through this section, I discussed the myriad of wonderful and effective activities available to help us promote healing and lasting well-being in traumatized children.

Framing interventions for abandoned children as butterfly-metamorphosis stages is useful as with each stage of butterfly life significant changes take place in the butterfly both internally—biologically as it matures—and externally—in response to its environment. These are similar to the changes that occur in the life of the human child.

Figure 14.1 describes how interventions delivered through the framework of PERMA help children heal from the trauma of parental abandonment. Clockwise, each cell depicts the alignment between the human development cycle from infant to adulthood with that of the butterfly. The

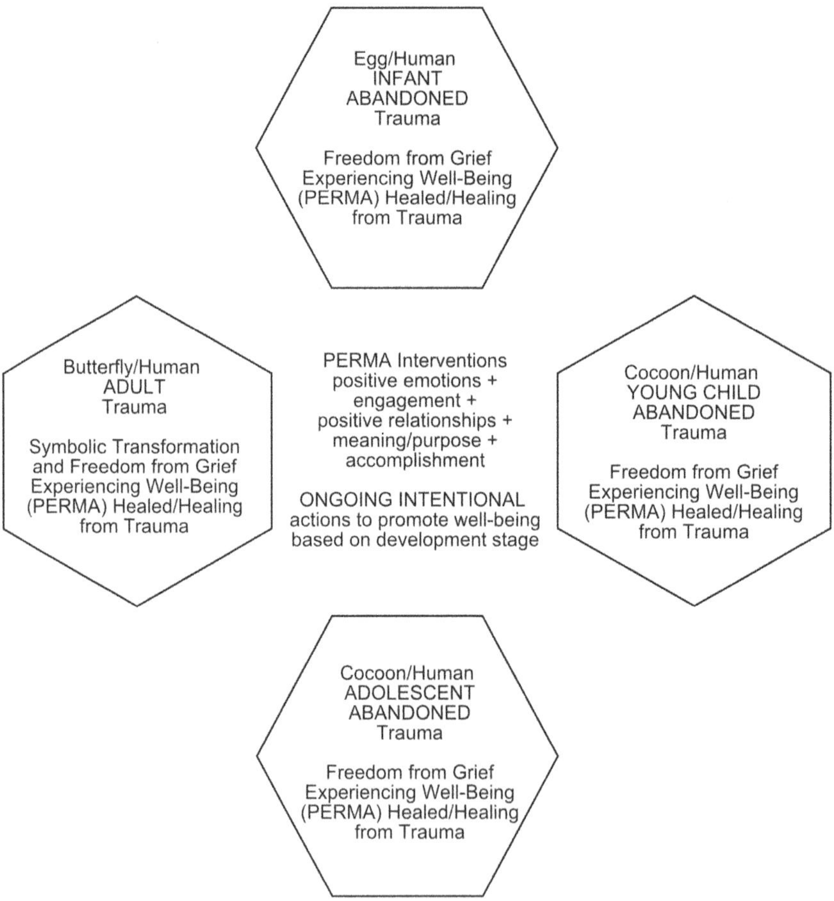

Figure 14.1 PERMA model.

center anchors the four cells indicating intentional and developmentally appropriate practices to facilitate healing.

Figure 14.2 describes the optimal environment for the butterfly's healthy growth from egg to pre-cocoon and the essential protective environments with PERMA interventions that foster healthy fetus growth to thriving pre-adolescent child.

Figure 14.2b depicts the complexity of changes that occur during the third and fourth stages of metamorphosis. In the third stage, the cocoon,

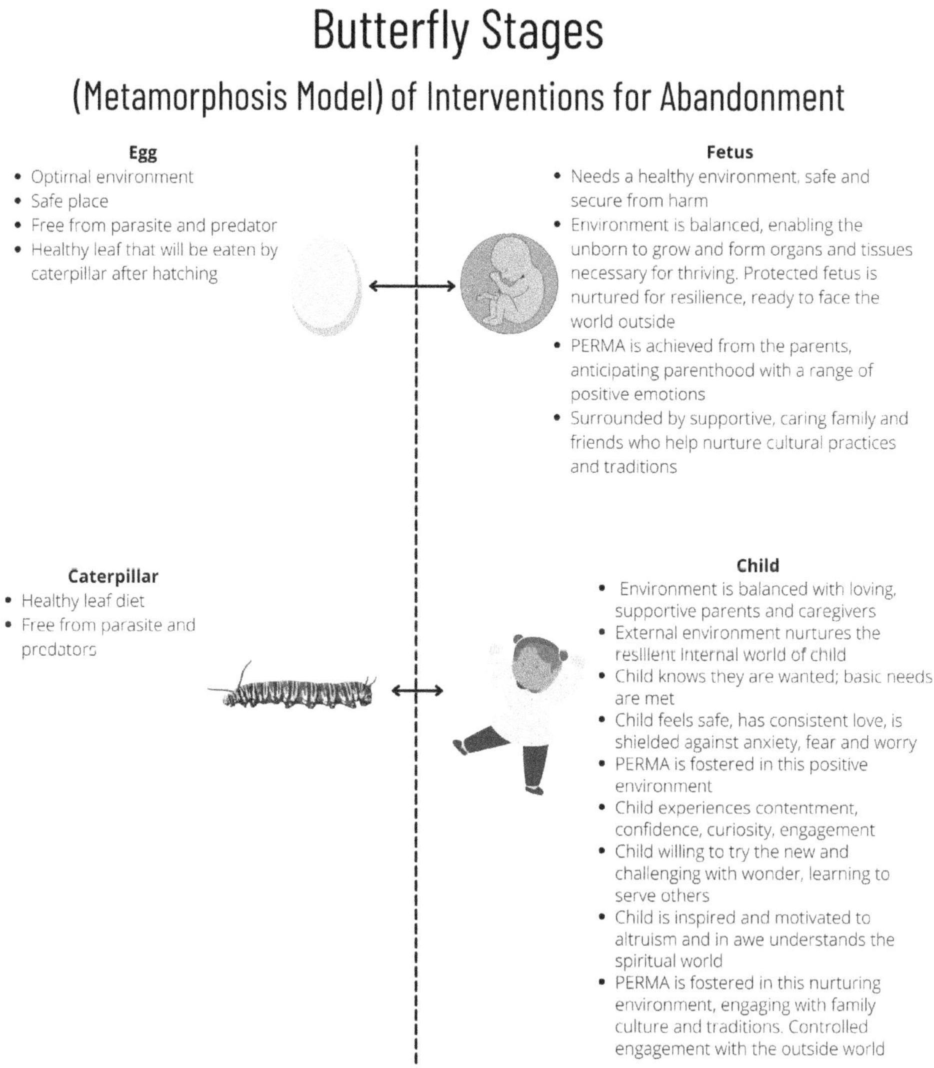

Figure 14.2a Butterfly Stages model. Created by Imani Francis. Reproduced with permission.

encased in its' hard protective shell is experiencing extraordinary "secret" reshaping in preparation for it emergence as a fully formed butterfly.

The adolescent is also undergoing incredible physical, emotional and psychological change. Like the cocoon, much of the metamorphosis at this stage is also in "secret," hidden away as maturation occurs. Parents and caregivers are essential in giving the adolescent space to grow while staying close and with intentionality use PERMA to help support the adolescent's emergence into a healthy, thriving adult.

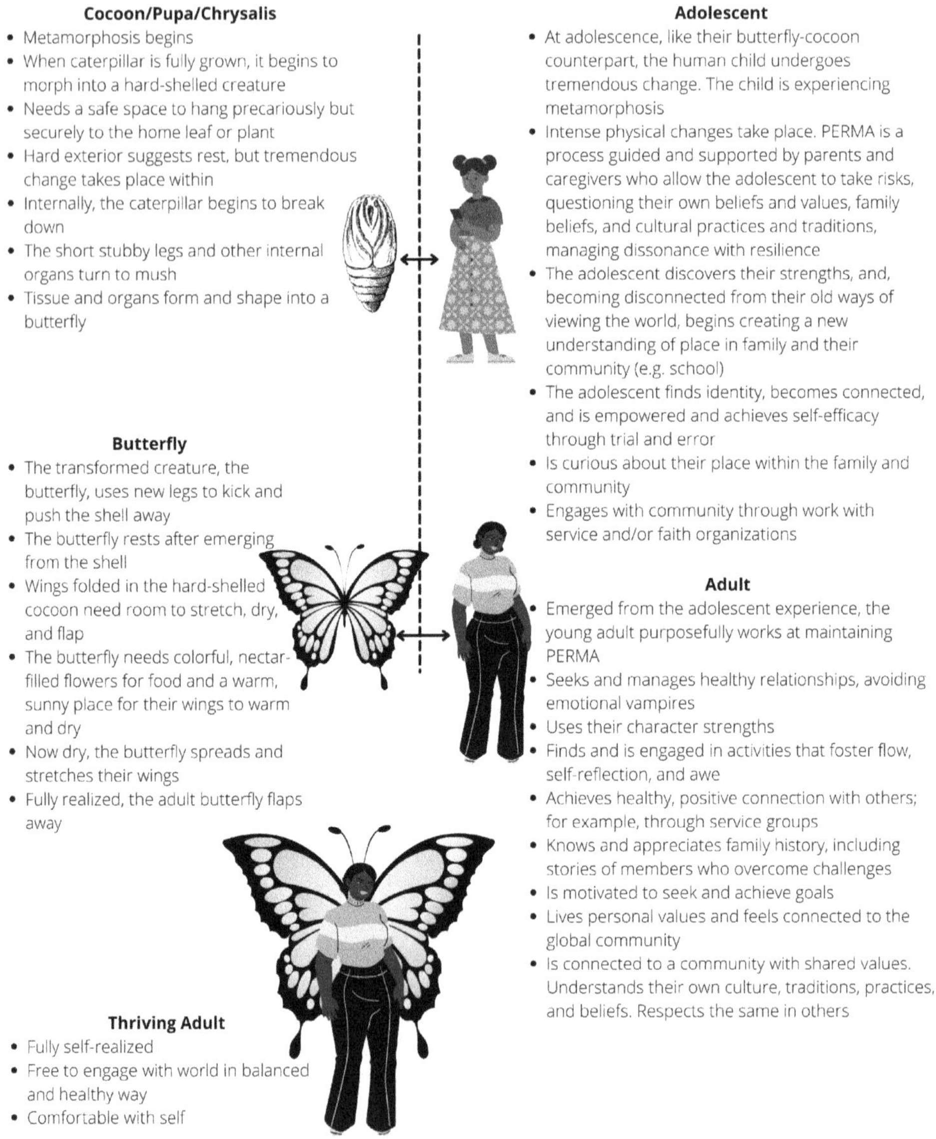

Figure 14.2b Butterfly Stages model. Created by Imani Francis. Reproduced with permission.

PART V

Conclusion: The Circle of Support

15

My Story: Full Circle

"I'm sorry you got pregnant with me," I mumbled to my mother. I was an adult with my own children, and after mustering up the courage, decided to apologize to my mother for being the cause of her martial and personal misery. I was responsible. It was my fault. Her pregnancy with me caused her ill-fated marriage and her subsequent sufferings with my father. I carried an irrational guilt all my childhood, when at adolescence, as some children do in their search for meaning and identity, I calculated my conception date from the date of my parents' marriage. A shotgun wedding! I was the reason for all the misery. My guilt, though irrational, was nonetheless real to me and shaped my behavior of perfectionism and wanting not to ever be the cause of further distress and worry for my mother.

"What?" my mother asked, startled. I repeated that I was sorry that she became pregnant with me and had to marry my father and as a result suffered a life of misery with him. She stared at me for a while, then said, "I always wanted you, from the moment I got pregnant. We got married because we wanted to. How things worked is between your father and me. I saw the signs from his behavior before we got married, but I wanted to marry him. I always wanted you and your brothers and sisters. It's your father I can't stand now."

So my mother separated her feelings for my father from her feelings for me and my siblings. Although, from time to time, she would tell us that she sees our father in us, especially when we behaved in a way that annoyed or upset her. This comment was especially directed to my younger brothers, who greatly resembled my father and were often mischievous.

Knowing I was loved and wanted made me feel relieved and grateful. Were all those years of guilt and anxiety wasted? Those were years that I did not know that I was not the cause of my parents' unhappiness. And although I knew in my head the irrationality of my feelings of guilt and deep sense of responsibility for my parents' acrimonious marriage, my heart needed to hear those words—that I was loved and wanted. Her words did not reduce my feelings of being abandoned by my father—my mother wanted me—but was I the reason my father left? At least one parent wanted us. My mother's words made me feel like I mattered and that I was worth the grief and pain.

My strong feelings of guilt and anxiety about my parents' relationship certainly helps me to understand the feelings of the young people I work with at school and in private practice. Young people who are abandoned by a parent need to know that they are wanted and loved by someone—the remaining parent, grandparent(s), or caregiver. They need to know that they matter. The guilt I felt is not isolated to me. The guilt that children feel is one of the many strong emotions experienced by children who are abandoned, that it is somehow their fault that the abandoning parent left them. For me this guilt and feelings of being responsible fostered my perfectionist behaviors.

The pressure I put on myself to do things "right" was also influenced by my not wanting to add to the strain my single mother was going through as she tried to parent the five of us on her own. In addition, culturally, as the first born of five, I had the responsibility of setting an example for my younger siblings of not only model behavior but the expectation of stellar academic performance. To further compound the already emotionally layered situation, I am the firstborn and female. At that time, growing up in Jamaica meant domestic chores that positioned me as a "little mama."

I remember myself as a reserved child but even more so a reserved and quiet adolescent. I held myself to an extremely high standard of behavior and academic excellence. I brooded about my parents' lives, my father's repeated rejections to provide for my siblings and myself, and wondered about my worth. I would often drift off in daydreams. While I did not create scenarios of my father caring for me as some of the young people I work with do, I did imagine and yearn for a home where my mother was happy and my siblings and I had our all needs met without the strain of my mother's daily disparaging of my father's failings and his lack of care.

BETTER BUT STILL HEALING

I will describe my journey to healing using the butterfly model (Figure 14.2a, 14.2b) that explains the needs of children as they mature from childhood into adulthood. I will contextualize the concept of PERMA (which did not exist when I was growing up) and describe how family history and culture and spirituality, my belief in something bigger than myself, inspired awe and gave my life purpose and meaning.

I start with the butterfly model of child development, explained in Chapter 14—and framed by the natural developmental stages described by Erikson. Because with my many years working in the school system, mostly for middle-grade students, I see the young child's innocent and voracious absorption of the world around as akin to the caterpillar working its way from experience to experience. At adolescence, there is the turning inward and the internal metamorphosis occurring at puberty, the quest for identity and meaning hidden, very much like the changes occurring within the hard-shelled yet vulnerable cocoon. The third stage, young adulthood, heralds the miraculous emergence of the transformed beautiful creature at high school and beyond, like the butterfly ready to fly, to take on the world. When I attend high school graduations, the symbolic emergence of butterflies, I often do not recognize the lumpy, gangly, pimply students I knew at the adolescent–cocoon middle school stage. Their wonderful physical change is delightful to see, and their maturity shows me that psychological healing has occurred.

For me, as a young child, I struggled to make sense of my parents' tumultuous relationship and had a frequent memory of the one major violent interaction between them that led to my father finally leaving us. I suffered the twoness that kept that memory in my mind, easily conjured. I escaped in play with siblings and was influenced by songs and stories told in Jamaica of magical creatures from the African–Caribbean culture like Anansi and River Mumma tales. I had frequent flights of fancy, imagined fantastical creatures like fairies and elves in our garden. I believed they existed and hid from me because I was not quick enough to catch sight of them. As a therapist, I believe that children's belief in magical creatures helps them with healing through imaginative play. As an adult, I collect folktales and legends from Africa and believe in the healing power of fantasy. I am a member of the Northmoor Project, affiliated with J. R. R. Tolkien's home in Oxford, England, now the Oxford Center for Fantasy.[1] As a child, magical dreams were a delightful escape. I had an imaginary playmate. My mother told me the relationship did not last very long, since Jerry and I had some kind of falling-out. She recalls my running indoors crying and complaining that Jerry hit me for no reason at all. Was I reliving my parents' violent physical interaction? Or as Bouldin and Pratt[2] suggest, my imaginary friend helped me "alleviate loneliness and promoted [my] emotional and cognitive growth" in a positive environment. In addition, I had some measure of control over my opposite gender common in creative girls.[3] My imaginary companion was an important part of my childhood play. It made my troubled childhood happier and distracted me from my inner turmoil of self-doubt. This type of play is an aspect of current theory-of-the-mind research on how children cope and is considered an important part of their social development.[4]

Within the framework of PERMA, my childhood memory of the trauma of my father abandoning me was blanketed by play, both with my siblings and with an imaginary companion. Also at this time, I was immature, like a caterpillar in my small world, not yet fully aware of my mother's struggles to provide for us. I recall the (P) positive emotions of contentment, engaged (E) outdoor play with positive relationships (R) with my siblings, neighbors, and the cousins of my extended family. In my caterpillar stage, I had little awareness of the meaning and purpose (M) of my life, nor any concern or care for achievement (A).

In contrast, my adolescent years were tumultuous. These years from late primary to high school were marked by anxiety and stress, coinciding with the very difficult social and economic years in Jamaica. Food scarcity, high inflation, low wages, increased crime fueled by political conflicts added to my mother's daily concern of making ends meet. My father's absence and lack of care for us were keenly felt by me as the eldest as I became my mother's confidant. I understood the strain of our single mother trying to feed five growing children. I was also very disturbed that our father ignored our mother's and our appeals for help with basic needs.

I pondered the meaning of life and considered my own value and worth. Was I a burden to my mother? What was the meaning of love? Why did our father not care for or love us or love me? Some financial support from him would have eased the endless round of my mother borrowing money from friends to repaying them at end of the month only to borrow again mid-month. I recall our mother taking us to find our father, when he left us he went back to his childhood home with my paternal grandparents. I recall our grandfather's indifference to us and his noninterference in my mother's requests for our father to give financial help.

This lack of care and concern for our well-being from our paternal side made a deep impression on me and made me deeply sad. My mother sacrificed her own well-being to give me all the school supplies and extra classes I needed to succeed. I noticed she slept for long periods, was often irritable, and had bouts of rage. In hindsight, I now know my mother was suffering from depression. We learned to live with our depressed mother and to accept the neglect from our father. I understood her helplessness and limited options in Jamaica at that time.

ONSET OF SELF-INJURIOUS BEHAVIOR

Adolescence was difficult. I suffered high anxiety and began the self-injurious behaviors of body-focused repetitive behaviors (BFRBs)—in particular nail biting—and I remember the onset of trichotillomania.[5] At that time, 1970s Jamaica, entrance to a prestigious high school was limited to the few children who obtained scholarships by passing the national Common Entrance Examination. Failure to pass this extremely rigorous examination taken at the end of the primary years meant parents had to pay fees for the children to attend private secondary school or a government secondary school. My mother saved and sacrificed to send me to "extra lessons" designed to sharpen academic skills and to give additional insight (outside of regular classes) into the possible questions on the examination paper. This sacrifice all for me to have a chance of attending one of Jamaica's superior all-girls Catholic schools.

I remember my mother pleading with me to pass the examination as she could not afford to pay for private secondary education out of pocket. My father did not offer support. I had no power over the contents of the examination paper, but I studied hard and tried to prepare for what was to come. But I was really powerless. As the exam loomed closer, I recall feelings of increasing dread and extreme anxiety. One day, alone worrying about the exam, I became lost in the panicked thought that repeated over and over in my head—"What if I did not pass the Common Entrance?" My panic overwhelmed me as I ruminated and chastised myself about my failings, about the shame and the stress my failure would cause—my one way of not giving my mother another bill to pay. There began the self-injurious but self-soothing act of hair pulling. I was distracted from my overwhelming thoughts, and as I pulled my hair, I felt myself calm. This was one action that made me feel better. Ironically, as I journeyed through adolescence, the damage I did by hair pulling made me self-conscious and increased my anxiety. It was also during the time my mother left us for work in the United States and my father continued to stay away. I had to navigate the demands of school, social relationships, and the reality of two absent parents and the haranguing of our disapproving aunt, who was stuck as caregiver to five children.

RESCUED BY SPIRITUALITY, FRIENDS, ACHIEVEMENTS, AND H[ER]ISTORY

As an adolescent, I was reserved and brooding. I escaped into self-injury and focused on academic work. The welcome relief of my passing the Common Entrance Examination for one of the most prestigious all-girls schools in Jamaica proved the turning point. In the context of PERMA, passing the examination was a major accomplishment. It also brought deep gratitude, and my awareness of the many hundreds of children who did not pass the exam humbled me.

During the hard cocoon stage of adolescence, I protected myself and retreated into books, became a voracious reader and subsequent literature major. I was a reserved, quiet person who hardly spoke in public and did more listening than talking. Attending an all-girls school allowed me to retreat without the additional worry of interaction with the opposite gender—for whom I had deep distrust. My religious school offered me many close friendships and also opened the door of spirituality for me. It fostered my belief that my life had meaning and purpose. Spirituality is seen as a major cross-cultural human developmental milestone by researchers interested in well-being.[6] In addition, before she left us, my mother insisted I become involved in church activities. I attended regular meetings at my church youth organization and made friends with other young people, some older, some younger than me. We did volunteer work for the community, including summer workshops and mentoring younger children. I learned to relax and to accept and cherish the many friendships offered to me.

Over time, I became less painfully self-conscious, but my deep anxiety and feelings of insecurity never left me. I continued self-injury in secret. I was only later able to manage my trichotillomania because very short cropped hair is consistently fashionable in the black community. In keeping my hair very short, I removed the stimuli for self-soothing. I had made good and lasting friends, those positive relationships of close bonds with a few special people who knew my failings but loved and supported me.

Finally, by understanding my identity within the context of both my paternal side but more my maternal family helped heal my self-doubts, anxieties, and fears. In college as a young adult, I began to pay attention to my ancestral roots. As a literature major, the works of brilliant writers of the African diaspora and the English canon inspired me to learn more about myself as I analyzed the behavior of characters of the many books I read in pursuit of an undergraduate degree in English literature. I asked my mother to tell me about her family, in essence my family. I learned about her grandmother—Granny Lizzie. Granny Lizzie's parents were children kept captive while the formerly enslaved fled to the mountains after the abolition of slavery in Jamaica. My mother does not know if Granny Lizzie's grandparents had died or if they fled and left their children; but my maternal great-grandmother was born on a former slave estate and as a child was required to stand for hours waving a frond to keep the mistress cool from the tropical heat.

My mother told me that when Granny Lizzie's parents finally left the plantation, she was not allowed to leave with them because the mistress refused to let her go although slavery had been long abolished. At thirteen, she ran away and made her way to the city. It is not known how she managed and who helped her, but Granny Lizzie sold produce in the market, pulling her cart without a donkey. Over time, she was able to purchase a donkey and soon had an employee who delivered her goods to the market for her. By the time my grandmother was born, Granny Lizzie had property, married a Cuban cigar maker, and was an independent woman of means.

How did Granny Lizzie's story, her-story, help me heal? I thought often and still think often of her courage and determination to be independent and physically free. When I think of what she must have suffered first with the forced fanning of the mistress and then the loss of her parents, I feel that I too can do hard things. Her-story is my story. My genogram begins with her parents abandoning her, and yet she was brave and managed through grit and belief in God. My mother, who has childhood memories Granny Lizzie, noted her devotion to God. This devotion and spiritual faith were passed on to my maternal grandmother, to my mother and my siblings and me. There is a force bigger than me that gives me purpose, and I am grateful.

MY FATHER REFLECTS

I asked my father to give advice to young fathers. He is now an old man, and my siblings and I are his caretakers. In asking my father's advice, I was seeking both my own reconciliation and to satisfy my curiosity about his perspective after fifty-five years of fatherhood in absentia. Living in the Caribbean, alone and often making long-distance calls to the United States to my siblings and myself, "just to check in on [you] children," my father began philosophically, alluding to the transience of life speaking in Jamaican, "Man is like a tree leaf. Now you see him, then he disappear. Do the best you can, while you can."

He went on to advise that a father must be warm and caring, never be afraid to show his children love and affection. He emphasized that it is the father's responsibility to take care of the family, making sure everyone is happy, feel safe and protected. Fathers should not be afraid to help care for the children, including cooking meals or doing bath-time chores. Further, he added, the father should encourage social connections, including church and the extended family. He continued, "When a child is born, the child eyes search for both mother and father." So fathers are an integral part of nurturing of child. "A father," he added, "should spend time with the children, playing with them, buying treats for them like ice cream." My father concluded by stressing the importance of the father supporting the mother in creating a home where there is accountability and compromise. "There must be respect and love."

As I listened to my father opine, I wondered how my siblings and my life would have been like had he remained with us and tried to be the father he advised—I will never know. For my part, I know that my experience of grief and longing led me to my insight into the need that children have for their father and mother. My experience made me kinfolk with abandoned children and their families. My kinship makes me keenly aware of my role in helping abandoned children forgive and heal.

Afterword

The following are brief updates on the lives of some the children whose experiences I described when I discussed the reasons parents leave and the impact on their children. Although the names have been changed, parents and caregivers gave permission for the stories to be told.

Christopher

Christopher remained angry for a long time. His anger made it difficult for him to fit in with his aunt, her husband, and his cousin James. His family remained loving, although they had to enforce strict house rules. At middle school, he was defiant and involved with a group of students who engaged in several acts of vandalism. Attempts to connect him to school and community activities failed. Christopher also refused to engage in therapy sessions, so much so that his therapist terminated their meetings, explaining that Christopher was not yet ready to process his feelings about his past traumas. In addition, he was frequently sent home as a disciplinary consequence for behavior at school; and as a result, he missed several days of instruction. However, because of his high intelligence, Christopher passed to high school.

High school gave Christopher the chance to be different. He joined the ROTC (Reserve Officers Training Corps), and the training helped him quiet his mind through the discipline and high expectations of behavior and academic performance. He also made friends and was popular. Maturation and the loving, consistent commitment of his family helped. Christopher thoroughly enjoyed a recent family vacation to Jamaica. However, when his mother greeted him with cries of joy, he responded with cool detachment. Now in the eleventh grade and college bound, perhaps with time Christopher will understand mental illness and his mother's behavior.

Tye (Too-Young Mother of Baby Julianna)

Tye graduated high school and is now training to be an esthetician. Reports are that she has been taking her medication consistently but does not believe that psychotherapy is necessary for her at this time. She visits Julianna occasionally and sometimes feels regret and guilt that she gave her up for adoption. Although her baby is with Dain's parents, when Tye looks at Julianna, she wants to take her home. She wants to say, "I am your mother. I carried you in me." These thoughts are fleeting, however, as the reality of mothering Julianna would be too much to handle.

Dain (Too-Young Father of Baby Julianna)

Dain is a freshman in college, pursuing a degree in accounting. He lives on campus, but when he goes home, he sometimes runs into Tye on the rare occasion that she visits baby Julianna. He is not interested in therapy or to unpack his experience of young fatherhood. He is happy that his mother and father are Julianna's parents. He feels free to date and to enjoy college life without the responsibility of caring for her. He loves Julianna, but she is like his little sister; he often forgets how she came into his life.

Cassie and Lucas

After four years of stable, loving parenting and consistent psychotherapy, the children are thriving. They are creative, happy, and optimistic. Cassie and Lucas have many friends and made honor roll three years in a row. Lucas was identified as gifted.

Dominik

In high school, Dominik thrived. He tried out for the football team in the ninth grade, and although he was not selected to play, he was chosen the team manager. He completed his tasks with pride, setting up the drills for the coach such as laying out cones, cleaning up after practice, or delivering water to the players. Dominik bonded with the team and was popular. He became an integral part of the team because of his sense of humor and worked hard to keep team morale high. In the tenth grade, he got his chance to play. Reports are that Dominik was not overly talented as a wide receiver on the field, but his playful spirit and his happiness at belonging to the team made him a favorite with both the football players and the student body.

Grace

Although Grace managed to graduate from high school, it was a difficult journey. She had deficiencies in math and resisted group work. Grace also was simultaneously sexually involved with a number of male and female students. These intimacies caused emotional turmoil—hurts, anger, and jealousy as Grace did not demonstrate commitment to any of her partners. After graduating from high school, she enrolled in esthetician training at the community college in her area.

Notes

Introduction

1. U.S. Dept. of Health and Human Services, "Preliminary FY 2016 Estimates as of Oct. 20, 2017, No. 24," p. 2. https://www.acf.hhs.gov/sites/default/files/documents/cb/afcarsreport24.pdf. Accessed December 20, 2022.

2. U.S. Dept. of Health and Human Services, "Trends in Foster Care and Adoption: FY 2010–FY 2019," June 20, 2023. https://www.acf.hhs.gov/sites/default/files/documents/cb/trends_fostercare_adoption_10thru19.pdf. Accessed December 20, 2022.

3. U.S. Dept. of Health and Human Services. "Preliminary FY 2016 Estimates."

4. National Conference of State Legislatures, "Disproportionality and Disparity in Child Welfare." NCSL, August 28, 2020. https://www.ncsl.org/research/human-services/disproportionality-and-disparity-in-child-welfare.aspx. Accessed December 20, 2022.

5. U.S. Census Bureau, "The Majority of Children Live with Two Parents, Census Bureau Reports," November 17, 2016. https://www.census.gov/newsroom/press-releases/2016/cb16-192.html#. Accessed December 20, 2022.

6. M. Ungar et al., "Unique Pathways to Resilience across Cultures. *Adolescence* 42, no. 166 (2007): 287–310. https://pubmed.ncbi.nlm.nih.gov/17849937/. Accessed February 4, 2023.

7. Darcia F. Narvaez, "Believing 'Children Are Resilient' May Be a Fantasy," *Psychology Today*, June 13, 2011. https://www.psychologytoday.com/us/blog/moral-landscapes/201106/believing-children-are-resilient-may-be-fantasy. Accessed December 20, 2022.

8. W. E. B. Du Bois, *The Souls of Black Folk; Essays and Sketches* (Chicago: A. C. McClurg, 1903).

9. U.S. Department of Health and Human Services, Jeffrey Rosenberg and W. Wilcox Bradford, "The Importance of Fathers in the Healthy Development of Children" (2006). https://www.childwelfare.gov/pubpdfs/fatherhood.pdf. Accessed February 4, 2023.

10. Haley A. Hamilton, "Extended Families and Adolescent Well-Being," *Journal of Adolescent Health* 36, no. 3 (2005): 260–266. https://doi.org/10.1016/j.jadohealth.2004.02.022. Accessed February 4, 2023.

Chapter 1

1. Family Systems Therapy, *GoodTherapy*, updated July 3, 2015. https://www.goodtherapy.org/learn-about-therapy/types/family-systems-therapy. Accessed December 20, 2022.
2. John F. Butler, "The Family Diagram and Genogram: Comparisons and Contrasts," *The American Journal of Family Therapy* 36 no. 3 (June 2008): 169–180, https://doi.org/10.1080/01926180701291055. Accessed December 20, 2022.
3. Monica McGoldrick, Randy Gerson, and Sueli Petry, *Genograms, Assessment and Intervention* (New York: W. W. Norton, 2008).
4. Patricia Minuchin, Jorge Colapinto, and Salvador Minuchin, "Working with Families of the Poor," in Michael P. Nichols, ed., *The Guilford Family Therapy Series*, vol. 15 (Guilford Press, 1998).
5. Minuchin et al., "Working with Families of the Poor," p. 23.
6. Mary Sykes Wylie, "Do We Still Need Attachment Theory? Jerome Kegan, Daniel Siegel and Salvador Minuchin Weigh In," *Psychotherapy Networker* (blog), excerpted from *The Attuned Therapist*, March/April 2011. https://www.psychotherapynetworker.org/article/attuned-therapist. Accessed September 12, 2020.

Chapter 2

1. Christopher Peterson and Martin Seligman, *Character Strengths and Virtues: A Handbook and Classification* (Oxford, UK: American Psychological Association/Oxford University Press, 2004).
2. Neal H. Mayerson, "The Character Strengths Response: An Urgent Call to Action," *Frontiers in Psychology* 11, no. 2106 (2020). https://doi.org/10.3389/fpsyg.2020.02106. Accessed December 20, 2022.
3. Mayerson, "The Character Strengths Response."
4. Mayerson, "The Character Strengths Response."
5. Emily Schondelmyer, "Demographics and Living Arrangements: 2013," U.S. Census Bureau, *Current Population Reports*, P70BR-148, Washington, DC (2017). https://www.census.gov/content/dam/Census/library/publications/2017/demo/p70br-148.pdf. Accessed December 18, 2022.
6. U.S. Census Bureau, "The Majority of Children Live with Two Parents," November 17, 2016. https://www.census.gov/newsroom/press-releases/2016/cb16-192.html. Accessed December 18, 2022.
7. Melanie Mallers, Susan Charles, Shevaun Neupert, and David Almeida. "Perceptions of Childhood Relationships with Mother and Father; Daily Emotional and Stressor Experiences in Adulthood," *Developmental Psychology* 46 no 6 (November 2010): 1651–1661. https://doi.org/10.1037/a0021020. Accessed December 20, 2022.

8. Peggy Drexler, "When Mothers Leave: Freedom of Choice Does Not Necessarily Mean Freedom from Stigma," *Psychology Today*, August 8, 2011. https://www.psychologytoday.com/us/blog/our-gender-ourselves/201108/when-mothers-leave. Accessed June 20, 2018.

9. Timothy Grall, "Custodial Mothers and Fathers and Their Child Support: 2013," U.S. Census Bureau, Current Population Reports, January 2016. https://www.census.gov/content/dam/Census/library/publications/2016/demo/P60-255.pdf. Accessed February 4, 2023.

10. Crystal Ponti, "The Rise in Walk-Away Moms," *FilterFree Parents* (blog), December 18, 2020. http://mommifried.com/the-rise-of-walk-away-moms. Accessed December 20, 2022.

11. Cristina Munroe, "Moms Reveal the Heartbreaking Reasons Why They Abandoned Their Kids," *Rebel Circus* (blog), January 28. 2018. https://www.rebelcircus.com/blog/moms-reveal-heartbreaking-reasons-abandoned-kids. Accessed August 8, 2018.

12. Kathy Parker, "Walking Away from My Children Wasn't My Biggest Failure as a Mother," Body and Soul, news.com.au, May 10, 2019. https://www.bodyandsoul.com.au. Accessed January 26, 2023.

13. *Bad Moms*, directed by Jon Lucas and Scott Moore (STX films, 2016).

14. "A Talk with Konrad Lorenz," *New York Times*, July 5, 1970. https://www.nytimes.com/1970/07/05/archives/a-talk-with-konrad-lorenz.html?searchResultPosition=2. Accessed December 18, 2022.

15. Saul McLeod, "Konrad Lorenz's Imprinting Theory," *Simply Psychology*, 2018. https://www.simplypsychology.org/Konrad-Lorenz.html. Accessed December 20, 2022.

16. McLeod, "Konrad Lorenz's Imprinting Theory."

17. Marga Vicedo, "The Father of Ethology and the Foster Mother of Ducks: Konrad Lorenz as Expert on Motherhood," *Isis* 100, no. 2. (June 2009): 266–291. https://doi.org/10.1086/599553. Accessed December 20, 2022.

18. McLeod, "Konrad Lorenz's Imprinting Theory."

19. Charles Patrick Davis, "Medical Definition of Imprinting, Psychological," MedicineNet, n.d. https://www.medicinenet.com/imprinting_psychological/definition.htm. Accessed December 20, 2022.

20. Vicedo, "The Father of Ethology."

21. Frank van der Horst, Helen LeRoy, and René van de Veer, "'When Strangers Meet': John Bowlby and Harry Harlow on Attachment Behavior," *Integrative Psychological and Behavioral Science* 42, no. 4 (September 3, 2008): 370–388. https://doi.org/10.1007/s12124-008-9079-2. Accessed December 20, 2022.

22. Harry F. Harlow, "Love in Infant Monkeys," *Scientific American* 200, no. 6 (1959): 68–75. http://www.jstor.org/stable/26309508. Accessed December 18, 2022.

23. Ellen Herman, "Harry F. Harlow, Monkey Love Experiments," The Adoption History Project. https://pages.uoregon.edu/adoption/studies/HarlowMLE.htm. Accessed December 18, 2022.

24. Harlow, "Love in Infant Monkeys," 70, 72–73, 74.

25. John Bowlby. "Attachment and Loss," in *Attachment*, vol. 1 (New York: Basic Books, 1969/1982).

26. Van der Horst et al., "When Strangers Meet."

27. Jean Piaget and Barbel Inhelder, *The Psychology of the Child* (New York: Basic Books, 1969), pp. 13–15.

28. Mary D. Ainsworth, "Individual Differences in Strange-Situational Behaviour of One-Year-Olds, in H. R. Shaffer, *The Origins of Human Social Relations* (New York: Academic Press, 1971). https://files.eric.ed.gov/fulltext/ED056742.pdf. Accessed December 20, 2022.

29. Mary Main, "Cross-Cultural Studies of Attachment Organization: Recent Studies, Changing Methodologies, and the Concept of Conditional Strategies," *Human Development* 33, no. 1 (1990): 48–61. https://www.karger.com/Article/Abstract/276502. Accessed December 20, 2022.

30. Jerome Kagan, "The One Thing That's Missing from Attachment Theory: Challenging a Therapeutic Cornerstone," *Psychotherapy Networker* (blog), excerpted from "Bringing Up Baby" by Jerome Kagan. The full version is available in the March/April 2011 issue, *The Great Attachment Debate: How Important Is Early Experience?* https://www.psychotherapynetworker.org/blog/details/617/the-one-thing-thats-missing-from-attachment-theory. Accessed December 20, 2022.

31. Yoo Rha Hong and Jae Sun Park, "Impact of Attachment, Temperament and Parenting on Human Development," *Korean Journal of Pediatrics* 55, no. 12 (2012): 449–454.

32. "Adopted Romanian Orphans Still Suffering in Adulthood," BBC News, February 22, 2017. https://www.bbc.com/news/health-39055704. Accessed December 20, 2022.

33. Harold P. Blum, "Separation-Individuation Theory and Attachment Theory," *Journal of American Psychoanalytic Association* 52, no. 2 (Spring 2004): 535–553. https://pubmed.ncbi.nlm.nih.gov/15222460/. Accessed December 20, 2022.

34. Margaret Mahler, "On the First Three Phases of the Separation-Individuation Process," *International Journal of Psychoanalysis* 53 (1972): 333–338.

35. Anna R. Brandon, Sandra Pitts, Wayne H. Denton, C. Allen Stringer, and H. M. Evans, "A History of the Theory of Prenatal Attachment," *Journal of Prenatal and Perinatal Psychological Health* 23, no. 4 (Summer 2009): 201–222. https://www.ncbi.nlm.nih.gov/pmc/articles/PMC3083029. Accessed December 20, 2022.

36. Brandon et al., "A History of the Theory of Prenatal Attachment."

37. Brandon et al., "A History of the Theory of Prenatal Attachment."

38. Brandon et al. "A History of the Theory of Prenatal Attachment."

39. Mary Sykes Wylie and Lynn Turner, "The Attuned Therapist," *Psychotherapy Networker*, March/April 2011. https://www.psychotherapynetworker.org/article/attuned-therapist

40. Jorge Colapinto, "Structural Family Therapy," in Arthur M. Horne and Merle M. Ohlsen, eds., *Family Counseling and Therapy* (Itasca, IL: F. E. Peacock, 1982), p. 11. http://www.colapinto.com/files/SFT1982.pdf. Accessed December 19, 2022.

41. Colapinto, "Structural Family Therapy."

42. Colapinto, "Structural Family Therapy."

43. BeeGees, "How Can You Mend a Broken Heart?" 1971, Barry Gibb/Robin Gibb. Notting Hill Lyrics. Universal Music Publishing Group.

Chapter 3

1. Lieselotte Ahnet and Sarah J. Schoppe-Sullivan, "Fathers from an Attachment Perspective," *Attachment and Human Development* 22, no. 1 (2020): 1–3. https://doi.org/10.1080/14616734.2019.1589054. Accessed December 20, 2022.

2. John T. Condon, "The Parental-Foetal Relationship—a Comparison of Male and Female Expectant Parents," *Journal of Psychosomatic Obstetrics and Gynecology* 4, no. 4. (1985): 271–284. Published online July 7, 2009. https://doi.org/10.3109/01674828509016729. Accessed December 20, 2022.

3. Hedwig Von Bakel, A. Janneke Maas, Charlotte Vreeswik, and Ad Vingerhoets, "Pictorial Representation of Attachment: Measuring the Parent-Fetus Relationship in Expectant Mothers and Fathers," *BMC Pregnancy and Childbirth* 13, no. 138 (June 27, 2013). https://bmcpregnancychildbirth.biomedcentral.com/articles/10.1186/1471-2393-13-138. Accessed December 20, 2022.

4. John Condon, Carolyn Corkindale, Phillip Boyce, and Elizabeth Gamble, "A Longitudinal Study of Father-to-Infant Attachment: Antecedents and Correlates," *Journal of Reproductive and Infant Psychology* 31, no. 1 (2013). https://www.tandfonline.com/doi/abs/10.1080/02646838.2012.757694. Accessed December 20, 2022.

5. Er-Mei Chen, Meei-Ling Gau; Chieh-Yu Liu, and Tzu-Ying Lee, "Effects of Father-Neonate Skin-to-Skin Contact on Attachment: A Randomized Controlled Trial," *Nursing Research and Practice* 2017, Article ID 8612024, https://doi.org/10.1155/2017/8612024. Accessed December 20, 2022.

6. George Tarabulsy, Rejean Tessier, Jocelyne Gagun, and Christine Piche, "Attachment Classification and Infant Responsiveness during Interactions," *Infant Behaviors and Development* 19 (1996): 131–143.

7. Binta Alleyne-Green, Claudette Grinnell-Davis, Trenette Clark, Camille Quinn, and Qiana Cryer, "Father Involvement, Dating Violence, and Sexual Risk Behavior among a National Sample of Adolescent Females," *Journal of Interpersonal Violence* 31 no. 5, (2016): 810–830. https://doi.org/10.1177/0886260514556762. Accessed December 20, 2022.

8. Michael Lamb, "How Do Fathers Influence Children's Development? Let Me Count the Ways," in *The Role of the Father in Child Development* (New York: Wiley and Sons, 2010), p. 3.

9. Richard Fletcher, Jennifer St. George, Chris May, and Phillip Morgan, "Fathers' Perception of Rough-and-Tumble Play: Implications for Early Childhood Services," *Australasian Journal of Early Childhood* 36, no. 4 (2011): 131–138. https://www.researchgate.net/publication/258207422_Fathers'_perceptions_of_rough-and-tumble_play_Implications_for_early_childhood_services. Accessed December 20, 2022.

10. Angela Duckworth, *Grit* (New York: Simon and Schuster, 2016).

11. Joseph Flanders, Vanessa Leo, Daniel Paquette, Robert Pihl, and Jean Seguin, "Rough-and-Tumble Play and Regulation: An Observational Study of Father Child Play Dyads," *Aggressive Behavior* 35, no. 4. July/August (2009), https://www.ncbi.nlm.nih.gov/pmc/articles/PMC3283567. Accessed December 19, 2022.

12. Bruce Ellis, John Bates, Kenneth Dodge, David Fergusson, L. John Horwood, Gregory Pettit, and Lianne Woodward, "Does Father Absence Place Daughters at Special Risk for Early Sexual Activity and Teenage Pregnancy?" *Child Development* 74, no. 3 (May–June 2003): 801–821. https://www.ncbi.nlm.nih.gov/pmc/articles/PMC2764264/. Accessed December 19, 2022.

13. U.S. Dept. of Health and Human Services, National Responsible Fatherhood Clearing House, "Dad Stats." https://www.fatherhood.gov/content/dad-stats. Accessed February 4, 2023.

14. U.S. Dept. of Health and Human Services, Jeffrey Rosenberg and W. Wilcox Bradford, "The Importance of Fathers in the Healthy Development of Children," 2006. https://www.childwelfare.gov/pubpdfs/fatherhood.pdf. Accessed December 19, 2022.

15. Lauren Porter, "Is Primary Attachment Better Than Secondary Attachment?" *Fathers—Secondary Attachment Issue. Journal of Attachment Parenting International* 10 (Summer 2007): 3. http://theattachedfamily.com/membersonly/?p=1259. Accessed December 19, 2022.

16. See Figure 3.1, p. 21, A basic genogram of a female child including the extended family (maternal and paternal grandparents).

17. Monica McGoldrick, Randy Gerson, and Sueli Petry, *Genograms, Assessment and Intervention* (New York: W. W. Norton, 2008).

18. Martin Seligman, *Authentic Happiness* (New York: Simon and Schuster, 2002).

19. Lawrence Kohlberg, *The Psychology of Moral Development: The Nature and Validity of Moral Stages* (Essays on Moral Development, vol. 2) (New York: Harper & Row, 1984).

20. Carol Gilligan, "In a Different Voice: Women's Conceptions of Self and of Morality," *Harvard Educational Review* 47, no. 4 (1977): 481–517. https://sfonline.barnard.edu/sfxxx/documents/gilligan.pdf. Accessed December 19, 2022.

21. Michael Murray, "Roughhousing with Dad Crucial for Development, Say Researchers," *ABC News*. June 17, 2011. https://abcnews.go.com/Health/dads-roughhousing-children-crucial-early-development/story?id=13868801. Accessed February 4, 2023.

22. Murray, "Roughhousing with Dad."
23. Ellis et al., "Does Father Absence Place Daughters at Special Risk?"

Chapter 4

1. Alfred Bandura, "Social Learning Theory" (Palo Alto, CA: Stanford University, General Learning Cooperation, 1971), p. 29. http://www.asecib.ase.ro/mps/Bandura_SocialLearningTheory.pdf. Accessed February 4, 2023.
2. Saul McLeod, "Albert Bandura—Social Learning Theory," *Simply Psychology*, updated 2016. https://www.simplypsychology.org/bandura.html. Accessed December 20, 2022.
3. McLeod, "Albert Bandura."
4. Alfred Bandura, "Self Efficacy," *The Corsini Encyclopedia of Psychology*, 2010, Wiley Online. https://doi.org/10.1002/9780470479216. Accessed February 4, 2023.
5. Tahereh Ataei, Reza Zeighami, Nezai Azh, and Maryam Mafi, "Factors Affecting Adolescents' Risk-Taking in Single-Child Families," *Social Health and Behavior* 2, no. 4 (2019): 151–157. https://doi.org/10.4103/SHB.SHB_20_19. Accessed February 4, 2023.
6. Mayo Clinic Staff, "Single Parent? Tips for Raising A Child Alone," in *Healthy Lifestyle: Children's Health*. https://mcpress.mayoclinic.org/parenting/single-parent-go-from-surviving-to-thriving/
7. Sheri Madigan, Dillon Browne, Nicole Racine, Camille Mori, and Suzanne Tough, "Association between Screen Time and Children's Performance on a Developmental Screening Test," *JAMA Pediatrics* 173, no. 3 (2019): 244–250. https://pubmed.ncbi.nlm.nih.gov/30688984/. Accessed December 18, 2022.
8. Jennifer Martin-Biggers, G. Alleman, N. Haugu, J. Worobey, and Carol Byrd-Bredbenner, "Beliefs and Barriers to Limiting Screentime Behavior by Parents of Preschoolers," *Journal of Nutrition Education and Behavior* 47, no. 4 (July 1, 2015).
9. Bandura, "Social Learning Theory."
10. James Steyer, *The Other Parent: The Inside Story of the Media's Effect on Our Children* (New York: Atria Books, 2002).
11. Madigan et al., "Association between Screen Time and Children's Performance."
12. Dana Goldstein, Adam Popescu, and Nikole Hannah-Jones, "As School Moves Online Many Students Stay Logged Out," *New York Times*, April 6, 2020. https://www.nytimes.com/2020/04/06/us/coronavirus-schools-attendance-absent.html. Accessed December 18, 2022.
13. Erik Erikson, *Identity, Youth and Crisis* (New York: W. W. Norton, 1950/1963).
14. Erikson, *Identity, Youth and Crisis.*
15. Brigid Schulte and Stravroula Pabst, "Combating Burnout as a Single Working Parent," *Harvard Business Review*, June 29, 2021, https://hbr.org/2021/06/combating-burnout-as-a-single-working-parent. Accessed December 18, 2022.
16. Bandura, "Social Learning Theory."

17. Alan Sroufe and Daniel Siegel, "The Verdict Is In: The Case for Attachment Theory," *Psychotherapy Networker,* March/April 2011. https://www.metanoia.ac.uk/media/1524/sroufe-a-siegel-d-the-verdict-is-in-the-case-for-attachment-theory.pdf. Accessed December 18, 2022.

18. Sroufe and Siegel, "The Verdict Is In."

19. D. Siegel, "Secure Attachment: Parenting from the Inside Out," *U.S. News & World Report,* January 9, 2017. https://health.usnews.com/wellness/for-parents/articles/2017-01-09/secure-attachment-parenting-from-the-inside-out. Accessed December 21, 2022.

20. D. Siegel, "Secure Attachment."

Chapter 5

1. Cathy Schen, "When Mothers Leave Their Children Behind," *Harvard Review of Psychiatry* 13, no. 4 (2005): 233–243.

2. U.S. Census Bureau, 2016 Current Population Survey. Annual Social and Economic Supplement. www.census.gov/hhes/families/. "Living Arrangements of Children under 18." https://www.census.gov/library/visualizations/2016/comm/cb16-192_living_arrangements.html. Accessed February 4, 2023.

3. U.S. Census Bureau, "The Majority of Children Live with Two Parents," November 17, 2016. https://www.census.gov/newsroom/press-releases/2016/cb16-192.html. Accessed December 18, 2022.

4. Eli Rapoport et al., "Family Well-Being in Grandparent- versus Parent-Headed Households," *Pediatrics* 146, no. 3 (September 2020). https://doi.org/10.1542/peds.2020-0115. Accessed December 18, 2022.

5. Elizabeth Gilbert, *Eat, Pray, Love: One Woman's Search for Everything across Italy, India and Indonesia* (New York: Viking, 2006).

6. Cheryl Strayed, *Wild: From Lost to Found on the Pacific Crest Trail* (New York: Alfred A. Knopf, 2012).

7. African Diaspora News Channel, "Eat Love Migrate Interview." Hosted by Phillip Scott. "ES, from the Eat Love Migrate YouTube Channel, joins us to talk about what made her leave America, transitioning into a life on the Motherland, and what she noticed about the African family." https://youtu.be/o1CbiulYarY.

8. Gretchen Livingston, "The Rise of Single Fathers: A Ninefold Increase since 1960," Pew Research Center. Social and Demographic Trends, July 2, 2013. https://www.pewsocialtrends.org/2013/07/02/the-rise-of-single-fathers/. Accessed December 19, 2022.

9. Crystal Ponti, "The Rise in Walk-Away Moms," *FilterFree Parents* (blog), December 18, 2020. http://mommifried.com/the-rise-of-walk-away-moms. Accessed February 4, 2023.

10. Cristina Munroe, "Moms Reveal the Heartbreaking Reasons Why They Abandoned Their Kids," *Rebel Circus* (blog), January 28. 2018. https://www.magzin.net/moms-reveal-the-heartbreaking-reasons-why-they-abandoned-their-kids. Accessed February 4, 2023.

11. Anne Reneau, "To the Mom on the Brink of Breaking," *ScaryMommy* (blog). https://www.scarymommy.com/motherhood-mom-on-brink-breaking. Accessed December 20, 2022.

12. Peggy Drexler, "Why There Are More Walk-Away Moms." *Special to CNN*. May 6, 2013. https://www.cnn.com/2013/05/04/opinion/drexler-mothers-leaving/index.html. Accessed December 20, 2022.

13. Marina Kamenev, "Why Three Women Made the Tough Decision to Leave Their Children," *The Sunday Herald*, March 17, 2018. https://www.smh.com.au/lifestyle/life-and-relationships/why-three-women-made-the-tough-decision-to-leave-their-children-20180315-p4z4im.html. Accessed December 20, 2022.

14. Alison Squire Smith, "Shameless: The Unrepentant Mother Who Walked Out on her Five Children and Husband and Began a New Family," *Daily Mail Online*, August 5, 2009. https://www.dailymail.co.uk/femail/article-1204334/Shameless-The-unrepentant-mother-walked-children-husband-began-new-family.html. Accessed December 20, 2022.

15. Bunmi Sofola, "Abandoned Child Never Get Over the Mother Who Walks Away," *Vanguard News*, January 18, 2020. https://www.vanguardngr.com/2020/01/abandoned-children-never-get-over-the-mother-who-walks-away. Accessed December 20, 2022.

16. "When Mother Walks Out," *The Irish Times*, August 28, 1998. https://www.irishtimes.com/culture/when-mother-walks-out-1.146944. Accessed December 20, 2022.

17. Lane Vasquez, "20 Parents Share Why They Left Their Kids Behind: Not Everyone Can Bring Themselves to Stay," Moms Online Magazine, October 12, 2018. https://www.moms.com/20-parents-share-why-they-left-their-kids-behind. Accessed December 20, 2022.

18. Sarah Glynn. "Breadwinning Mothers Continue to Be the U.S. Norm," Center for American Progress, May 10, 2019. https://www.americanprogress.org/issues/women/reports/2019/05/10/469739/breadwinning-mothers-continue-u-s-norm. Accessed December 20, 2022.

19. Caryn Medved, "The New Female Breadwinner: Discursively Doing and Undoing Gender Relations," *Journal of Applied Communication Research* 44, no. 3 (2016): 236–255. https://doi.org/10.1080/00909882.2016.1192286. Accessed December 20, 2022.

20. Leah Boustan and William Collins, "The Origins and Persistence of Black-White Differences in Women's Labor Force Participation." National Bureau of Economic Research, Working Paper 19040. May 2013. 8,10. https://www.nber.org/papers/w19040.pdf. Accessed December 20, 2022.

21. Sharin N. Elkholy, "Feminism and Race in the United States," The Internet Encyclopedia of Philosophy, July 27, 2020. https://iep.utm.edu/fem-race/. Accessed December 20, 2022.

22. Jennifer Hallam, "The Slave Experience: Men, Women, and Gender," *Slavery and the Making of America*. Thirteen/WNET New York, 2004. Educational Broadcasting Corporation. https://www.thirteen.org/wnet/slavery/experience/gender/history.html. Accessed December 20, 2022.

23. Kirsten E. Wood, "Gender and Slavery," in Mark Smith and Robert Paquette, eds., *The Oxford Handbook of Slavery in the Americas* (Oxford, UK: Oxford University Press, 2012), pp. 2–3. https://www.oxfordhandbooks.com/view/10.1093/oxfordhb/9780199227990.001.0001/oxfordhb-9780199227990-e-24. Accessed February 4, 2023.

24. Wood, "Gender and Slavery."

25. Data and Statistics, 100 Years of Working Women. U.S. Dept. of Labor. https://www.dol.gov/agencies/wb/date. Accessed February 4, 2023.

26. Data and Statistics, 100 Years of Working Women.

27. Martin Abraham, Sabastian Behr, and Mark Trappmann, "Gender Differences in Willingness to Move for Interregional Job Offers," *Demographic Research* 40 (January–June 2019): 1571–1572. https://www.demographic-research.org/volumes/vol40/53/40-53.pdf. Accessed December 21, 2022.

28. Guy Standing, "Global Feminization through Flexible Labor: A Theme Revisited," *World Development* 27 no. 3 (1999): 600.

29. Standing, "Global Feminization through Flexible Labor."

30. Jeanne Batalova, "Immigrant Women and Girls in the United States in 2018," Migration Policy Institute, March 24, 2020. https://www.migrationpolicy.org/article/immigrant-women-and-girls-united-states. Accessed December 20, 2022.

31. Batalova, "Immigrant Women and Girls."

32. Batalova, "Immigrant Women and Girls."

33. BBC, "Windrush Generation: Who Are They and Why Are They Facing Problems?" November 24, 2021. https://www.bbc.com/news/uk-43782241. Accessed December 20, 2022.

34. BBC, "Windrush Generation."

35. Prachi Mishra, "Emigration and Brain Drain: Evidence from the Caribbean," International Monetary Fund, WP/06/05, January 1, 2006. https://www.imf.org/external/pubs/ft/wp/2006/wp0625.pdf. Accessed December 20, 2022.

36. Charmaine Crawford, "Sending Love in a Barrel: The Making of Transnational Families in Canada," *Canadian Women Studies/Les Cahiers de la Femme* 22, nos. 3–4 (2003). https://cws.journals.yorku.ca/index.php/cws/article/view/6420. Accessed December 20, 2022.

37. Crawford, "Sending Love in a Barrel."

38. Melissa Noel, "Jamaica's Barrel Children Often Come Up Empty with a Parent Abroad," *NBC News*, December 27, 2017. https://www.nbcnews.com/news/nbcblk/jamaica-s-barrel-children-often-come-empty-parent-abroad-n830636. Accessed December 20, 2022.

39. Noel, "Jamaican Barrel Children."

40. Noel, "Jamaican Barrel Children."

41. "Bodies on the Doorstep: Jamaica in the 1970's," A Moment in U.S. Diplomatic History. ADST, Association for Diplomatic Studies and Training, December 27, 2017. https://adst.org/2016/12/bodies-doorstep-jamaica-late-1970s/. Accessed December 20, 2022.

42. Noel, "Jamaican Barrel Children."

43. Centers for Disease Control and Prevention. Reproductive Health: Teen Pregnancy. "About Teen Pregnancy." Last reviewed March 1, 2019. https://www.cdc.gov/teenpregnancy/about/index.htm. Accessed December 20, 2022.

44. Fatemeh Abdollahi, Mouloud Agajani-Delavar, Mehran Zarghami, and Munn-Sann Lye, "Postpartum Mental Health in First-Time Mothers: A Cohort Study," *Iranian Journal of Psychiatry and Behavioral Science* 10 no. 1 (2016): e426. https://doi.org/10.17795/ijpbs-426. Accessed December 20, 2022.

45. See Sara Agnafors, Marie Bladh, Carl Göran Svedin, and Gunilla Sydsjö, "Mental Health in Young Mothers, Single Mothers and Their Children," *BMC Psychiatry*, April 11, 2019. https://bmcp sychiatry.biomedcentral.com/articles/10.1186/s12888-019-2082-y; also see Vanessa Reid and Mikki Meadows-Oliver, "Postpartum Depression in Adolescent Mothers: An Integrative Review of the Literature," *Journal of Pediatric Health* 21, no. 5 (September 1, 2007). https://www.jpedhc.org/article/S0891-5245(06)00329-4/fulltext. Accessed February 4, 2023.

46. Reid and Meadows-Oliver, "Postpartum Depression in Adolescent Mothers."

47. Mayo Clinic, "Postpartum Depression." https://www.mayoclinic.org/diseases-conditions/postpartum-depression/symptoms-causes/syc-20376617. Accessed February 4, 2023.

48. Tommy Rowan and Joseph Gambardello, "Police Charge 15-Year-Old Philadelphia Mom after Newborn Found Dumped in Trash," *Philadelphia Enquirer*, January 2, 2019. https://www.inquirer.com/news/baby-dead-fetus-swampoodle-north-philadelphia-new-years-eve-teen-mother-20190102.html. Accessed February 4, 2023.

49. Elvia Malagón, "Teen Mother Allowed to Stay in Mother's Home with Baby Left in Alley Last Month," *Chicago Tribune*, June 24, 2019. https://www.chicagotribune.com/news/breaking/ct-met-teen-parents-alley-baby-20190614-story. html. Accessed February 4, 2023.

50. For extended discussion of grandparenting across the globe, see David W. Shwalb and Ziarat Hossain, eds., *Grandparents in Cultural Context* (London: Routledge, 2018), pp. 12–15.

51. Center for Behavioral Health Statistics and Quality, *Serious Mental Health Challenges among Older Adolescents and Young Adults* (Rockville, MD: Substance Abuse and Mental Health Services Administration, 2014). https://www.samhsa.gov/data/sites/default/files/sr173-mh-challenges-young-adults-2014/sr173-mh-challenges-young-adults-2014/sr173-mh-challenges-young-adults-2014.htm. Accessed February 4, 2023.

52. Center for Behavioral Health Statistics and Quality, *Serious Mental Health Challenges.*

53. "One in Four People Worldwide Affected by Mental Disorder, UN Health Agency Says," UN News Global Perspective Human Stories, United Nations, October 4, 2001. https://news.un.org/en/story/2001/10/16612. Accessed February 4, 2023.

54. Women's Mental Health: An Evidence Based Review. Mental Health Determinants and Populations. Department of Mental Health and Substance Dependence. World Health Organization. Geneva 2000. https://apps.who.int/iris/bitstream/handle/10665/66539/WHO_MSD_MDP_00.1.pdf. Accessed February 4, 2023.

55. Lynne McCormack, Sarah White, and José Cuenca, "A Fractured Journey of Growth: Making Meaning of a "Broken" Childhood and Parental Mental Ill-Health," *Community, Work and Family* 20, no. 3 (2017). https://doi.org/10.1080/13668803.2015.1117418. Accessed December 20, 2022.

56. McCormack et al., "A Fractured Journey of Growth."

57. Kathleen C. Basile, Sharon G. Smith, Matthew Breiding, Michele C. Black, and Reshma R. Mahendra, "Sexual Violence Surveillance: Uniform Definitions and Recommended Data Elements, Version 2.0," Centers for Disease Control and Prevention, 2014, p. 11. https://www.cdc.gov/violenceprevention/pdf/sv_surveillance_definitionsl-2009-a.pdf. Accessed December 20, 2022.

58. John Bradshaw, *Family Secrets: What You Don't Know Can Hurt You* (London: Piatkus Books, 1995).

59. Martin R. Huecker, Kevin C. King, Gary A. Jordan, and William Smock, "Domestic Violence," *StatsPearls*, June 26, 2020. https://www.ncbi.nlm.nih.gov/books/NBK499891/. Accessed December 20, 2022.

60. Katie Zezima, Deanna Paul, Steven Rich, Julie Tate, and Jennifer Jenkins, "Murder with Impunity. Domestic Slayings: Brutal and Foreseeable," *Washington Post*, December 9, 2018. https://www.washingtonpost.com/graphics/2018/investigations/domestic-violence-murders/. Accessed February 4, 2023.

61. UNODC, *Global Study on Homicide 2019* (Vienna, 2019), p. 29.

62. UN Women, *Press Release: UN Women Raises Awareness of the Shadow Pandemic of Violence against Women during COVID-19,* May 27, 2020. https://www.unwomen.org/en/news/stories/2020/5/press-release-the-shadow-pandemic-of-violence-against-women-during-covid-19. Accessed February 4, 2023.

63. National Coalition Against Domestic Violence, "Why Do Victims Stay?" https://ncadv.org/why-do-victims-stay. Accessed February 4, 2023.

64. The Sentencing Project, "Incarcerated Women and Girls," May 12, 2022. https://www.sentencingproject.org/publications/incarcerated-women-and-girls. Accessed February 4, 2023.

65. The Sentencing Project, "Incarcerated Women and Girls."

66. Pew Trust, "Breaking the Cycle of Incarceration by Keeping Mothers and Children Together," https://www.pewtrusts.org/en/research-and-analysis/blogs/stateline/2017/09/13/breaking-the-cycle-of-incarceration-by-keeping-mothers-and-children-together. Accessed February 4, 2023.

67. Marc Mauer and Virginia McCalmont, "A Lifetime of Punishment: The Impact of the Felony Drug Ban on Welfare Benefits," The Sentencing Project, November 14, 2013. https://www.sentencingproject.org/publications/a-lifetime-of-punishment-the-impact-of-the-felony-drug-ban-on-welfare-benefits. Accessed December 20, 2022.

68. The Sentencing Project. "A Lifetime of Punishment."

69. The Sentencing Project. "A Lifetime of Punishment."

70. Lucius Couloute and Daniel Kopf, "Out of Prison & Out of Work: Unemployment among Formerly Incarcerated People," Prison Policy Initiative. https://www.prisonpolicy.org/reports/outofwork.html. Accessed December 20, 2022.

71. Dan Levin, "As More Mothers Fill Prisons, Children Suffer a Primal Wound," *New York Times*, December 28, 2019. https://www.nytimes.com/2019/12/28/us/prison-mothers-children.html. Accessed December 20, 2022.

72. U.S. Citizen Children Impacted by Immigration Enforcement. Fact Sheet. American Immigration Council. June 24, 2021. https://www.americanimmigrationcouncil.org/research/us-citizen-children-impacted-immigration-enforcement. Accessed February 4, 2023.

Chapter 6

1. Bureau of Justice Statistics, *Prison Inmates Characteristics. Terms and Definitions.* https://www.bjs.gov/index.cfm/dataonline/content/pub/pdf/index.cfm?ty=tdtp&tid=141. Accessed December 20, 2022.

2. World Prison Brief (WPB), "Highest to Lowest—Prison Population Rate," June 2020. https://www.prisonstudies.org/highest-to-lowest/prison_population_rate?field_region_taxonomy_tid=All. Accessed February 4, 2023.

3. Bureau of Justice Statistics, "Parents in Prison and Their Minor Children," 2010. https://bjs.ojp.gov/content/pub/pdf/pptmc.pdf. Accessed December 20, 2022.

4. Bureau of Justice, "Recidivism of Prisoners Released in 24 States in 2008: A 10-year Follow-Up Period (2008–2018)," Summary, NCJ 256094, September 2021. https://bjs.ojp.gov/sites/g/files/xyckuh236/files/media/document/rpr24s0810yfup0818_sum.pdf

5. *Nightline*, "Children of Prisoners Reunite with Their Fathers behind Bars for a Day," *ABC News*. Aired December 12, 2015. https://www.youtube.com/watch?v=i5VV0og-a7w. Accessed February 4, 2023.

6. *Nightline*, "Children of Prisoners Reunite."

7. Federal Bureau of Investigation. "Crime in the United States: Property Crime." https://ucr.fbi.gov/crime-in-the-u.s/2010/crime-in-the-u.s.-2010/property-crime. Accessed February 4, 2023.

8. Mathew R. Durose, Alexia D. Cooper, and Howard N. Snyder, "Recidivism of Prisoners Released in 30 States in 2005: Patterns from 2005 to 2010," *U.S. Dept. of Justice. Special Report*, April 2014. https://bjs.ojp.gov/content/pub/pdf/rprts05p0510.pdf. Accessed February 4, 2023.

9. Mark T. Berg and Beth Huebner, "Reentry and the Ties That Bind: An Examination of Social Ties, Employment and Recidivism," *Justice Quarterly* 28, no. 2 (April 2011): 402.

10. Lucius Couloute and Daniel Kopf, "Out of Prison & Out of Work: Unemployment among Formerly Incarcerated People," Prison Policy Initiative. https://www.prisonpolicy.org/reports/outofwork.html. Accessed December 20, 2022.

11. Couloute and Kopf, "Out of Prison & Out of Work."

12. Kathryn Edin and Timothy Nelson, *Doing the Best I Can: Fatherhood in the Inner City* (Berkeley: University of California Press, 2013), p. 83.

13. Ann Adalist-Estrin, "Homecoming: Children's Adjustment to Parent's Parole." Original presentation at the Child Welfare League of America Annual Conference, 1996. Updated 2002. https://nrccfi.camden.rutgers.edu/files/Homecoming.pdf. Accessed February 4, 2023.

14. Laura Tach and Kathryn Edin, "The Relationship Contexts of Young Disadvantaged Men," *Annals of the American Academy of Political and Social Science* 635, no. 1 (May 2011): 76–94. https://doi.org/10.1177/0002716210393680. Accessed February 4, 2023.

15. Bureau of Justice Statistics, "Parents in Prison and Their Minor Children."

16. Edin and Nelson, *Doing the Best I Can.*

17. Thomas Sowell, "The Scapegoat for Strife in the Black Community," *National Review*, July 7, 2015. https://www.nationalreview.com/2015/07/slavery-didnt-cause-todays-black-problems-welfare-did. Accessed February 4, 2023.

18. Della V. Mosely, Kathryn Hanes Owen, Sharon Scales Rostosky, and Robert J. Reese, "Contextualizing Behaviors Associated with Paranoia: Perspectives of Black Men," *Psychology of Men & Masculinity* 18, no 2 (2017): 165–175. https://doi.org/10.1037/men0000052

19. U.S. Census Bureau, "Family Structure and Children's Living Arrangements in Census Bureau Data," June 13, 2012. https://www2.census.gov/about/partners/sdc/events/steering-committee/2012-06/2012-kreider.pdf. Accessed February 4, 2023.

20. The 1619 Project, *New York Times Magazine*, August 2019. https://www.nytimes.com/interactive/2019/08/14/magazine/1619-america-slavery.html. Accessed February 4, 2023.

21. W. E. B. Du Bois, ed., "The Negro American Family; A Social Study," made by Atlanta University under the patronage of the Trustees of the John F. Slater Fund (Atlanta: Atlanta University Press, 1908), p. 9.

22. "The Negro American Family; A Social Study," p. 9.

23. "The Negro American Family; A Social Study," p. 39.

24. Patterson, Orlando, *Rituals of Blood: Consequences of Slavery in Two American Centuries* (Washington, DC: Civitas, 1998), p. 27.

25. Patterson, *Rituals of Blood*, p. 27.

26. Patterson, *Rituals of Blood*, p. 25.

27. Theodore Dwight Weld, *American Slavery as It Is: Testimony of a Thousand Witnesses,* American Anti-Slavery Society, January 1, 1839, New York. https://docsouth.unc.edu/neh/weld/weld.html. Accessed February 4, 2023.

28. Tawanda Greer and Klaus Cavalhieri, "The Role of Coping Strategies in Understanding the Effects of Institutional Racism on Mental Health Outcomes for African American Men," *Journal of Black Psychology* 45, no. 5 (July 2019). https://journals.sagepub.com/doi/full/10.1177/0095798419868105. Accessed December 20, 2022.

29. Bryan Stevenson, "Why American Prisons Owe Their Cruelty to Slavery—The 1619 Project," *New York Times Magazine*, August 14, 2019. https://www.nytimes.com/interactive/2019/08/14/magazine/prison-industrial-complex-slavery-racism.html. Accessed February 4, 2023.

30. Associated Press, "Six Times as Many Black Men in Prison as Whites," December 4, 2019. https://www.courthousenews.com/six-times-as-many-black-men-in-prison-as-whites. Accessed February 4, 2023.

31. Mikaela Pitcan, Jennie Park-Taylor, and Janelle Hayslett, "Black Men and Racial Microaggressions at Work," *Career Development Quarterly* 66, no. 4 (December 6, 2018): 300–314. https://onlinelibrary.wiley.com/doi/full/10.1002/cdq.12152. Accessed February 4, 2023.

32. Harriet Jacobs, *Incidents in the Life of a Slave Girl* (New York: Dover 2001/1861), pp. 11, 12.

33. Jacobs, *Incidents in the Life of a Slave Girl*, p. 12.

34. Thomas Foster, *Rethinking Rufus: Sexual Violations of Enslaved Men* (Athens: University of Georgia Press, 2019).

35. D. C. Klein, E. Fencil-Morse, and M. E. Seligman, "Learned Helplessness, Depression, and the Attribution of Failure," *Journal of Personality and Social Psychology*, 33, no. 5 (1976): 508–516. https://doi.org/10.1037/0022-3514.33.5.508. Accessed February 4, 2023.

36. Martin Seligman, *Authentic Happiness* (New York: Atria Paperbacks, 2002), p. 90.

37. Kendra Cherry, "What Is Learned Helplessness and Why Does It Happen?" *VeryWell Mind*. June 7, 2020.

38. Christopher Peterson and Martin Seligman, "Learned Helplessness and Victimization," *Journal of Social Issues* 39, no. 2 (Summer 1983): 103–116. https://doi.org/10.1111/j.1540-4560.1983.tb00143.x. Accessed February 4, 2023.

39. Patterson, *Rituals of Blood*, p. 41.

40. "Slaves Resist," *Black Chronicle*, September 1, 1831, 3. p. 3.

41. Nola C. Veazie, "*You Belong to Me*: An African American Narrative," *Journal of Psychological Issues* 6, no. 4 (April 6, 2016). https://onlinelibrary.wiley.com/doi/pdf/10.1002/jpoc.21201. Accessed December 20, 2022.

42. Wilma King, "Prematurely Knowing of Evil Things: The Sexual Abuse of African American Girls and Young Women in Slavery and Freedom," *Journal of African American History* 99, no. 3 (Summer 2014): 173–196.

43. Foster, *Rethinking Rufus*.

44. Henry Louis Gates Jr., *The Classic Slave Narratives: Narrative of the Life of Frederick Douglass* (New York: Signet, 1987), p. 340.

45. History.com Editors, "Slavery in America," The History Channel, July 6, 2020. https://www.history.com/topics/black-history/slavery. Accessed December 20, 2022.

46. "They Sold Human Beings Here," 1619 Project, *New York Times Magazine*, February 12, 2020. https://www.nytimes.com/interactive/2020/02/12/magazine/1619-project-slave-auction-sites.html. Accessed February 4, 2023.

47. Moses Roper, *Narrative of My Escape from Slavery* (New York: Dover, 2003/1838).

48. Roper, *Narrative of My Escape*, pp. 1–2.

49. "A Chronology of Moses Roper's Life." http://www.roperld.com/RoperMoses.htm. Accessed December 20, 2022.

50. "A Chronology of Moses Roper's Life."

51. "Letters to R.C. Bullard Regarding Slave Woman Abuse," Historical Documents, Georgia Public Broadcasting. https://www.pbs.org/wgbh/aia/part4/4h3436.html. Accessed February 4, 2023.

52. Nancy Clanton, "Sally Hemmings, Mother of 6 of Jefferson's Children, Was Also His Property," *Atlanta Journal Constitution*, February 7, 2019. https://www.ajc.com/news/national/sally-hemings-mother-six-thomas-jefferson-children-was-also-his-property/oKIBF28ni64Yv4i6x2NHJM/. Accessed February 4, 2023.

53. "Thomas Jefferson and Sally Hemmings, A Brief Account." Monticello.org. https://www.monticello.org/thomas-jefferson/jefferson-slavery/thomas-jefferson-and-sally-hemings-a-brief-account. Accessed December 20, 2022.

54. "The Life of Sally Hemmings," Monticello.org. https://www.monticello.org/sallyhemings/. Accessed December 20, 2022.

55. William Thompson, enslaved in Virginia, interviewed in Ontario, Canada, 1855; in Benjamin Drew, *The Refugee: Or the Narratives of Fugitive Slaves in Canada*, 1856.

56. Tristan Stubbs, *Masters of Violence.* (Columbia: University of South Carolina Press, 2018).

57. Orlando Patterson, *Slavery and Social Death: A Comparative Study* (Cambridge, MA: Harvard University Press, 1982), p. 10.

58. "Report on the Apprenticeship System in the West Indies by James Williams," Collection Items: British Library. United Kingdom. https://www.bl.uk/collection-items/report-on-the-apprenticeship-system-in-the-west-indies-by-james-williams. Accessed September 24, 2020.

59. "Report on the Apprenticeship System in the West Indies."

60. Hazel Bennett and Phillip Sherlock, *Story of the Jamaican People* (Kingston, Jamaica: Ian Randle Caribbean Press, 1998), p. 234.

61. Bennett and Sherlock, *Story of the Jamaican People*, p. 234.

62. Jamaica Almanac, 1839: Assistant Judges and Magistrates. Parish of St. Mary.

63. Bennett and Sherlock, *Story of the Jamaican People.*

64. Edward Henry Stanley, Earl of Derby, "Claims and Resources of the West Indian Colonies: A Letter to the Rt. Hon. W.E Gladstone, M.P., Late Secretary of State for the Colonies" (T &W Boone, 1850), p. 106.

65. Jamaican Family Search Genealogy: Research Library. 1839 Jamaica Almanac http://www.jamaicanfamilysearch.com/Members/a/AL39Lis4.htm. Accessed February 4, 2023.

66. Chevannes, Barry, "Sexual Behaviour of Jamaicans: A Literature Review," *Social and Economic Studies* 42, no. 1 (1993): 1–45. http://www.jstor.org/stable/27865876. Accessed February 4, 2023.

67. Foster, *Rethinking Rufus*, p. 55.

68. Willie Williams, in *Federal Writers'* Project: *Slave Narratives Project, Vol. 16, Texas Part 4, Sanco-Young, 1936*, Manuscript/Mixed Material. https://www.loc.gov/resource/mesn.164/?sp=195. Accessed February 4, 2023.

69. Foster, *Rethinking Rufus*, p. 61.

70. Foster, *Rethinking Rufus*, p. 57.

71. Ida Blackshear Hutchinson, in *Federal Writers' Project: Slave Narrative Project, Vol. 2, Arkansas, Part 3, Gadson-Isom*, 1936, Manuscript/Mixed Material. https://www.loc.gov/item/mesn023/. Accessed February 4, 2023.

72. Sam and Louisa Elliot, in *Federal Writers' Project: Slave Narrative Project, Vol. 3, Florida, Anderson—Wilson with Combined Interviews of Others*, 127, 1936, Manuscript/Mixed Material. https://www.gutenberg.org/files/12297/12297-h/12297-h.htm#EverettSamLouisa. Accessed February 4, 2023.

73. Foster, *Rethinking Rufus*, p. 57.

74. Hutchinson, in *Federal Writers' Project.*

75. Hutchinson, in *Federal Writers' Project.*

76. Edin and Nelson, *Doing the Best I Can*, p. 226.

77. Edin and Nelson, *Doing the Best I Can*, p. 226.

78. Patterson, *Rituals of Blood*, p. 28.

79. Patterson, *Rituals of Blood*, p. 28.

80. Patterson, *Rituals of Blood*, p. 28.

81. Patterson, *Rituals of Blood*, pp. 34–35.

82. Aramide Tinubu, "How Many Children Does Future Have and from How Many Different Women?" *Show Biz Cheat Sheet*. https://www.cheatsheet.com/entertainment/how-many-children-does-future-have-and-from-how-many-different-women.html. Accessed December 20, 2022.

83. Patterson, *Rituals of Blood*, p. 174.

84. Patterson, *Rituals of Blood*, p. 28.

85. Edin and Nelson, *Doing the Best I Can*, p. 174.

86. Edin and Nelson, *Doing the Best I Can*, p. 213.

87. Edin and Nelson, *Doing the Best I Can*, p. 213.

88. Edin and Nelson, *Doing the Best I Can*, p. 82.

89. Edin and Nelson, *Doing the Best I Can*, p. 82.

90. Mark Aguiar, Mark Bils, Kerwin Kofi Charles, and Erik Hurst, "Leisure Luxuries and the Labor Supply of Young Men," July 4, 2017. NBER Working Paper No. w23552. https://ssrn.com/abstract=2996308. Accessed February 4, 2023.

91. Edin and Nelson, *Doing the Best I Can*, p. 174.

92. Roy F. Baumeister, "Fathers Who Leave: How Could a Man Leave His Family for Another Woman?" *Psychology Today*, June 23, 2008. https://www.psychologytoday.com/us/blog/cultural-animal/200806/fathers-who-leave. Accessed February 4, 2023.

93. Gretchen Livingston, "The Changing Profile of Unmarried Parents; A Growing Share Live with a Partner," Pew Research Center, Social and Demographic Trends, April 25, 2018.

94. Sarah Schoppe-Sullivan, Miranda Berrigan, and Michael Wells, "Rivalry in Coparenting at the Transition to Parenthood," in Sybil Hart and Nancy Jones, eds., *Psychology of Emotions* (New York: Nova Science Publishers, 2018), pp. 217–238.

95. Chad Prevost, "Why This Is the End of the Dumb Dad Era," *On Parenting* (blog), *Washington Post*, May 7, 2015. https://www.washingtonpost.com/news/parenting/wp/2015/05/07/why-this-is-the-end-of-the-dumb-dad-era. Accessed February 4, 2023.

96. Elissa Strauss, "Gatekeeping: Why Moms Won't Let Dads Help," *CNN Health*, December 6, 2017. https://www.cnn.com/2017/12/06/health/maternal-gatekeeping-strauss/index.html. Accessed February 4, 2023.

97. Peg Streep, "Unloved Daughters and the Dark Side of Maternal Gatekeeper: How Traditional Values Can Mask and Normalize Toxic Behavior," *Psychology Today*, March 15, 2019. https://www.psychologytoday.com/us/blog/tech-support/201903/unloved-daughters-and-the-dark-side-maternal-gatekeeping. Accessed February 4, 2023.

98. Sarah Schoppe-Sullivan, Lauren Altenburger, Meghan Lee, Daniel Bower, and Claire Kamp Dush, "Who Are the Gatekeepers? Predictors of Maternal Gatekeeping," *Parenting Science and Practice* 15, no. 3 (July 31, 2015): 166–186. https://doi.org/10.1080/15295192.2015.1053321. Accessed February 4, 2023.

99. Schoppe-Sullivan et al., "Who Are the Gatekeepers?"

100. Melissa Byers, "Maternal Gatekeeping & Why It Matters for Children," The Father Factor, National Fatherhood Initiative, November 9, 2017. https://www.fatherhood.org/fatherhood/maternal-gatekeeping-why-it-matters-for-children. Accessed December 20, 2022.

101. Christopher Brown, "350 Practitioners on the Challenge of Maternal Gatekeeping," The Father Factor, National Fatherhood Initiative, February 15, 2017. https://www.fatherhood.org/fatherhood/350-practitioners-on-the-challenge-of-maternal-gatekeeping. Accessed December 20, 2022.

102. Bruce Hawthorne and C. J. Lennings, "The Marginalization of Nonresident Father: Their Postdivorce Roles, *Journal of Divorce and Remarriage* 49, no. 3 (October 11, 2008): 191–209. https://doi.org/10.1080/10502550802232419. Accessed February 4, 2023.

103. Julia Arroyo, Barbara Zsembik, and Chuck Peek, "Ain't Nobody Got Time for Dad? Racial-Ethnic Disproportionalities in Child Welfare Casework Practice with Nonresident Fathers," *Child Abuse and Neglect* 93 July 2019. 182–196.

104. Christian Campbell, Douglas Howard, Brett Rayford, and Derrick Gordon, "Fathers Matter: Involving and Engaging Fathers in the Child Welfare System Process," *Child and Youth Services Review* 53 (June 1, 2015): 84–91.

105. Hawthorne and Lennings, "The Marginalization of Nonresident Father."

106. John M. O'Donnell, Waldo E. Johnson Jr., Lisa Easley D'Aunno, and Helen L. Thornton, "Fathers in Child Welfare: Caseworkers' Perspectives," *Child Welfare: Journal of Policy, Practice, and Program* 84, no. 3 (2005): 387–414.

107. O'Donnell et al., "Fathers in Child Welfare."

108. Arroyo et al., "Ain't Nobody Got Time for Dad?"

109. Nehami Baum, "Gender-Sensitive Interventions to Improve Work with Fathers in Child Welfare Services," *Child and Family Social Work* 22, no. 1 (February 2017): 419–427. https://doi.org/10.1111/cfs.12259. Accessed December 21, 2022.

110. Donald Harris, "Reflections of a Jamaican Father," WordPress.com, September 26, 2018. https://guyaneseonline.files.wordpress.com/2020/08/kamala-harris-by-donald-harris.pdf?fbclid=IwAR3yTn8MKB5P_80j5NogYtAhV-bXPO6Y06kcUH6P0qZu0rpapo0z28xI7Fw. Accessed February 4, 2023.

111. Andrea Miller, "Gender Roles Highlight Gender Bias in Judicial Decisions," *ScienceDaily*, April 3, 2018. https://www.sciencedaily.com/releases/2018/04/180403085049.htm. Accessed December 21, 2022.

112. U.S. Bureau of Labor Statistics, *Labor Force Characteristics by Race and Ethnicity*, BLS Reports, December 2020. https://www.bls.gov/opub/reports/race-and-ethnicity/2019/home.htm. Accessed February 4, 2023.

113. Demetra Smith Nightingale and Stephen Wandner, "Informal and Nonstandard Employment in the United States: Implications for Low-Income Working Families," The Urban Institute, Brief 20, August 2011. https://webarchive.urban.org/publications/412372.html. Accessed February 4, 2023.

114. Martin Abraham, Sabastian Behr, and Mark Trappmann, "Gender Differences in Willingness to Move for Interregional Job Offers," *Demographic Research* 40 (January–June 2019): 1571–1572. www.jstor.org/stable/26727042. Accessed December 21, 2022.

115. Abraham et al., "Gender Differences in Willingness to Move," p. 1571.

116. Abraham et al., "Gender Differences in Willingness to Move," p. 1571.

117. Andrew Chamberlain, "Metro Movers; Where Are American Moving for Jobs, and Is It Worth It?" Glassdoor Research Report, May 2018. https://www.glassdoor.com/research/app/uploads/sites/2/2018/05/GD_ResearchReport_MetroMovers_Draft4.pdf. Accessed February 4, 2023.

118. U.S. Bureau of Labor Statistics, "Foreign-Born Workers: Labor Force Characteristics—2021," May 8, 2022. https://www.bls.gov/news.release/pdf/forbrn.pdf. Accessed February 4, 2023.

119. U.S. Bureau of Labor Statistics, "Foreign-Born Workers."

120. Maggie Kirkman, Kate Bourne, Jane Fisher, Louise Johnson, and Karin Hammarburg, "Gamete Donor's Expectations and Experiences of Contact with Their Donor Offspring," *Human Reproduction* 29, no. 4 (2014): 731–738.

121. Gregory C. Elliott, Melissa F. Colangelo, and Richard J. Gelles, "Mattering and Suicide Ideation: Establishing and Elaborating a Relationship," *Social Psychology Quarterly* 68, no. 3 (2005): 223–238. https://doi.org/10.1177/019027250506800303. Accessed December 21, 2022.

122. S. Isaksson, G. Sydsjo, A. Skoog Svanberg, and C. Lampic, "Disclosure Behaviour and Intentions among 111 Couples Following Treatment with Oocytes or Sperm for Identity Release Donors: Follow-up at Offspring Age 1–4 Years," *Human Reproduction* 27, no. 10. (October 2012): 2998–3007. https://www.ncbi.nlm.nih.gov/pmc/articles/PMC3442633/. Accessed December 21, 2022.

123. Elena Llioi, Lucy Blake, Vasanti Jadva, Gabriela Roman, and Susan Golombok, "The Role of Age of Disclosure of Biological Origins in the Psychological Wellbeing of Adolescents Conceived by Reproductive Donation: A Longitudinal Study from Age 1 to Age 14," *Journal of Child Psychology and Psychiatry* 58, no. 3 (2016). https://doi.org/10.1111/jcpp.12667. Accessed December 21, 2022.

124. Rosanna Hertz, Margaret Nelson, and Wendy Kramer, "Donor-Conceived Offspring Conceive of the Donor: The Relevance of Age, Awareness and Family Form," *Social Science and Medicine* 86 (June 2013): 52–65. https://www.researchgate.net/publication/236265189_Donor_Conceived_Offspring_Conceive_of_the_Donor_The_Relevance_of_Age_Awareness_and_Family_Form. Accessed December 21, 2022.

125. Kirkman et al., "Gamete Donor's Expectations."

126. S. Graham, T. Freeman, and V. Jadva, "A Comparison of the Characteristics, Motivations, Preferences, and Expectations of Men Donating Sperm Online or through a Sperm Bank," *Human Reproduction* 34, no. 11 (2019): 2208–2218. https://pdfs.semanticscholar.org/2653/a6d5d758290f6b577753843d3e1a4a46f7e6.pdf. Accessed December 21, 2022.

127. Graham et al., "A Comparison of the Characteristics."

128. A. Ravelingien, V. Provoost, and G. Pennings, "Donor-Conceived Children Looking for Their Sperm Donor: What Do They Want to Know?" *Facts, Views and Vision in Obgyn* 5, no. 4 (2013). https://www.ncbi.nlm.nih.gov/pmc/articles/PMC3987373. Accessed December 21, 2022.

129. Alana Newman, "The Overlooked Fatherless: One Donor-Conceived Woman's Story" (blog), *Institute for Family Studies*, October 26, 2016. https://ifstudies.org/blog/the-overlooked-fatherless-one-donor-conceived-womans-story. Accessed December 21, 2022.

130. Margaret K. Nelson, Rosanna Hertz, and Wendy Kramer, "Gamete Donor Anonymity and Limits on Numbers of Offspring: The Views of Three Stakeholders," *Journal of Law and the Biosciences* 3 no. 1 (October 29, 2015): 39–67. https://doi.org/10.1093/jlb/lsv045. Accessed December 21, 2022.

131. Ravelingien et al., "Donor-Conceived Children."

132. Stephanie Pappas, "Genetics Testing and Family Secrets," *Monitor on Psychology* 49, no. 6 (June 2018): 50. https://www.apa.org/monitor/2018/06/cover-genetic-testing. Accessed December 21, 2022.

133. Pappas, "Genetics Testing," p. 50.

134. Pappas, "Genetics Testing," p. 46.

135. Mayo Clinic, "Sperm Donation—Overview," 1998–2021 Mayo Foundation for Medical Education and Research (MFMER). https://www.mayoclinic.org. Accessed February 4, 2023.

136. Bureau of Justice Statistics, "Parents in Prison and Their Minor Children," 2010. https://bjs.ojp.gov/content/pub/pdf/pptmc.pdf. Accessed December 20, 2022.

137. Campbell et al., "Fathers Matter."

138. U.S. Dept. of Health and Human Services. "Multi-Site Family Study on Incarceration, Parenting and Partnering: Change in Couple Relationships before,

during and after Incarceration," March 2016. https://aspe.hhs.gov/system/files/pdf/202081/MFSIP_CoupleRelation.pdf. Accessed December 20, 2022.

139. Edin and Nelson, "Doing the Best I Can," p. 83.

140. Strauss, "Gatekeeping: Why Moms Won't Let Dads Help."

141. Schoppe-Sullivan et al., "Who Are the Gatekeepers?"

142. Patterson, *Rituals of Blood.*

143. Foster, *Rethinking Rufus*, p. 55.

144. Foster, *Rethinking Rufus*, p. 67.

145. Brandon et al., "A History of the Theory of Prenatal Attachment."

146. Pappas, "Genetic Testing and Family Secrets," p. 55.

Chapter 7

1. Nikita Stewart, "He Is 16 and His Mother Died of Covid-19. What Happens to Him Now?" *New York Times*, August 13, 2020. https://www.nytimes.com/2020/08/13/nyregion/coronavius-ny-parents-dead.html. Accessed December 20, 2022.

2. David Ovalle, "For Helping Coronavirus Patients, a South Florida Doctor Lost Custody of Her Daughter," *Miami Herald*, April 13, 2020, updated April 14, 2020. https://www.miamiherald.com/news/coronavirus/article241974676.html. Accessed February 4, 2023.

3. Megan Twohey, "New Battle for Those on Coronavirus Front Lines: Child Custody," *New York Times*, April 7, 2020, https://www.nytimes.com/2020/04/07/us/coronavirus-child-custody.html. Accessed December 20, 2022.

4. Twohey, "New Battles for Those on the Coronavirus Front Lines."

5. Bari Weiss, "Doctors Are Writing Their Wills," *New York Times*, March 26, 2020, Opinion. https://www.nytimes.com/2020/03/26/opinion/sunday/doctors-coronavirus-safety.html. Accessed December 20, 2022.

6. Weiss, "Doctors Are Writing Their Wills."

7. Rianna Mohammed-Roberts and Sarah McCune, "In Liberia, Providing Comfort for Kids in the Aftermath of the Ebola Crisis," World Bank Blogs. July 20, 2017, https://blogs.worldbank.org/health/liberia-providing-comfort-kids-aftermath-ebola-crisis. Accessed December 20, 2022.

8. Mercy Corps, *Chapter 6: The Effects of an Ebola Outbreak on the Children of Africa*. Mercy Corps Blog. March 2019. https://www.mercycorps.org/blog/ebola-outbreaks-africa-guide/chapter-6. Accessed December 20, 2022.

Chapter 8

1. Vincent J. Felitti, Robert F. Anda, Dale Nordenberg, David F. Williamson, Alison M. Spitz, Valerie Edwards, Mary P. Koss, and James S. Marks, "Relationship of Childhood Abuse and Household Dysfunction to Many of the Leading Causes of Death in Adults: The Adverse Childhood Experiences (ACE) Study," *American Journal of Preventive Medicine* 14, no. 3 (May 1, 1998): 245–258. https://www.ajpmonline.org/article/S0749-3797(98)00017-8/pdf. Accessed December 20, 2022.

2. Laurie Leitch, "Action Steps Using ACEs and Trauma-Informed Care: A Resilience Model," *Health Justice*, April 28, 2017. https://www.ncbi.nlm.nih.gov/pmc/articles/PMC5409906/. Accessed December 20, 2022.

3. Felitti et al., "Relationship of Childhood Abuse and Household Dysfunction."

4. Andrew Curry, "Parents' Emotional Trauma May Change Their Children's Biology: Studies in Mice Show," *Science*, July 18, 2019. https://www.science.org/content/article/parents-emotional-trauma-may-change-their-children-s-biology-studies-mice-show-how. Accessed February 4, 2023.

5. Dora L. Costa, Noelle Yetter, and Heather DeSomer, "Intergenerational Transmission of Paternal Trauma among US Civil War ex-POWs," *Proceedings of the National Sciences of the United States of America (PNAS)* 115, no. 44 (October 15, 2018): 11215–11220. https://doi.org/10.1073/pnas.1803630115. Accessed December 20, 2022.

6. Costa et al., "Intergenerational Transmission of Paternal Trauma."

7. Costa et al., "Intergenerational Transmission of Paternal Trauma."

8. Jessica Wolf, "Civil War Data Reveals That Fathers' Trauma Can Be Passed On to Sons," UCLA Newsroom, October 22, 2018. https://newsroom.ucla.edu/releases/civil-war-data-fathers-trauma-can-be-passed-on-to-children. Accessed December 20, 2022.

9. Joy DeGruy, *Post Traumatic Slave Syndrome: America's Legacy of Enduring Injury and Healing* (Portland, OR: Joy DeGruy Publications, 2017).

10. James Davis, Janell Penha, Omar Mbowe, and Deborah A. Taira, "Prevalence of Single and Multiple Leading Causes of Death by Race/Ethnicity among People Aged 60 to 70 years," *Preventing Chronic Diseases* 14 (October 19, 2017): 16024. https://www.cdc.gov/pcd/issues/2017/16_0241.htm. Accessed December 20, 2022.

11. U.S. Dept. of Health and Human Services, Office of Minority Health, "Profile: Black/African Americans." Last modified August 22, 2019. https://www.minorityhealth.hhs.gov/omh/browse.aspx?lvl=3&lvlid=61. Accessed December 20, 2022.

12. Hilary McD. Beckles, *Britain's Black Debt: Reparations for Slavery and Native Genocide* (Kingston, Jamaica: University of the West Indies Press, 2013).

13. CSPAN UCTV, "Sir Hilary Beckles," November 1, 2017. YouTube video. https://www.youtube.com/watch?v=FVIrVMJhehI. Accessed December 20, 2022.

14. R. Yehuda, J. Schmeidler, M. Wainberg, K. Binder-Brynes, and T. Duvdevani, "Vulnerability to Posttraumatic Stress Disorder in Adult Offspring of Holocaust Survivors," *American Journal of Psychiatry* 155, no. 9 (September 1998): 1163–1171.

15. Martha Henriques, "Can the Legacy of Trauma Be Passed Down the Generations?" *BBC Future*, March 26, 2019. https://www.bbc.com/future/article/20190326-what-is-epigenetics. Accessed December 20, 2022.

16. Christopher Green, "The Nature of Love" by Harry F. Harlow, 1958, in *Classics in the History of Psychology*," March 2000, York University, Toronto. https://psychclassics.yorku.ca/Harlow/love.htm#f1. Accessed December 20, 2022.

17. K. Gapp, G. van Steenwyk, P. L. Germain, W. Matsushima, K. L. M. Rudolph, F. Manuella, M. Roszkowski, G. Vernaz, T. Ghosh, P. Pelczar, I. M. Mansuy, and E. A. Miska, "Alterations in Sperm Long RNA Contribute to the Epigenetic Inheritance of the Effects of Postnatal Trauma," *Molecular Psychiatry* 25 (2020): 2162–2174. https://doi.org/10.1038/s41380-018-0271-6. Accessed December 20, 2022.

18. Gapp et al., "Alterations in Sperm Long RNA."

19. Irene Lacal and Rossella Ventura, "Epigenic Inheritance: Concepts, Mechanisms and Perspectives," *Frontiers in Molecular Neuroscience*, September 28, 2018. https://doi.org/10.3389/fnmol.2018.00292. Accessed December 20, 2022.

20. Leitch, "Action Steps Using ACEs and Trauma-Informed Care."

Chapter 9

1. The Theory of Twoness is by Andrea Francis.

2. W. E. B. Du Bois, "Strivings of the Negro People," *The Atlantic,* August 1897. https://www.theatlantic.com/magazine/archive/1897/08/strivings-of-the-negro-people/305446/. Accessed December 20, 2022.

3. Du Bois, "Strivings of the Negro People."

4. American Psychiatric Association, "What Are Dissociative Disorders?" Physician Review by Philip Wang, August 2018. https://www.psychiatry.org/patients-families/dissociative-disorders/what-are-dissociative-disorders. Accessed December 20, 2022.

5. American Psychiatric Association, "What Are Dissociative Disorders?"

6. American Psychiatric Association, "What Are Dissociative Disorders?"

7. B. A. van der Kolk, "The Body Keeps the Score: Memory and the Evolving Psychobiology of Posttraumatic Stress," *Harvard Review of Psychiatry* 1, no. 5 (Jan. Feb. 1994): 254 265. https://doi.org/10.3109/10673229409017088. Accessed December 20, 2022.

8. "Daydreaming Is Good. It Means You're Smart," Georgia Tech News Center October 24, 2017, Atlanta, Georgia. https://news.gatech.edu/news/2017/10/24/daydreaming-good-it-means-youre-smart. Accessed February 4, 2023.

9. Bence Nanay, "The Psychology of Shipping," *Psychology Today*, July 25, 2018. https://www.psychologytoday.com/us/blog/psychology-tomorrow/201807/the-psychology-shipping. Accessed December 20, 2022.

10. Windrush, discussed in detail in Chapter 5, is the name of the ship that brought Caribbean people to England to work in rebuilding cities devastated during World War II. Many Jamaican and other Caribbean people settled in London and Birmingham.

11. Paula Erizanu, "What Really Matters? An Interview with Rebecca Goldstein," *Institute of Art and Ideas. An Online Magazine of Big Ideas*, September 3, 2018. https://iai.tv/articles/rebecca-goldstein-on-what-really-matters-auid-1141. Accessed December 20, 2022.

12. David B. Feldman, "Why Daydreaming Is Healthy for Us," *Psychology Today*, December 19, 2017. https://www.psychologytoday.com/us/blog/supersurvivors/201712/why-daydreaming-is-good-us. Accessed December 20, 2022.

13. Joseph Stromberg, "The Benefits of Daydreaming," *SmithsonianMag.com*, April 3, 2012. https://www.smithsonianmag.com/science-nature/the-benefits-of-daydreaming-170189213/?no-ist. Accessed December 20, 2022.

14. Catarina Lino, *Positive Psychology: An Introduction,* October 2, 2016. https://positivepsychology.com/positive-psychology-an-introduction-summary/. Accessed December 20, 2022.

15. Lisa Firestone, "A Guide to the Fantasy Bond," *Psychology Today*, July 20, 2017. https://www.psychologytoday.com/us/blog/compassion-matters/201707/guide-the-fantasy-bond. Accessed December 20, 2022.

16. Robert Firestone, "Destructive Effects of the Fantasy Bond in Couple and Family Relationships," *Psychotherapy* 24, no. 2 (Summer 1987): 233–239. https://psycnet.apa.org/record/1988-01258-001. Accessed December 20, 2022.

Chapter 10

1. Haruv Institute, The Hebrew University of Jerusalem, "Van de Kolk—Childhood Adversity and Attachment Disruptions: Restoration by Establishing Synchrony," YouTube video, April 17, 2019. https://www.youtube.com/watch?v=r6p93kV054Q. Accessed February 4, 2023.

2. Gregory C. Elliott, Melissa F. Colangelo, and Richard J. Gelles, "Mattering and Suicide Ideation: Establishing and Elaborating a Relationship," *Social Psychology Quarterly* 68, no. 3 (2005): 223–238. https://doi.org/10.1177/019027250506800303. Accessed December 21, 2022.

3. Elliot et al., "Mattering and Suicidal Ideation."

4. Erik Erikson, *Identity, Youth and Crisis* (New York: W. W. Norton, 1968).

5. Jocelyn Block and Melinda Smith, "Co-Parenting Tips for Divorced Parents. Making Joint Custody Work after a Divorce or Separation," *HelpGuide*, June 2019. https://www.helpguide.org/articles/parenting-family/co-parenting-tips-for-divorced-parents.htm. Accessed December 21, 2022.

6. Armin Brott, "Ask Mr. Dad: Parenting through Divorce," *Mercury News*, June 16, 2016. https://www.mercurynews.com/2016/06/16/ask-mr-dad-parenting-through-divorce. Accessed December 21, 2022.

7. Brott, "Ask Mr. Dad."

8. Perri Klass, "Rethinking Covid-19 in Children," *New York Times*, May 12, 2020. https://www.nytimes.com/2020/05/12/well/family/coronavirus-children-covid-19.html. Accessed December 21, 2022.

9. Elizabeth Chuck, "Sheltering in Place—with Your Ex-Wife? Pandemic Poses Extra Challenges for Divorced Parents," *NBC News*, April 14, 2020. https://www.nbcnews.com/news/us-news/sheltering-place-your-ex-wife-pandemic-poses-extra-challenges-divorced-n1182831. Accessed December 21, 2022.

10. Valarie King and Juliana M. Sobolewski, "Nonresident Fathers' Contributions to Adolescent Well-Being," *Journal of Marriage and Family* 68, no. 3 (2006): 537–557. https://www.ncbi.nlm.nih.gov/pmc/articles/PMC2239255/. Accessed December 21, 2022.

11. Jenny Radesky, Caroline Kistin, Barry Zukerman et. al., "Patterns of Mobile Device Use by Caregivers and Children during Meals in Fast Food Restaurants," *Pediatrics* 133, no. 4 (April 2014): e843–849. https://pubmed.ncbi.nlm.nih.gov/24616357/. Accessed December 21, 2022.

12. Dona Matthews, "Why Parents Really Need to Put Down Their Phones," *Psychology Today*, November 23, 2017. https://www.psychologytoday.com/ca/blog/going-beyond-intelligence/201711/why-parents-really-need-put-down-their-phones. Accessed February 4, 2023.

13. Matthews, "Turn Off That Smartphone."

14. Brandon McDaniel, "Parent Distraction with Phones, Reasons for Use, and Impacts on Parenting and Child Outcomes: A Review of the Emerging Research," *Human Behavior and Emerging Technologies*, April 26, 2019. https://onlinelibrary.wiley.com/doi/full/10.1002/hbe2.139. Accessed December 21, 2022.

15. McDaniel, "Parent Distraction with Phones."

16. Jay Caspian Kang, "I Play Video Games with My 4-Year-Old, and That's OK," Opinion, *New York Times*, December 9, 2021. https://www.nytimes.com/2021/12/09/opinion/video-games-kids.html. Accessed December 21, 2022.

17. Karen Reivich and Andrew Shatté, *The Resilience Factor: 7 Keys to Finding Your Inner Strengths and Overcoming Life's Hurdles* (New York: Three Rivers Press, 2003).

Chapter 11

1. David Shwalb and Ziarat Hossain, eds., *Grandparents in Cultural Context* (New York: Taylor & Francis Group, 2018).

2. Shwalb and Hossain, *Grandparents in Cultural Context.*

3. Shwalb and Hossain, *Grandparents in Cultural Context.*

4. Lois Collins, *When Fear Drives Parenting, What Happens to the Kids? Deseret-News.* December 20, 2016. https://www.deseret.com/2016/12/20/20602719/when-fear-drives-parenting-what-happens-to-the-kids. Accessed December 21, 2022.

5. Shwalb and Hossain, *Grandparents in Cultural Context.*

6. Jenny Taitz, "He's No Longer My Ex-Husband, He's My Co-Grandparent," *New York Times*, April 13, 2018. https://www.nytimes.com/2018/04/13/well/family/hes-no-longer-my-ex-husband-hes-my-co-grandparent.html. Accessed December 21, 2022.

7. Centers for Disease Control, "COVID-19 Recommendations for Older Adults," September 11, 2020. https://www.cdc.gov/aging/covid19-guidance.html. Accessed January 31, 2023.

Chapter 12

1. Ann Meier, Kelly Musick, Sarah Flood, and Rachel Dunifon, "Mothering Experiences: How Single Parenthood and Employment Structure the Emotional Valence of Parenting," *Demography* 53, no. 3 (May 5, 2016): 649–674. https://read.dukeupress.edu/demography/article/53/3/649/167602/Mothering-Experiences-How-Single-Parenthood-and. Accessed February 4, 2023.

2. Maria Chiu, Simone Vigod, Farah Rahman, Cindy Lau, John Cairney, and Paul Kurdyak, "Mortality in Single Fathers Compared with Single Mothers and Partnered Parents: A Population-Based Cohort Study," *The Lancet* 3, no. 3 (February 2018): E115–E123. https://doi.org/10.1016/S2468-2667(18)30003-3. Accessed February 4, 2023.

3. Susan J. Kelley, Deborah M. Whitley, and Peter Campos, "Differential Impact of an Intervention for Grandmothers Raising Grandchildren," *Journal of Intergenerational Relationships* 17, no. 2 (May 2019): 141–162. https://doi.org/10.1080/15350770.2018.1535351. Accessed December 18, 2022.

4. PERMA Theory of Well-Being and PERMA Workshops, Positive Psychology Center. University of Pennsylvania. https://ppc.sas.upenn.edu/sites/default/files/permawellbeing.pdf. Accessed February 4, 2023.

5. Martin Seligman, "PERMA and the Building Blocks of Well-Being," *Journal of Positive Psychology*, February 16, 2018. https://ppc.sas.upenn.edu/sites/default/files/permawellbeing.pdf. Accessed December 18, 2022.

6. B. L. Fredrickson. "The Role of Positive Emotions in Positive Psychology: The Broaden-and-Build Theory of Positive Emotions," *American Psychologist* 56, no. 3 (March 2001): 218–226. http://dx.doi.org/10.1037/0003-066X.56.3.218. Accessed December 18, 2022.

7. Fredrickson, "The Role of Positive Emotions."

8. Robert A. Emmons and Michael E. McCullough, "Counting Blessing versus Burdens: An Experimental Investigation of Gratitude and Subjective Well-Being in Daily Life," *Journal of Personality and Social Psychology* 84, no. 2 (September 2003); 377–389. Accessed December 18, 2022.

9. Martin Seligman, "Three Blessings," Reflectivehappiness.com. https://www.youtube.com/watch?v=RT2vKMyIQwc. Accessed December 18, 2022.

10. Daniela Ramirez-Duran, "Savoring in Positive Psychology: 21 Tools to Appreciate Life," February 5, 2021. Positive Emotion. Positive Psychology.com https://positivepsychology.com/savoring/. Accessed February 4, 2023.

11. Nicholas Van Dam et al., "Mind the Hype: A Critical Evaluation and Prescriptive Agenda for Research on Mindfulness and Meditation," *Perspectives in Psychological Science* 13, no. 1 (October 2017): 36–61. https://doi.org/10.1177/1745691617709589. Accessed December 22, 2022.

12. Tania Singer, "What Type of Meditation Is Best For You?" *Greater Good Magazine*, July 2, 2018. https://greatergood.berkeley.edu/article/item/what_type_of_meditation_is_best_for_you. Accessed February 4, 2023.

13. Ilias Kamitsis and Andrew J. P. Francis, "Spirituality Mediates the Relationship between Engagement with Nature and Psychological Wellbeing,"

Journal of Environmental Psychology 36 (December 2013): 136–143. https://doi.org/10.1016/j.jenvp.2013.07.013. Accessed December 22, 2022.

14. Mark Holder, Ben Coleman, and Judi M. Wallace, "Spirituality, Religiousness, and Happiness in Children Aged 8–12 Years," *Journal of Happiness Studies* 11, no. 2 (April 2010): 131–150. https://www.researchgate.net/publication/46537115_Spirituality_Religiousness_and_Happiness_in_Children_Aged_8-12_Years. Accessed December 22, 2022.

15. Bridget Grenville-Cleave, "Five Reasons to Focus on Flow," *Positive Psychology News*, February 26, 2013. https://positivepsychologynews.com/news/bridget-grenville-cleave/2013022625517. Accessed December 22, 2022.

16. Amy Muise, Emily Christofides, and Serge Desmarais, "More Information than You Ever Wanted: Does Facebook Bring Out the Green-Eyed Monster of Jealousy?" *Cyberpsychology and Behavior* 12, no. 4 (2009): 443.

17. Muise et al., "More Information than You Ever Wanted."

18. PERMA Theory of Well-Being and PERMA Workshops, Positive Psychology Center.

19. "What Is WOOP?" WOOP. https://woopmylife.org/en/home. Accessed December 22, 2022.

Chapter 13

1. Maryam Abdullah, "With Kids, Love Is in the Little Things: Researcher Barbara Frederickson Explains How a Parent's Love Helps Kids Thrive," *Greater Good Magazine*, June 18, 2019. https://greatergood.berkeley.edu/article/item/with_kids_love_is_in_the_little_things. Accessed February 4, 2023.

2. Abdullah, "With Kids, Love Is in the Little Things."

3. Abdullah, "With Kids, Love Is in the Little Things."

4. Martin Seligman, "PERMA and the Building Blocks of Well-Being," *Journal of Positive Psychology*, February 16, 2018. https://ppc.sas.upenn.edu/sites/default/files/permawellbeing.pdf. Accessed December 22, 2022.

5. Kenneth R. Ginsburg, "The Importance of Play in Promoting Healthy Child Development and Maintaining Strong Parent-Child Bonds," *Pediatrics* 119, no. 1 (2007): 182–191.

6. Marc Bekoff, "The Importance of Play: Having Fun Must Be Taken Seriously," *Psychology Today*, May 2, 2014. https://www.psychologytoday.com/us/blog/animal-emotions/201405/the-importance-play-having-fun-must-be-taken-seriously. Accessed December 22, 2022.

7. Darcia F. Narvaez, "Attachment Social Play for Self-Transformation: What Everyone Needs to Thrive and Reach Their Potential," *Psychology Today*, January 3, 2021. https://www.psychologytoday.com/us/blog/moral-landscapes/202101/attachment-social-play-self-transformation. Accessed December 22, 2022.

8. PERMA Theory of Well-Being and PERMA Workshops, Positive Psychology Center.

9. Harry F. Harlow, "Love in Infant Monkeys," *Scientific American* 200, no. 6 (1959): 68–75. http://www.jstor.org/stable/26309508. Accessed December 18, 2022.

10. Judy Kuriansky, "Resilience and Empowerment for Youth" (workshops presented at the Caribbean Well-Being Conference), Phillipsburg, St. Maarten, August 7–8, 2017.

11. Allie, "Dreaming of Dad," case info.

12. Jeanne Nakamura and Mihaly Csikszentmihalyi, "Flow Theory and Research," in C. R. Snyder and Shane J. Lopez, eds., *Handbook of Positive Psychology* (Oxford, UK: Oxford University Press, 2009), pp. 195–206.

13. Elizabeth Hawkey, "Media Use in Childhood: Evidence-Based Recommendations for Caregivers," *CYF News*, May 2019. https://www.apa.org/pi/families/resources/newsletter/2019/05/media-use-childhood. Accessed December 22, 2022.

14. Nansook Park and Christopher Peterson, "Character Strengths: Research and Practice," *Journal of College and Character* 10, no. 4 (2009). https://doi.org/10.2202/1940-1639.1042. Accessed December 22, 2022.

15. Martin Seligman, *Flourish: Positive Psychology and Positive Interventions.* The Tanner Lectures on Human Values, delivered at the University of Michigan, October 7, 2010. https://tannerlectures.utah.edu/_resources/documents/a-to-z/s/Seligman_10.pdf. Accessed December 22, 2022.

16. Seligman, *Flourish.*

17. Camille Piner, "Chris Peterson's Unfinished Masterwork—A Strengths-Based Perspective of Mental Illness" (blog), Center for Positive Organizations, December 4, 2013. https://positiveorgs.bus.umich.edu/blog/chris-petersons-unfinished-masterwork-a-strengths-based-perspective-of-mental-illness. Accessed December 22, 2022.

18. "Bring Your Strengths to Life & Live More Fully," Values in Action Free Survey. https://www.viacharacter.org/character-strengths. Accessed February 4, 2023.

19. "Bring Your Strengths to Life."

20. Piner, "Chris Peterson's Unfinished Masterwork."

21. Louise Bennett, *Selected Poems* (Kingston, Jamaica: Sangster's Book Stores, 1982), p. 10.

22. Beatrix Potter, "The Tale of Peter Rabbit," in *Peter Rabbit: Naturally Better. Classic Gift Set* (United Kingdom: Frederick Warne, 2009).

23. Peggy Appiah, *Tales of an Ashanti Father* (Boston: Beacon Press, 1969).

24. *Happily Ever After: Fairy Tales for Every Child*, directed by Bruce W. Smith et al. (Warner Bros. Television Distribution, 1995), Animation.

25. The 24 Character Strengths. https://www.viacharacter.org/character-strengths. Accessed February 4, 2023.

26. *StoryJumper*, Palo Alto, California, 2009. https://www.crunchbase.com/organization/storyjumper. Accessed December 22, 2022.

27. Matt Johnson, "How to Use Journaling as a Coping Tool," National Alliance on Mental Illness, January 30, 2019. https://www.nami.org/Blogs/NAMI-Blog/January-2019/How-to-Use-Journaling-as-a-Coping-Tool. Accessed December 22, 2022.

28. Christina Elgersma, "Parents, Here Is the Truth about Online Predators," *CNN Health*, August 3, 2017. https://www.cnn.com/2017/08/03/health/online-predators-parents-partner/index.html. Accessed December 22, 2022.

29. Eduardo Lima, "The Once and Future Hero: Understanding the Hero in Quest Fantasy," *Fafnir: Nordic Journal of Science Fiction and Fantasy Research* 4 no. 1, (2017): 7–19. http://journal.finfar.org/articles/the-once-and-future-hero-understanding-the-hero-in-quest-fantasy. Accessed December 22, 2022.

30. Emily Zobel Marshall, *Anansi's Journey: A Story of Jamaican Cultural Resistance* (Kingston, Jamaica: University of the West Indies Press, 2012).

31. PERMA Theory of Well-Being and PERMA Workshops, Positive Psychology Center.

32. Andrea Francis, "Adolescent Girls' Perspectives on their Relationship with Their Nonresident Fathers," Unpublished Dissertation (Walden University, 2012).

33. 'Celeb Dads Get Real," *People Magazine*, n.d. https://people.com/tag/celeb-dads-get-real/. Accessed February 4, 2023.

34. Lauren Knight, "5 Ways to Let a Little More Risk into Your Child's Day (and Why That's a Good Thing)," *Washington Post*, January 16, 2015. https://www.washingtonpost.com/news/parenting/wp/2015/01/16/5-ways-to-let-a-little-more-risk-into-your-childs-day-and-what-thats-a-good-thing. Accessed December 22, 2022.

35. Ellen Barry, "In Britain, Learning to Accept Risk and the Occasional 'Owie,'" *New York Times*, March 11, 2018.

36. Karyn B. Purvis, Erin Becker Razuri, Amanda R. Hiles Howard, Casey D. Call, Jamie Hurst DeLuna, Jordan S. Hall, and David R. Cross, "Behavioral Problems and Trauma Symptoms among At-Risk Adopted Children Following Trauma-Informed Parent Training Intervention," *Journal of Child and Adolescent Trauma* 8 (2015): J201–210. https://doi.org/10.1007/s40653-015-0055-y. Accessed December 22, 2022.

37. Helga Synnevåg, Løvoll, Knut-Willy Saether, and Mark Graves, "Feeling at Home in the Wilderness: Environmental Conditions, Well-Being and Aesthetic Experience," *Frontiers in Psychology*, March 13, 2020. https://doi.org/10.3389/fpsyg.2020.00402. Accessed December 22, 2022.

38. Sadie Dingfelder, "A Flying Start," *Washington Post*, August 26, 2020. https://www.washingtonpost.com/magazine/2020/08/26/forget-neflix-tune-feathered-soap-opera-outside-your-window/?arc404=true. Accessed February 4, 2023.

39. Dingfelder, "A Flying Start."

40. Jacey Fortin, "Birds Are Not on Lockdown and More People Are Watching Them," *New York Times*, May 29, 2020. https://www.nytimes.com/2020/05/29/science/bird-watching-coronavirus.html. Accessed December 22, 2022.

41. Synnevåg, et al., "Feeling at Home in the Wilderness."

42. Karen Weintraub, "Going Barefoot Is Good for the Sole," *Scientific American*, June 26, 2019. https://www.scientificamerican.com/article/going-barefoot-is-good-for-the-sole/. Accessed February 4, 2023.

43. Alex S. Holdaway, Aaron M. Luebbe, and Stephen P. Becker, "Rumination in Relation to Suicide Risk, Ideation, and Attempts: Exacerbation by Poor Sleep Quality?" *Journal of Affective Disorders* 236 (2018): 6–13. https://doi.org/10.1016/j.jad.2018.04.087. Accessed December 22, 2022.

44. Karen Reivich, "Thinking Traps Introduction. Definition and Demonstration," Coursera. https://es.coursera.org/lecture/positive-psychology-resilience/2-1-thinking-traps-introduction-OC0na. Accessed February 4, 2023.

45. Reivich, "Definition and Demonstration."

46. Reivich, "Definition and Demonstration."

47. Reivich, "Definition and Demonstration."

48. Karen J. Reivich, Martin E. P. Seligman, and Sharon McBride, "Master Resilience Training in the US Army," *American Psychologist* 66, no. 1 (January 2011): 25–34. https://ppc.sas.upenn.edu/sites/default/files/mrtinarmyjan2011.pdf. Accessed December 22, 2022.

49. Seligman, "The Three Blessings Exercise."

50. Reivich et al., "Master Resilience Training in the U.S. Army."

51. Robert A. Emmons, *Thanks! How Practicing Gratitude Can Make You Happier* (New York: Houghton Mifflin, 2007).

52. Emmons, *Thanks!*

53. The 24 Character Strengths.

54. Karen Reivich and Andrew Shatté, *The Resilience Factor: 7 Essential Skills for Overcoming Life's Inevitable Obstacles* (New York: Broadway Books, 2002).

55. Gabriele Oettingen, *Rethinking Positive Thinking: Inside the New Science of Motivation* (New York: Penguin Random House, 2014).

Chapter 14

1. The National Wildlife Federation, "Wildlife: Attracting Butterflies." https://www.nwf.org/Garden-for-Wildlife/Wildlife/Attracting-Butterflies. Accessed December 22, 2021.

2. National Wildlife Federation, "Wildlife: Attracting Butterflies."

3. National Wildlife Federation, "Wildlife: Attracting Butterflies."

4. Karen Oberhauser, Sonia Altizer, O. R. Taylor, and Daniel Vickerman, "MonarchWatch: Biology. Parasite Control: Ophryocystis elektroscirrha." https://monarchwatch.org/biology/control.htm. Accessed December 22, 20222.

5. Debbie Hadley, "Why Do Some Monarch Butterflies Have Crumpled Wings?" ThoughtCo., July 12, 2019. https://www.thoughtco.com/why-monarch-butterfly-have-crumpled-wings-1968187. Accessed December 22, 2022.

6. Hadley, "Why Do Some Monarch Butterflies."

7. Martin Seligman, *Flourish: Positive Psychology and Positive Interventions*. The Tanner Lectures on Human Values, delivered at the University of Michigan, October 7, 2010. https://tannerlectures.utah.edu/_resources/documents/a-to-z/s/Seligman_10.pdf. Accessed December 22, 2022.

8. Karen Reivich and Andrew Shatté, *The Resilience Factor: 7 Keys to Finding Your Inner Strengths and Overcoming Life's Hurdles* (New York: Three Rivers Press, 2003).

9. Reivich and Shatté, *The Resilience Factor.*

10. Kelly, "Butterfly Garden Tips," Joyful Butterfly. https://www.joyfulbutterfly.com, Accessed December 22, 2022.

11. Andrea Francis, Butterfly Model of Interventions for Children Traumatized by Parental Abandonment (June 24, 2019).

Chapter 15

1. The Oxford Centre for Fantasy. https://oxfordcentreforfantasy.org/. Accessed December 22, 2022.

2. Paula Bouldin and Chris Pratt, "Characteristics of Preschool and School-Age Children with Imaginary Companions," *Journal of Genetic Psychology: Research and Theory on Human Development* 160, no. 4 (1990): 397–410. https://www.tandfonline.com/doi/abs/10.1080/00221329909595553. Accessed December 21, 2022.

3. Eva V. Hoff, "Imaginary Companions, Creativity, and Self-Image in Middle Childhood," *Creativity Research Journal* 17, no. 2–3 (July 2005): 167–180. https://doi.org/10.1080/10400419.2005.9651477. Accessed December 21, 2022.

4. Espen Klausen and Richard Passman, "Pretend Companions (Imaginary Playmates): The Emergence of a Field," *Journal of Genetic Psychology* 168, no. 4 (2006): 349–364. https://doi.org/10.3200/GNTP.167.4.349-364. Accessed December 21, 2022.

5. The TLC Foundation for Body-Focused Repetitive Behaviors, "Hair Pulling." https://www.bfrb.org/learn-about-bfrbs/trichotillomania. Accessed December 21, 2022.

6. Peter L. Benson, Eugene C. Roehlkepartain, and Stacey P. Rude, "Spiritual Development in Childhood and Adolescence: Toward a Field of Inquiry," *Applied Developmental Science* 7, no. 3 (July 2003): 205–213. https://paulthompsontherapy.com/wp-content/uploads/2018/04/2003-BensonRPRude-ADS.pdf. Accessed December 21, 2022.

Resources

Character Strengths

Park, Nansook and Christopher Peterson. "Character Strengths: Research and Practice." *Journal of College and Character* 10, no. 4 (2009). https://doi.org/10.2202/1940-1639.1042

Forgiveness

Pellissier, Hank. "Why Teach Kids to Forgive?" *Great Schools*, updated July 27, 2022. https://www.greatschools.org/gk/articles/teach-kids-forgive/

Kindness

Sabky, Rebecca. "Check This Box if You're a Good Person." *The New York Times*, April 4, 2017. https://www.nytimes.com/2017/04/04/opinion/check-this-box-if-youre-a-good-person.html

Life-Satisfaction Scale

Diener, E., R. A. Emmons, R. J. Larsen, and S. Griffin. "The Satisfaction with Life Scale." *Journal of Personality Assessment* 49 (1985): 71–75.

Mindfulness and Deep Breathing

Li, Peng, Wiktor A. Janczewski, Kevin Yackle, Kaiwen Kam, Silvia Pagliardini, Mark A. Krasnow, and Jack L. Feldman. "The Peptidergic Control Circuit for Sighing." *Nature* 539 (2016): 293–297.

Reynolds, Gretchen. "Why Deep Breathing May Keep Us Calm." *The New York Times*, April 5, 2017. https://www.nytimes.com/2017/04/05/well/move/what-chill-mice-can-teach-us-about-keeping-calm.html/

Motivation and Goal-Setting

Oettingen, Gabriele. *Rethinking Positive Thinking: Inside the New Science of Motivation*. London: Current, 2014.

Penman, Maggie and Shankar Vedantam. "WOOP, There It Is! 4 Steps to Achieve Your Goals." *Hidden Brain*, May 10, 2016. National Public Radio. https://www.npr.org/2016/05/10/477379965/woop-there-it-is-four-steps-to-achieve-your-goals

Optimism

Aspinwall L. G., L. Richter, and R. R. Hoffman, III. "Understanding How Optimism Works: An Examination of Optimists' Adaptive Moderation in Belief and Behavior." In E. C. Chang, ed., *Optimism and Pessimism: Implications for Theory, Research, and Practice*, pp. 217–238. Washington, DC: American Psychological Association, 2001.

Brody, Jane E. "A Positive Outlook May Be Good for Your Health." *The New York Times*, March 27, 2017. https://www.nytimes.com/2017/03/27/well/live/positive-thinking-may-improve-health-and-extend-life.html

Brody, Jane E. "Turning Negative Thinkers into Positive Ones." *The New York Times*, April 3, 2017. https://www.nytimes.com/2017/04/03/well/live/turning-negative-thinkers-into-positive-ones.html

Carver, Charles S. and Michael F. Scheier. "Optimism," in C. R. Snyder and S. J. Lopez, eds., *Handbook of Positive Psychology*. Oxford, UK: Oxford University Press, 2002, pp. 231–243.

Peterson, Christopher and Tracy A. Steen. "Optimistic Explanatory Style," in C. R. Snyder and S. J. Lopez, eds., *Handbook of Positive Psychology*, 2nd ed. Oxford, UK: Oxford University Press, 2009.

Sin, Nancy L. and Sonja Lyubomirsky, S. "Enhancing Well-Being and Alleviating Depressive Symptoms with Positive Psychology Interventions: A Practice-Friendly Meta-Analysis." *Journal of Clinical Psychology* 65, no. 5 (May 2009): 467–487. http://doi.org/10.1002/jclp.20593

Play

Bekoff, Marc. "The Importance of Play: Having Fun Must Be Taken Seriously." *Psychology Today*, May 2, 2014. https://www.psychologytoday.com/blog/animal-emotions/201405/the-importance-play-having-fun-must-be-taken-seriously

Gray, Peter. "Risky Play: Why Children Love It and Need It." *Psychology Today*, April 7, 2014. https://www.psychologytoday.com/blog/freedom-learn/201404/risky-play-why-children-love-it-and-need-it

Rabin, Roni Caryn Rabin. "Teenagers Aren't Getting Enough Exercise at School, or Anywhere." *The New York Times*, December 9, 2015. https://well.blogs.nytimes.com/2015/12/09/teenagers-arent-getting-enough-exercise-at-school-or-anywhere/

Reynolds, Gretchen. "Child's Play Is Good for All of Us." *The New York Times*, May 3, 2017. https://www.nytimes.com/2017/05/03/well/move/childs-play-is-good-for-all-of-us.html

Positivity

Brody, Jane E. "A Positive Outlook May Be Good for Your Health." *The New York Times*, March 27, 2017. https://www.nytimes.com/2017/03/27/well/live/positive-thinking-may-improve-health-and-extend-life.html

Brody, Jane E. "Turning Negative Thinkers into Positive Ones." *The New York Times*, April 3, 2017. https://www.nytimes.com/2017/04/03/well/live/turning-negative-thinkers-into-positive-ones.html

Technology

Divecha, Diana. "Five Tips for Helping Teens Manage Technology." *Greater Good Magazine*, June 25, 2014. https://greatergood.berkeley.edu/article/item/five_tips_for_helping_teens_manage_technology

Feiler, Bruce. "When Tech Is a Problem Child." *The New York Times*, November 19, 2016. https://www.nytimes.com/2016/11/20/fashion/children-technology-limits-smartphones.html

Teens Overestimate the Bad Behavior of Peers

Helms, Sarah W. "Teens Overestimate the Bad Behavior of Peers." *Greater Good Magazine*, November 25, 2016. https://greatergood.berkeley.edu/article/item/teens_overestimate_bad_behavior_peers

Using Genograms

McGoldrick, M., R. Gerson, and S. Shellenberger. *Genograms: Assessment and Intervention*. New York: W. W. Norton, 2008.

The Value of Gratitude

Froh, Jeffrey J., William J. Selfick, and Robert A. Emmons. "Counting Blessings in Early Adolescence: An Experimental Study of Gratitude and Subjective Well-Being. *Journal of School Psychology* 46, no. 2 (April 2008): 213–233. http://doi.org/10.1016/j.jsp.2007.03.005

Walker, J., T. Gilovich, and A. Kumar. "Cultivating Gratitude and Giving through Experiential Consumption." *Emotions* 16, no. 8 (2016): 1126–1136. https://psycnet.apa.org/doiLanding?doi=10.1037%2Femo0000242

Index

Note: Page numbers followed by *f* indicate figures.

About the Author

ANDREA FRANCIS, PhD, is a psychotherapist and former school counselor. She is in private practice, specializing in intergenerational trauma in children, adolescents, and families. She earned a BA in English literature from the University of the West Indies and a PhD from Walden University, where her doctoral work focused on the relationship between adolescent girls and their nonresident fathers. Francis also holds MA and MEd degrees from Columbia University in New York, where she specialized in counseling psychology. As a middle school counselor, she was recognized as counselor of the year, and she conducts workshops for practitioners in the field.

www.ingramcontent.com/pod-product-compliance
Ingram Content Group UK Ltd.
Pitfield, Milton Keynes, MK11 3LW, UK
UKHW021907150926
475560UK00003B/237

9 781440 877964